Microsoft® Excel 97

ILLUSTRATED PROJECTS™

Carol M. Cram

Capilano College, North Vancouver, B.C.

ONE MAIN STREET, CAMBRIDGE, MA 02142

COURSE TECHNOLOGY

an International Thomson Publishing company I(T)P®

Cambridge • Albany • Bonn • Boston • Cincinnati • London • Madrid • Melbourne • Mexico City
New York • Paris • San Francisco • Singapore • Tokyo • Toronto • Washington

COURSE TECHNOLOGY

Microsoft® Excel 97 — Illustrated Projects™

is published by Course Technology.

Managing Editor:	Nicole Jones Pinard
Product Manager:	Jeanne Herring
Production Editor:	Catherine G. DiMassa
Composition House:	GEX, Inc.
Quality Assurance Tester:	Brian McCooey
Text Designer:	Joseph Lee Design
Cover Designer:	Joseph Lee Design

© 1997 by Course Technology
A Division of International Thomson Publishing —I(T)P®

For more information contact:

Course Technology
One Main Street
Cambridge, MA 02142

International Thomson Editores
Campos Eliseos 385, Piso 7
Col. Polanco
11560 Mexico D.F. Mexico

International Thomson Publishing Europe
Berkshire House 168-173
High Holborn
London WC1V 7AA
England

International Thomson Publishing GmbH
Königswinterer Strasse 418
53277 Bonn
Germany

Thomas Nelson Australia
102 Dodds Street
South Melbourne, 3205
Victoria, Australia

International Thomson Publishing Asia
211 Henderson Road
#05-10 Henderson Building
Singapore 0315

Nelson Canada
1120 Birchmount Road
Scarborough, Ontario
Canada M1K 5G4

International Thomson Publishing Japan
Hirakawacho Kyowa Building, 3F
2-2-1 Hirakawacho
Chiyoda-ku, Tokyo 102
Japan

Trademarks

Disclaimer

Course Technology reserves the right to revise this publication and make changes from time to time in its content without notice.

ISBN 0-7600-5125-9

Printed in the United States of America

10 9 8 7 6 5 4 3 2

From the Illustrated Series™ Team

At Course Technology we believe that technology will transform the way that people teach and learn. We are very excited about bringing you, instructors and students, the most practical and affordable technology-related products available.

The Development Process

Our development process is unparalleled in the educational publishing industry. Every product we create goes through an exacting process of design, development, review, and testing.

Reviewers give us direction and insight that shape our manuscripts and bring them up to the latest standards. Every manuscript is quality tested. Students whose backgrounds match the intended audience work through every keystroke, carefully checking for clarity and pointing out errors in logic and sequence. Together with our own technical reviewers, these testers help us ensure that everything that carries our name is as error-free and easy to use as possible.

The Products

We show both how and why technology is critical to solving problems in the classroom and in whatever field you choose to teach or pursue. Our time-tested, step-by-step instructions provide unparalleled clarity. Examples and applications are chosen and crafted to motivate students.

The Illustrated Series Team

The Illustrated Series Team is committed to providing you with the most visual introduction to microcomputer applications. No other series of books will get you up to speed faster in today's changing software environment. This book will suit your needs because it was delivered quickly, efficiently, and affordably. In every aspect of business, we rely on a commitment to quality and the use of technology. Each member of the Illustrated Series Team contributes to this process. The names of all our team members are listed below.

Cynthia Anderson	Pam Conrad	Meta Hirschl	Neil Salkind
Chia-Ling Barker	Mary-Terese Cozzola	Jane Hosie-Bounar	Gregory Schultz
Donald Barker	Carol M. Cram	Steven Johnson	Ann Shaffer
David Beskeen	Kim Crowley	Bill Lisowski	Dan Swanson
Ann Marie Buconjic	Catherine G. DiMassa	Tara O'Keefe	Marie Swanson
Rachel Bunin	Linda Eriksen	Harry Phillips	Jennifer Thompson
Joan Carey	Jessica Evans	Nicole Jones Pinard	Sasha Vodnik
Patrick Carey	Lisa Friedrichsen	Katherine T. Pinard	Jan Weingarten
Sheralyn Carroll	Michael Halvorson	Kevin Proot	Christie Williams
Pat Coleman	Jamie Harper	Elizabeth Eisner Reding	Janet Wilson
Brad Conlin	Jeanne Herring	Art Rotberg	

Preface

Welcome to *Microsoft Exel 97—Illustrated Projects*. This highly visual book offers a wide array of interesting and challenging projects designed to reinforce the skills learned in any beginning Excel book. The Illustrated Projects Series is for people who want more opportunities to practice important software skills.

Organization and Coverage

This text contains a total of six units. Each unit contains three projects followed by four Independent Challenges and a Visual Workshop. In these units, students practice creating, editing, and formatting worksheets in addition to working with charts, lists, and the data analysis features of Excel.

About this Approach

What makes the Illustrated Projects approach so effective at reinforcing software skills? It's quite simple. Each activity in a project is presented on two facing pages, with the step-by-step instructions on the left page, and large screen illustrations on the right. Students can focus on a single activity without having to turn the page. This unique design makes information extremely accessible and easy to absorb. Students can complete the projects on their own and because of the modular structure of the book, can also cover the units in any order.

Each two-page spread, or "information display," in an Illustrated Projects book contains the following elements:

Road map–It is always clear which project and activity you are working on.

Introduction–Concise text that introduces the project and explains which activity within the project the student will complete. Procedures are easier to learn when they fit into a meaningful framework.

Hints and Trouble comments–Hints for using Microsoft Excel 97 more effectively and trouble shooting advice to fix common problems that might occur. Both appear right where students need them, next to the step where they might need help.

Numbered steps–Clear step-by-step directions explain how to complete the specific activity. These steps get less specific as students progress to the third project in a unit.

Time To checklists–Reserved for basic skills that students should do frequently such as previewing, printing, saving, and closing worksheets.

ONE-PAGE RESUME FOR MARY MCDONALD

activity:

Enter Text

You will first enter all the data required for the resume. To save time you will enter this data without worrying about formatting. You will also use the Tables feature to quickly enter the data required for the Education, Work Experience, and Volunteer Experience sections of the resume.

Hint
Always select the Show/Hide button so you can easily identify font size changes and notice when you accidentally press the spacebar twice between words.

Trouble
If the value in cell E2 is *not* $110,000.00 or if #NAME? appears, check your formula and try again.

steps:

1. Launch Word and, if necessary, click the Show/Hide button ¶ on the Standard toolbar to select it, then click the Page Layout View button 🔲
   End of paragraph marks ¶ and dots between each word appear. Next, start entering the text for the resume.

2. Type the name and address as shown in Figure P1-2, press [Enter] twice, type **Objective**, press [Enter], type **To apply my organizational and computer skills as an Administrative Assistant in a service-based company or organization**, then press [Enter] twice
   Employers appreciate an Objective statement at the beginning of a resume. Now you are ready to enter the information about Mary's educational background. You could use the tab feature to separate the dates from the descriptions. However, you will save time by creating a table and then copying it for subsequent entries.

3. Type **Education**, press [Enter] twice, click the Insert Table button 🔳 and drag the mouse to create a table that is 2 columns by 4 rows, then reduce the width of column 1 to 1 inch
   To reduce the column width, you point the mouse between columns 1 and 2 and drag the ↔ until the marker on the Ruler Bar appears at 1.

4. Enter the text for the first two entries as shown in Figure P1-3, then save the resume as **Mary McDonald's Resume** to the disk where you plan to store all the files for this book
   Mary McDonald does not have any more entries for education. Often you will find that you have created a table that contains more rows than you need.

5. Point the mouse to the left of row 3, click the **left mouse button** and drag the mouse to select rows 3 and 4, click the **right mouse button** in one of the selected rows, then click **Delete Rows**

6. Press [Enter] once following the table, type **Work Experience**, then press [Enter] twice
   Next, save time by copying the table you created for the Education entries below Work Experience.

7. Click anywhere in the table, click Table on the menu bar, click **Select Table**, click the **Copy button** 📋, click at the paragraph mark below Work Experience, then click the **Paste button** 📋

8. Enter the text for Work Experience in the table as shown in Figure P1-4, press [Enter] after the table, type **Volunteer Experience**, then press [Enter] twice
   To replace existing text, click on the cell to select it, then start typing the new text.

9. Copy the Work Experience table, enter the text required for Volunteer Experience, type the remaining text as shown in Figure P1-4, then click the **Spelling and Grammar button** 📝
   Don't worry if the text of the resume extends to two pages. You will fix this problem later.

Time To
✓ Save
✓ Print
✓ Close

The Projects

The two-page lesson format featured in this book provides students with a powerful learning experience. Additionally, this book contains the following features:

▶ **Meaningful Examples**—This book features projects that students will be excited to create, including an expense report, a vacation planning budget, and a car loan analysis. By producing relevant documents that will enhance their own lives, students will more readily master skills.

▶ **Different Levels of Guidance**—the three projects in each unit provide varying levels of guidance. In Project 1, the guidance level is high, with detailed instructions keeping the student on track. Project 2 provides less guidance, and Project 3 provides minimal help, encouraging students to work more independently. This approach gets students in the real-world mindset of using their experiences to solve problems.

▶ **Start from Scratch**—To truly test if a student understands the software and can use it to reach specific goals, the student should start from scratch. This adds to the book's flexibility and real-world nature.

▶ **Outstanding Assessment and Reinforcement**—Each unit concludes with four Independent Challenges. These Independent Challenges offer less instruction than the projects, allowing students to explore various software features and increase their critical thinking skills. The Visual Workshop follows the Independent Challenges and broadens students' attention to detail. Students see a completed worksheet, and must recreate it on their own.

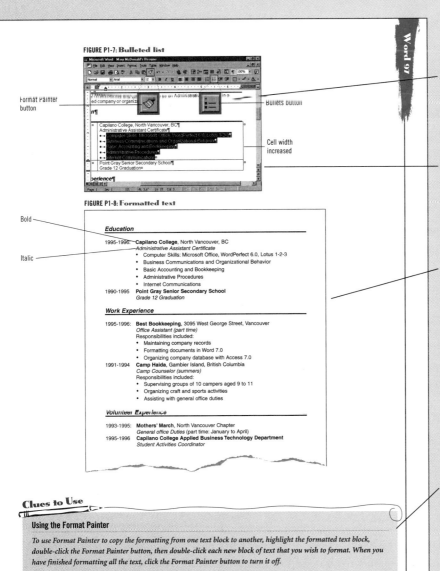

FIGURE P1-7: Bulleted list

FIGURE P1-8: Formatted text

Callouts and enlarged buttons—The innovative design draws the students' eyes to important areas of the screen.

Screen shots—Every activity features large representations of what the screen should look like as students complete the numbered steps.

Completed worksheet—At the end of every project, there is a picture of how the worksheet will look when printed. Students can easily assess how well they've done.

Clues to Use Boxes—Many activities feature these sidebars, providing concise information that either explains a skill or concept that is covered in the steps or describes an independent task or feature that is in some way related to the steps. These often include both text and screen shots.

Clues to Use

Using the Format Painter

To use Format Painter to copy the formatting from one text block to another, highlight the formatted text block, double-click the Format Painter button, then double-click each new block of text that you wish to format. When you have finished formatting all the text, click the Format Painter button to turn it off.

Instructor's Resource Kit

The Instructor's Resource Kit is Course Technology's way of putting the resources and information needed to teach and learn effectively into your hands. With an integrated array of teaching and learning tools that offer you and your students a broad range of instructional options, we believe this kit represents the highest quality and most cutting edge resources available to instructors today. Visit us on the Web at http://www.course.com. Briefly, the resources available with this text are:

Course Faculty Online Companion

This new World Wide Web site offers Course Technology customers a password-protected Faculty Lounge where you can find everything you need to prepare for class. These periodically updated items include lesson plans, graphic files for the figures in the text, additional problems, updates and revisions to the text, links to other Web sites, and access to Student Disk files. This new site is an ongoing project and will continue to evolve throughout the semester. Contact your Customer Service Representative for the site address and password.

Course Student Online Companion

The Student Online Companion is a place where students can access challenging, engaging, and relevant exercises. They can find a graphical glossary of terms found in the text, an archive of meaningful templates, software, hot tips, and Web links to other sites that contain pertinent information. We offer student sites in the broader application areas as well as sites for specific titles. These new sites are also ongoing projects and will continue to evolve throughout the semester.

Instructor's Manual

This is quality assurance tested and includes:
- ► *Solutions to end-of-unit material*
- ► *Lecture notes which contain teaching tips from the author*
- ► *Extra Projects*

Clues to Use

The Illustrated Family of Products

This book that you are holding fits into the Illustrated Projects Series—*one series of three in the Illustrated family of products. The other two series are the* Illustrated Series *and the* Illustrated Interactive Series. The Illustrated Series *consists of concepts and applications texts that offer the quickest, most visual way to* build software skills. The Illustrated Interactive Series *is our line of computer-based training multimedia products that offer the novice user a quick, visual and interactive learning experience. All three series are committed to providing you and your students with the most visual and enriching instructional materials.*

Contents

Microsoft
► Excel
Projects

Worksheet Building

In This Unit You Will Create:

PROJECT 1 ► **Projected Budget**

PROJECT 2 ► **Loan Amortization**

PROJECT 3 ► **Planning Budget**

Microsoft Excel provides you with the tools you need to make effective planning decisions. For example suppose you want to take a two-week vacation to the Caribbean. You have allocated $2,000 for all your trip expenses. To find out if you have enough money to cover your expenses, you can set up a simple worksheet that will list all your expenses for airfare, accommodations, food, entertainment, etc. Once you have totaled all your expenses, you may find that they exceed your $2,000 budget. Rather than cancel your trip, you could then try to determine which expenses you can decrease. You could decide to stay at a less expensive hotel or allocate a reduced amount for your shopping needs. When you use a worksheet as a planning tool, you identify and evaluate different courses of action and then select the actions that will best meet your personal or business needs. ► In this unit you will learn how to use Microsoft Excel to determine worksheet categories, build arithmetic formulas, and, most important, ask relevant "What if?" questions designed to help you develop worksheets that you can then use as planning tools.

OVERVIEW

Projected Budget for Cape Cod Arts Council

The Cape Cod Arts Council is a small, nonprofit organization that teaches arts and crafts classes in a converted boathouse located in the Cape Cod area. You will create the Cape Cod Arts Council's budget for the first six months of 1999, based on figures obtained from the 1998 budget, and then ask a series of "What if?" questions to determine realistic planning goals for the second half of 1999.

The following four activities are required to complete the six-month budget for the Cape Cod Arts Council:

Project Activities

Enter and Enhance Labels

You can easily present worksheet data in an attractive and easy-to-read format. In Figure P1-1, the labels in the top five rows are centered across columns and enhanced with various font styles and sizes, while a white-on-black effect is used to highlight two of the worksheet titles.

Calculate Totals

You can either use the AutoSum button or enter a formula when you need to add values in a spreadsheet. You use the AutoSum method when you want to add the values in cells that appear consecutively in a column or row and then display the total directly below or to the right of the added values. You enter a formula when you want to calculate values that do not appear in consecutive cells. For example, you would enter the formula =A1+A3 if you wished to add the values in cells A1 and A3. You can also use the SUM formula. For example, you would enter the function =SUM(A1..A6) if you wished to add all the values in cells A1 through A6 and display the result in a nonadjacent cell.

Ask "What if?" Questions

One of the most useful tasks you can perform with a spreadsheet program is to change values in a worksheet to see how the totals are affected. For example, you can ask yourself: "*If we spend $2,000 a month on payroll instead of $4,500, how much money will we save over six months?*" As soon as you change the values entered in the Payroll row, the totals are automatically updated. To complete Project 1, you will ask three "What if?" questions.

Format and Print the Budget

You will use a variety of the features in the Page Setup dialog box to produce an attractive printed version of your budget that includes a customized header and footer.

When you have completed the activities above, your budget will appear as shown in Figure P1-1.

FIGURE P1-1: Cape Cod Arts Council projected budget

Comma style

Currency style

Labels centered across columns

White text on black background

Border styles

Cape Cod Arts Council

North Shore Boathouse, R.R. #2, Mattapoisett, MA 02739

Projected Budget
January to June 1999

10/8/98

	January	February	March	April	May	June	Totals
Income							
Course Fees	$ 26,875.00	$ 26,875.00	$ 26,875.00	$ 26,875.00	$ 34,937.50	$ 34,937.50	$ 177,375.00
Grants	1,000.00	1,000.00	1,000.00	1,000.00	1,000.00	1,000.00	6,000.00
Donations	400.00	400.00	400.00	400.00	400.00	4,800.00	6,800.00
Total Income	$ 28,275.00	$ 28,275.00	$ 28,275.00	$ 28,275.00	$ 36,337.50	$ 40,737.50	$ 190,175.00
Expenses							
Payroll	$ 5,520.83	$ 5,520.83	$ 5,520.83	$ 5,520.83	$ 5,520.83	$ 5,520.83	$ 33,125.00
Lease	600.00	600.00	600.00	600.00	600.00	600.00	3,600.00
Course Supplies	1,200.00	1,200.00	1,200.00	1,200.00	1,000.00	1,000.00	6,800.00
Maintenance	900.00	900.00	900.00	900.00	400.00	400.00	4,400.00
Computer Lease	400.00	400.00	400.00	400.00	400.00	400.00	2,400.00
Advertising	700.00	700.00	3,000.00	700.00	700.00	700.00	6,500.00
Total Expenses	$ 9,320.83	$ 9,320.83	$ 11,620.83	$ 9,320.83	$ 8,620.83	$ 8,620.83	$ 56,825.00
Profit	$ 18,954.17	$ 18,954.17	$ 16,654.17	$ 18,954.17	$ 27,716.67	$ 32,116.67	$ 133,350.00

activity:

Enter and Enhance Labels

You need to enter and enhance the name and address of the organization, the worksheet title, the current date, and the first series of labels.

steps:

1. Open a new worksheet, click the blank box to the left of the **A** at the top left corner of the worksheet to select the entire worksheet, click the **Font Size list arrow**, then click **12**

   A font size of 12 is selected for the entire worksheet.

2. Click cell **A1**, type **Cape Cod Arts Council**, press **[Enter]**, type the remaining labels as shown in Figure P1-2, then save your worksheet as **Projected Budget for Cape Cod Arts Council** on the disk where you plan to store all the files for this book.

   Next, you can enhance the labels you have typed with new fonts, font sizes, colors, and fills. You'll start by enhancing "Cape Cod Arts Council" in cell A1.

3. Click cell **A1**, click the **Font list arrow**, select **Comic Sans MS**, if it is available, or select **Britannic Bold**, click the **Font Size list arrow**, then select **24**

   Next, enhance cells A4 and A5 with a font size of 18.

Hint

Allthough the text extends into columns B and C, you only need to select cells A4 and A5—where the text originated.

4. Select cells **A4** and **A5**, click the **Font Size list arrow**, then select **18**

   Your next step is to center cells A1 to A5 across several columns, then add a fill color to selected cells.

5. Select cells **A1** to **H5** as shown in Figure P1-3, right-click on the selection, click **Format Cells**, click the **Alignment tab**, click the **Horizontal list arrow**, click **Center Across Selection**, click **OK**, select cells **A4** to **H5**, click the **Fill Color list arrow**, click the **black box**, then click away from the cells to deselect them

   You can no longer see the labels in cells A4 and A5. Next, change their color to white.

6. Select cells **A4** and **A5**, click the **Font Color list arrow**, then click the **white box**

   Next, use the Today function to enter the current date.

7. Click cell **A7**, click the **Paste Function button** ![fx] on the Standard toolbar, select **Date & Time** from the list under Function Category, select **Today** from the list under Function Name (you'll need to scroll down), click **OK**, click **OK**, select cells **A7** to **H7**, then click the **Merge and Center button** ![icon] on the Formatting toolbar

   Next, use the automatic fill feature to enter the labels for the months of the year from January to June.

8. Click cell **B9**, type **January**, press **[Enter]**, click cell **B9** again, position the mouse pointer over the handle in the lower, right corner, drag the ╋ to cell **G9**, then click the **Center button** ![icon] on the Formatting toolbar

   The six months from January to June appear and are centered.

9. Click cell **A10**, enter the labels required for cells **A10** to **A25** and cell **H9** as shown in Figure P1-4, click the **Spelling button** ![icon] on the Standard toolbar, correct any spelling errors, then save your worksheet

   Next, you will link two sheets in the current workbook, then calculate the total income and expenses.

Click here to select
the whole worksheet

FIGURE P1-2: **Labels for cells A1 to A5**

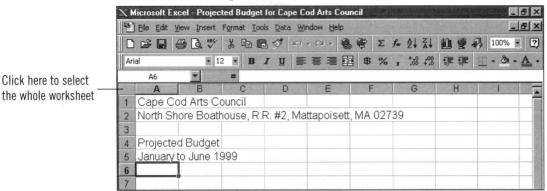

FIGURE P1-3: **Cells A1 to H5 selected**

Merge and Center
button

Fill Color list arrow

Font Color list arrow

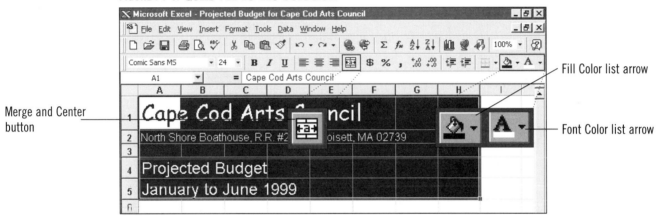

FIGURE P1-4: **Labels for cells A10 to A25 and H9**

Enter "Totals"
in cell H9

Labels for cells
A10 to A25

Clues to Use

Merging Cells

A merged cell is a single cell created by combining two or more cells. The cell reference for the merged cell is the upper, left cell in the original selected range. When you merge a range of cells, only the data in the upper, left cell of the range is included in the merged cell. If you want to center several rows of data across columns, select the cells, then use the Alignment tab in the Format Cells dialog box. If you want to center the data in only one cell across several columns, then you can use the Merge and Center button on the Formatting toolbar.

PROJECTED BUDGET FOR CAPE COD ARTS COUNCIL

activity:

Calculate Totals

You now need to enter the income and expenses that Cape Cod Arts Council expects in 1999. After you have entered the values, you will calculate the average monthly course fees collected and then the total income and expenses.

steps:

1. Position the mouse pointer on the column divider line between **A** and **B** on the worksheet frame so it changes to ✛, then double-click to increase the width of column A to fit all the labels in cells A10 to A25

   You are now ready to enter the values required for your budget.

2. Click cell **B12** then enter the values for January as shown in Figure P1-5

   Next, use the Fill feature to enter the same values for all six months.

3. Select cells **B12** to **B22**, position the mouse pointer over the handle in the lower right corner of cell **B22**, then drag across to cell **G22**

   The values in cells B12 to B22 appear in cells C12 to G22. Now you need to estimate the course fees you hope to make each month in 1999. You know that approximately 5,000 people took courses in 1998 in three payment categories: adults, children/seniors, and school groups. You will use a new blank worksheet to calculate the average course fee in each category for 1999, based on the total fees collected in 1998. Use a new worksheet to avoid cluttering the current worksheet with data that won't be printed.

Hint

You will need to use your mouse to widen column A so that the labels are clearly visible and then center and bold the labels in cells A1 to E1.

4. Click the **Sheet2 tab** at the bottom of your worksheet, then enter and enhance the labels and values as shown in Figure P1-6

   Next, calculate the course fees for each category.

5. Click cell **E2**, enter the formula **=B2*C2*D2**, then press **[Enter]**

   You should see 110000 in cell E2. If not, check your formula and try again.

6. With cell **E2** selected, drag the corner handle down to cell **E4**, click cell **E5**, then double-click the **AutoSum button** Σ on the Standard toolbar

   The course fees collected should be 156250 or $156,250. Now you need to display the average *course fees for each month in Sheet1. You will first calculate the fees for January by entering a formula in cell B11 of Sheet1 that divides the value in cell E5 of Sheet2 by six (for six months).*

7. Click the **Sheet1 tab**, click cell **B11**, enter the formula **=Sheet2!E5/6**, press **[Enter]**, then drag the corner handle of cell **B11** across to cell **G11**

   Ooops! Cells C11 through G11 contain zeroes. Why? If you click cell C11 and look at the formula entered in the formula bar at the top of the worksheet, you will see =Sheet2!F5/6. There is no value in cell F5 of Sheet2. To correct this, you need to enter a formula that designates cell E5 as an absolute *value.*

8. Click cell **B11**, drag I across **E5** in the formula bar, press **[F4]**, press **[Enter]**, then fill cells **C11** to **G11** with the new formula   *absolute value $*

   You will see 26042 in cells B11 to G11. Next, calculate the total income and expenses.

Time To
✓ **Save**

9. Select cells **B11** to **H14**, click Σ, select cells **B17** to **H23**, then click Σ again

   The total income in cell H14 is 164650, and the total expenses in cell H23 are 46800, as shown in Figure P1-7. Go on to calculate the profit and ask a series of "What if" questions.

FIGURE P1-5: Values for cells B12 to B22

	A	B	C	D	E	F	G	H
9		January	February	March	April	May	June	Totals
10	Income							
11	Course Fees							
12	Grants	1000						
13	Donations	400						
14	Total Income							
15								
16	Expenses							
17	Payroll	4500						
18	Lease	600						
19	Course Supplies	1200						
20	Maintenance	400						
21	Computer Lease	400						
22	Advertising	700						
23	Total Expenses							
24								
25	Profit							

Sheet2 tab

Sheet1 / Sheet2 / Sheet3 /

Ready   NUM

Start   Microsoft Excel - Proj...   5:15 AM

FIGURE P1-6: Sheet2 labels and values

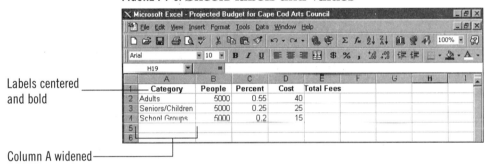

Microsoft Excel - Projected Budget for Cape Cod Arts Council

File Edit View Insert Format Tools Data Window Help

Arial   10   B   I   U

H19

	A	B	C	D	E	F	G	H	I
1	Category	People	Percent	Cost	Total Fees				
2	Adults	5000	0.55	40					
3	Seniors/Children	5000	0.25	25					
4	School Groups	5000	0.2	15					
5									
6									

Labels centered and bold

Column A widened

FIGURE P1-7: Worksheet completed with totals

	A	B	C	D	E	F	G	H
9		January	February	March	April	May	June	Totals
10	Income							
11	Course Fees	26042	26042	26042	26042	26042	26042	156250
12	Grants	1000	1000	1000	1000	1000	1000	6000
13	Donations	400	400	400	400	400	400	2400
14	Total Income	27442	27442	27442	27442	27442	27442	164650
15								
16	Expenses							
17	Payroll	4500	4500	4500	4500	4500	4500	27000
18	Lease	600	600	600	600	600	600	3600
19	Course Supplies	1200	1200	1200	1200	1200	1200	7200
20	Maintenance	400	400	400	400	400	400	2400
21	Computer Lease	400	400	400	400	400	400	2400
22	Advertising	700	700	700	700	700	700	4200
23	Total Expenses	7800	7800	7800	7800	7800	7800	46800
24								
25	Profit							

Total income

Total expenses

Sheet1 / Sheet2 / Sheet3 /

Ready   NUM

Start   Microsoft Excel - Proj...   5:34 AM

Clues to Use

Relative and Absolute References

*By default Microsoft Excel considers all values entered in formulas as relative values. That is, Excel will change all cell addresses in a formula when you copy it to a new location. If you do not want Excel to change the cell address of a value when you copy it, you must make the value **absolute**. To do this, you enter a dollar sign ($) before both the column and row designation in the address. You can also press [F4] to insert the symbol. For example, $C$26 tells Excel that the reference to cell C26 must not change, even if you copy the formula to a new location in the worksheet.*

PROJECTED BUDGET FOR CAPE COD ARTS COUNCIL

activity:

Ask "What if?" Questions

You need to calculate the profit you expect to make in each of the first six months of 1999, then perform the calculations required to answer three "What if?" questions.

steps:

Hint

To calculate percentage, multiply the total amount by the percentage amount expressed as a decimal. For example 300*.07 will calculate 7% of 300.

Hint

To enter new values in a cell that already contains values, just click on the cell and type the values. They will automatically replace the existing values.

1. Click cell **B25**, enter the formula **=B14-B23**, press [**Enter**], then copy the formula across to cell **H25** as shown in Figure P1-8

   The total profit for the first six months of 1998 is 117850 in cell H25. This profit will change when you make new calculations to answer the "What if?" questions. The first question is, "what if you raise the adult course fee to $60?" To answer this question you need to change the course fee entered in Sheet2.

2. Click the **Sheet2 tab**, click cell **D2**, type **60**, press [**Enter**], then click the **Sheet1 tab**

   Your total profit in cell H25 is 172850. Good news! However, a course fee increase could result in a 20% drop in the number of students you can expect in 1999. Next, display Sheet2 again and enter a formula that subtracts 20% of 5000 from the total number of adult course fees (5000).

3. Click the **Sheet2 tab**, click cell **B2**, enter the formula **=5000-(5000*.2)**, press [**Enter**], copy cell **B2** to cells **B3** and **B4** as shown in Figure P1-9, then click the **Sheet1 tab**

   The new profit is 130600—quite a reduction from 172850! Perhaps you shouldn't raise the adult course fees to $60, if the result is a 20% drop in the number of people who take courses.

4. Return to **Sheet2**, change the cost of the adult course fee to **40** and the number of people in cells **B2** to **B4** to **5000**, then return to **Sheet1**

   The results of the first "What if?" question led you to return to your original profit of 117850 in cell H25. The next question is, "What if you launch a $3,000 advertising campaign in March?"

5. Click cell **D22** in Sheet1, type **3000**, then press [**Enter**]

   Your total profit for the six months (cell H25) is now reduced to 115550 from 117850. However, a major advertising campaign launched in March could lead to a 30% increase in revenue from course fees in May and June. Next, edit the formula in cells F11 and G11 to reflect this projected 30% increase.

6. Click cell **F11**, click at the *end* of the formula displayed on the formula bar, type ***1.3**, press [**Enter**], then copy the formula to cell **G11**

   The new total profit in cell H25 is 131175. The next question is, "What if you hire a full-time administrative assistant for $24,500 per year?" You need to divide this amount by 12 to determine the monthly rate, then add the total to the values entered in the Payroll row.

7. Click cell **B17**, enter the formula **=(24500/12)+4500**, press [**Enter**], then copy the formula across to cell **G17**

   Your total profit is now 118925. Perhaps you should hire a part-time administrative assistant instead.

Trouble

If your results are different, ensure that your formula in cell B17 adds 4500 to 24500 divided by 2 *and* 12. Remember to use parentheses to control the order of operations.

8. Change the formula in cell **B17** so that it adds **4500** to *half* of **24500** divided by **12**, press [**Enter**], then copy the formula across to cell **G17**

   The value in cell B17 will be 5520.8, and the total profit in cell H25 will be 125050. Next, change some more values in the worksheet to reflect anticipated changes to the budget.

9. Increase Maintenance costs to **$900** per month from **January** through **April**, reduce Course Supplies costs to **$1000** per month in **May** and **June**, raise the course fee for School Groups to **$20**, then change the donation for **June** to **$4,800**

   Your total profit in cell H25 should now be 133350. Compare your worksheet with Figure P1-10.

FIGURE P1-8: Formula in cell B25 copied to cell H25

Microsoft Excel - Projected Budget for Cape Cod Arts Council

File Edit View Insert Format Tools Data Window Help

Arial 12

B25 = =B14-B23 —————————————— Formula in cell B25

	A	B	C	D	E	F	G	H
21	Computer Lease	400	400	400	400	400	400	2400
22	Advertising	700	700	700	700	700	700	4200
23	Total Expenses	7800	7800	7800	7800	7800	7800	46800
24								
25	Profit	19642	19642	19642	19642	19642	19642	117850
26								
27								

—— Total profit

FIGURE P1-9: Formula in cell B2 copied to cells B3 and B4

Microsoft Excel - Projected Budget for Cape Cod Arts Council

File Edit View Insert Format Tools Data Window Help

Arial 10

B2 = =5000-(5000*0.2) ————————————— Formula in cell B2

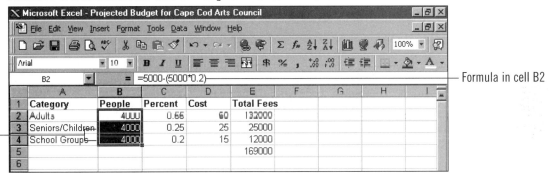

Formula copied to
cells B3 and B4

	A	B	C	D	E	F	G	H	I
1	Category	People	Percent	Cost	Total Fees				
2	Adults	4000	0.66	60	132000				
3	Seniors/Children	4000	0.25	25	25000				
4	School Groups	4000	0.2	15	12000				
5					169000				
6									

FIGURE P1-10: Worksheet with completed budget

	A	B	C	D	E	F	G	H
9		January	February	March	April	May	June	Totals
10	Income							
11	Course Fees	26875	26875	26875	26875	34937.5	34938	177375
12	Grants	1000	1000	1000	1000	1000	1000	6000
13	Donations	400	400	400	400	400	4800	6800
14	Total Income	28275	28275	28275	28275	36337.5	40738	190175
15								
16	Expenses							
17	Payroll	5520.8	5520.8	5520.8	5520.8	5520.83	5520.8	33125
18	Lease	600	600	600	600	600	600	3600
19	Course Supplies	1200	1200	1200	1200	1000	1000	6800
20	Maintenance	900	900	900	900	400	400	4400
21	Computer Lease	400	400	400	400	400	400	2400
22	Advertising	700	700	3000	700	700	700	6500
23	Total Expenses	9320.8	9320.8	11621	9320.8	8620.83	8620.8	56825
24								
25	Profit	18954	18954	16654	18954	27716.7	32117	133350

Sheet1 / Sheet2 / Sheet3 /

Ready NUM

Start Microsoft Excel - Proj... 5:54 AM

activity:

Format and Print the Budget

Now you need to display values in the Currency or Comma styles, add border lines to selected cells, use a variety of Page Setup features, and then print a copy of your budget.

Trouble

If the column widths did not automatically increase, click Format on the menu bar, point to Column, then click AutoFit Selection.

steps:

1. Select cells **B11** to **H11**, then click the **Currency Style button** on the Formatting toolbar

   The widths of columns B to H automatically increased.

2. Select cells **B12** to **H13**, click the **Comma Style button** on the Formatting toolbar, select cells **B14** to **H14**, then click

   Format the remaining cells.

3. Format cells **B18** to **H22** as **Comma style**, and format cells **B17** to **H17**, **B23** to **H23**, and **B25** to **H25** as **Currency style**

   Next, enclose selected cells with border lines.

Hint

You need to deselect the cell to see the borders.

4. Select cells **B14** to **H14**, click the **Borders list arrow** on the Formatting toolbar, then select the **Single top/Double bottom** border style as shown in Figure P1-11

   A single line appears above cells B14 to H14, and a double line appears below them.

5. Add the **Single top/Double bottom** border style to cells **B23** to **H23**, then add the **Double bottom** border style to cells **B25** to **H25**

6. Center and bold the heading "Totals" in cell **H9**, then enhance cells **B9** to **G9**, **A10**, **A14**, **A16**, **A23**, and **A25** to **H25** with **bold**

   Next, display your budget in the Print Preview screen, then select a variety of options from the Print Setup dialog boxes in order to format your budget attractively on the printed page.

7. Click the **Print Preview button** on the Standard toolbar, click **Setup**, click the **Landscape option button** and the **Fit to 1 page option button**, then click the **Margins tab**

   In the Margins dialog box, you will center the budget horizontally and vertically on the page and then display the Header/Footer dialog box.

Time To
✓ Save
✓ Print
✓ Close the workbook

8. Click the **Horizontal** and **Vertical check boxes**, click the **Header/Footer tab**, click **Custom Header**, enter the text for the header as shown in Figure P1-12, click **OK**, then click **OK** again

   The budget for the Cape Cod Arts Council is complete. Compare your print preview screen with Figure P1-13.

FIGURE P1-11: Border styles

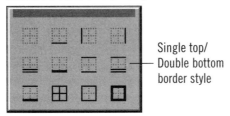

Single top/
Double bottom
border style

FIGURE P1-12: Custom header

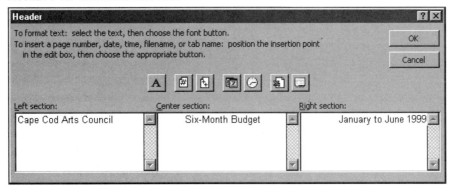

FIGURE P1-13: Completed worksheet in print preview

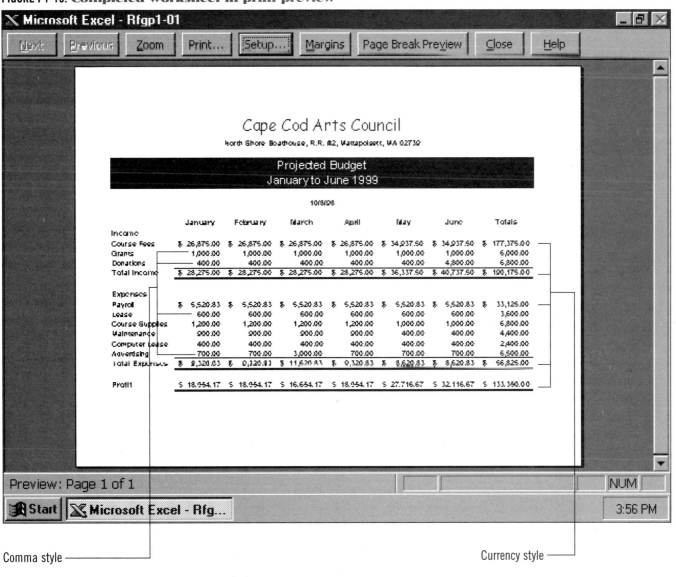

Comma style

Currency style

OVERVIEW

Loan Amortization to Lease or Buy a Car

You have decided to purchase a car that costs $12,400.00. Your monthly net income (after taxes) is $2,024.80. You need to decide whether to lease the car over three years or buy the car with the aid of a bank loan for $12,400.00. You will **Set Up a Loan Worksheet** and **Evaluate Options** to help you make an informed decision.

activity:

Set Up a Loan Worksheet

Hint

When you want to enter a value that you will then format as a percent, enter the value as a decimal. For example you would enter 10% as .1, then click the Percent Style button.

steps:

1. Open a new workbook, then set up the worksheet so that it appears as shown in Figure P2-1
Next, enter the interest rate percentage for the car lease option in cell B6.

2. Click cell **B6**, type **.18** press [**Enter**], click cell **B6** again, then click the **Percent Style button** 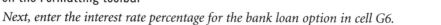 on the Formatting toolbar
Next, enter the interest rate percentage for the bank loan option in cell G6.

3. Click cell **G6**, type **.11**, press [**Enter**], then format cell **G6** in the **Percent Style**
Now that you know the retail price of the car ($12,400.00) and the interest rates for both a three-year lease and a bank loan, you need to calculate the total interest you will pay for each option. To calculate the total interest, you will multiply the Retail Price by the Interest Rate for both options.

4. Click cell **C6**, then enter the formula **=$A$6*B6** to calculate the total interest paid on the retail price for a three-year lease, then widen the column
The total interest you pay on a three-year lease is $2,232.00.

5. Copy cell **C6** to cell **H6**, then widen the column
The relative cell reference in the formula adjusted for cell H6, but the absolute reference to cell A6 remained constant. The total interest you will pay on a three-year loan is $1,364.00. Next, determine the monthly payment required for each option by adding the Retail Price to the Total Interest and dividing the total by 36.

6. Click cell **D6**, enter the formula **=($A$6+C6)/36**, press [**Enter**], then display the value in the **Currency Style**

7. Copy cell **D6** to cell **I6** to calculate the monthly payment on a bank loan
Compare your worksheet with Figure P2-2. As you can see, the monthly payment for a three-year lease is $406.44, while the monthly payment for a bank loan is $382.33. The monthly payment on a bank loan is less than the monthly payment on a three-year lease. However, what about resale value, and, more important, what about your monthly expenses? Can you really afford a new car?

8. Save your worksheet as **Car Planning Budget**

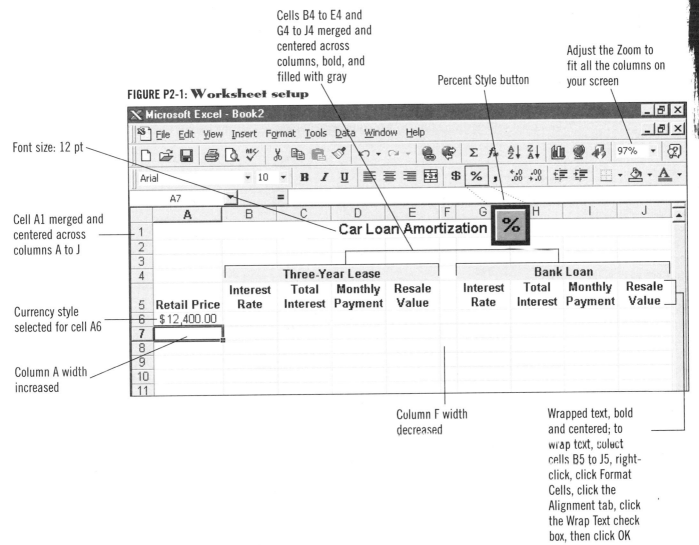

Cells B4 to E4 and G4 to J4 merged and centered across columns, bold, and filled with gray

Adjust the Zoom to fit all the columns on your screen

Percent Style button

FIGURE P2-1: **Worksheet setup**

Font size: 12 pt

Cell A1 merged and centered across columns A to J

Currency style selected for cell A6

Column A width increased

Column F width decreased

Wrapped text, bold and centered; to wrap text, select cells B5 to J5, right-click, click Format Cells, click the Alignment tab, click the Wrap Text check box, then click OK

FIGURE P2-2: **First row calculations added**

	Retail Price	Interest Rate	Total Interest	Monthly Payment	Resale Value		Interest Rate	Total Interest	Monthly Payment	Resale Value
			Three-Year Lease					Bank Loan		
6	$12,400.00	18%	$2,232.00	$406.44			11%	$1,364.00	$382.33	

I6 = =($A$6+H6)/36

PROJECT 2 LOAN AMORTIZATION TO LEASE OR BUY A CAR

activity:

Evaluate Options

The three-year lease plan includes a buyout feature. You can pay $2,000 at the end of three years to own your car. If you purchase the car with a bank loan, you will own the car outright. In both cases you need to determine how much your car will be worth at the end of three years.

Hint

Straight Line Depreciation is based on the assumption that depreciation of an asset (such as a car) depends only on time. The depreciable expense of the asset is therefore spread evenly over a period of time (such as three years). Another method is **accelerated depreciation**, where the expense is higher in the early years of the life of the asset.

steps:

1. Click cell **E6**, enter the formula =($A$6*0.2*3)-2000, press [Enter], then display the result in the **Currency Style** and widen the column

   The resale value is $5,440.00. The formula you entered calculates the straight line depreciation by multiplying the Retail Price by 20% and then multiplying this result by 3 (for three years). You subtracted the $2,000 from the resale value because you would pay an extra $2,000 at the end of three years to own the car. Next, calculate the resale value of the car for the bank loan option.

2. Click cell **J6**, enter the formula to multiply the retail price by **20%** and **3**, then press [Enter]

   The resale value will be $7,440.00. Next, calculate the loss you will sustain by selling the car.

3. Right-click in any cell in column **F**, click **Insert**, click the **Entire column** option button, click **OK**, type **Loss** in cell **F5**, then enter a formula in cell **F6** that subtracts the Resale Value from the sum of Total Interest, Retail Price, and $2,000

   The loss you will sustain is $11,192.00.

4. Type and enhance **Loss** in cell **L5**, click cell **L6**, enter the formula =(A6+I6)-K6 to calculate the loss you will sustain in the bank loan option, then extend the cell merge to cell **L4**

   The three-year lease option allows you to trade in your car at the end of three years and then lease a new car. You will always drive a new or near-new car—which may compensate for never owning a car. You could lose $6,324.00 when you try to sell the car you bought with the aid of a bank loan. But can you afford either option? Answer this question by creating a personal budget.

5. Click cell **A10**, enter and enhance the labels and values as shown in Figure P2-3 for Step 5, then widen columns as necessary

   The insurance on the new car will be $1,100 per year, and gas will be $840 a year. Start by determining whether you can afford to lease a car.

6. Click cell **B19**, type =D6 (the cell address of the monthly payment for a three-year lease), press [Enter], then enter the formulas shown in Figure P2-3 for cells B20 to B26 and format the cells

   Your surplus in cell B26 is a negative number: ($24.62). You obviously cannot afford to lease a car for $406.44 per month. Can you afford to buy a car with the aid of a bank loan?

7. Click cell **B19**, enter the cell address of the bank loan monthly payment, then press [Enter]

   The value in cell B26 is $1.90. Now find out what car you could afford based on your own monthly income and expenses.

Time To
✓ **Save**
✓ **Close your workbook**

8. Enter your own monthly expenses in cells **A14** to **A21** (add new rows if necessary), enter a variety of retail prices in cell **A6** until you find a price that you can afford, add the current date, then format and print your Car Planning Budget in landscape so that it appears similar to the illustration in Figure P2-4

   Note that your totals will differ, depending upon your monthly expenses and the retail price.

FIGURE P2-3: **Expense calculations**

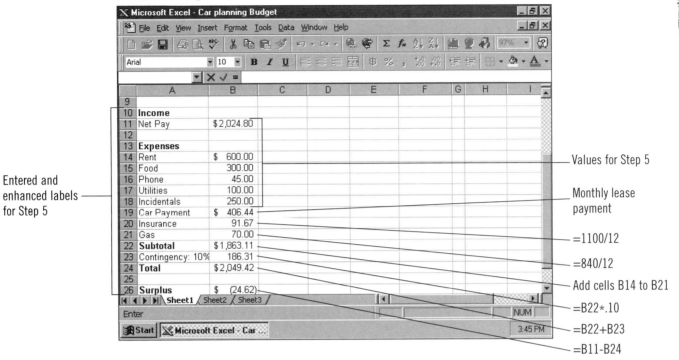

Entered and enhanced labels for Step 5

Values for Step 5

Monthly lease payment

=1100/12

=840/12

Add cells B14 to B21

=B22*.10

=B22+B23

=B11-B24

FIGURE P2-4: **Completed car planning budget**

Car Loan Amortization   Sheet1   [Your Name]

Car Loan Amortization

| | | Three-Year Lease | | | | | Bank Loan | | | |
Retail Price	Interest Rate	Total Interest	Monthly Payment	Resale Value	Loss	Interest Rate	Total Interest	Monthly Payment	Resale Value	Loss
$ 12,400.00	18%	$ 2,232.00	$ 406.44	$ 5,440.00	$ 11,192.00	11%	$ 1,364.00	$ 382.33	$ 7,440.00	$ 6,324.00

Income
Net Pay $ 2,024.80

Expenses

Rent	$ 600.00
Food	300.00
Phone	45.00
Utilities	100.00
Incidentals	250.00
Car Payment	$ 382.33
Insurance	91.67
Gas	70.00
Subtotal	$ 1,839.00
Contingency: 10%	183.90
Total	$ 2,022.90
Surplus	$ 1.90

Page 1

OVERVIEW

Planning a Budget for a European Vacation

You are planning a five-week trip to Europe with a friend. Your budget for the trip is $5,000. Before you buy your plane ticket, you need to determine how much you can spend on airfare, accommodations, food, entertainment, and transportation. You may *want* to stay in first-class hotels, but your $5,000 budget may not extend that far. What kind of trip can you really afford? For this project you will **Set Up a Vacation Planning Budget** and **Reduce Trip Costs** to create a spreadsheet that will help you to plan a European vacation that you will remember for a lifetime.

activity:

Set Up a Vacation Planning Budget

Hint

To right align the labels in cells D13 to D15, type the labels in these cells, then select them and click the Align Right button ≣.

Hint

Resize columns if necessary.

steps:

1. Set up your worksheet so that it appears as shown in Figure P3-1
   Next, vertically align the labels in cells B4 to E4.

2. Select cells **B4** to **E4**, click the **right mouse button**, click **Format Cells**, click the **Alignment tab**, make sure **Center** is selected in the Horizontal section, click **Top** in the Vertical section, drag the **red diamond** in the Orientation section down so the spin box shows -90 Degrees, as shown in Figure P3-2, then click **OK**
   Your next step is to enter the formulas required to calculate your total expenses.

3. Click cell **E5**, enter the formula =**C5*D5**, press [**Enter**], then copy the formula down to cell **E11**

4. Click cell **E13**, then double-click the **AutoSum button** Σ on the Standard toolbar to calculate the Subtotal

5. Click cell **E14**, calculate a **15%** contingency on the **Subtotal**, then click cell **E15** and add the **Subtotal** to the **Contingency** to determine your Total Expenses

6. Display the values in cells **E5**, **E13**, and **E15** in the **Currency Style** and the remaining values in column **E** in the **Comma Style**
   Compare your worksheet with Figure P3-3. Your total expenses in cell E15 are $6,563.05. You are $1,563.05 over your budget of $5,000.

7. Save your budget as **Europe Trip**
   Next, you will go on to perform a series of calculations to reduce your trip expenses to your $5,000 budget.

FIGURE P3-1: Worksheet setup

Font size: 24 pt ──

Font size: 14 pt ──

Display the value in cell C5 in the Currency style and the values in cells C6 to C11 in the Comma style

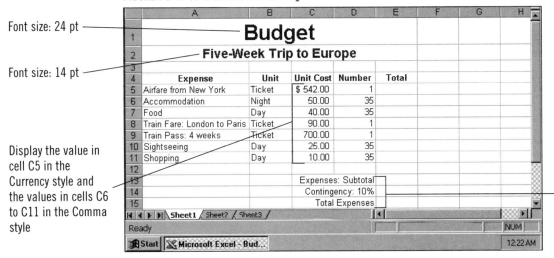

To right-align D13 to D15, select the cells and click the Align Right button

FIGURE P3-2: Format Cells dialog box

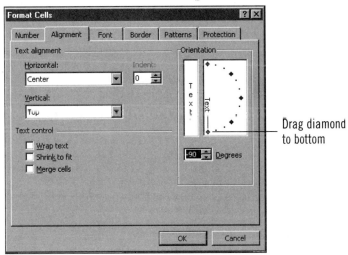

Drag diamond to bottom

FIGURE P3-3: Worksheet with expenses

	Expense	Unit	Unit Cost	Number	Total			
5	Airfare from New York	Ticket	$ 542.00	1	$ 542.00			
6	Accommodation	Night	50.00	35	1,750.00			
7	Food	Day	40.00	35	1,400.00			
8	Train Fare: London to Paris	Ticket	90.00	1	90.00			
9	Train Pass: 4 weeks	Ticket	700.00	1	700.00			
10	Sightseeing	Day	25.00	35	875.00			
11	Shopping	Day	10.00	35	350.00			
12								
13				Expenses: Subtotal	$5,707.00			
14				Contingency: 10%	856.05			
15				Total Expenses	$6,563.05			
16								

Ready

Start | Microsoft Excel - Bud... | 12:24 AM

PROJECT 3 **PLANNING A BUDGET FOR A EUROPEAN VACATION**

activity:

Reduce Trip Costs

To reduce the trip cost to $5,000, you will perform a variety of calculations to answer several "What if?" questions, then format and print your trip planning budget. As you perform the calculations in Steps 1 through 8, check the total in cell E15 against the totals provided. You will need to think carefully about the calculations required. For some steps you will need to insert new rows.

Hint

You may want to make a copy of the worksheet in Sheet2 in case you want to start over.

steps:

1. What if you reduce your sightseeing allowance to $20 a day?
   Total expenses are now $6,361.80.

2. What if you book a charter flight that costs $200 less than the current airfare?
   Total expenses are now $6,131.80.

3. What if you lease a car for four weeks at a cost of $435.72 per week, do not buy a train pass, and share the cost of the car lease with a friend?
   Total expenses are now $6,328.96.

4. What if you stay at campsites for 20 days ($22/night for two), stay in youth hostels for 10 days ($28.50/night for one), and then stay in hotels for the remaining 5 days ($120/night for two)?
   Note that you will need to insert two new rows for the various accommodation options. The total expenses are now $5,242.21.

5. What if you buy and cook your own food on the days that you camp, thereby reducing your food costs on those days to $25 a day?
   Note that your food costs will remain the same for the days that you do not camp. The total expenses are now $4,897.21.

6. If you lease a car, you will split gas costs with your friend during the four weeks that you have the car. You plan to drive approximately 3,000 kilometers; the car you plan to rent gets 12 kilometers to the liter; gas in Europe costs approximately $2.00 a liter
   The total expenses are now $5,184.71.

7. What if you decide not to go to England and save the cost of the train fare from London to Paris?
   The total expenses are now $5,081.21.

8. What if you reduce your contingency to 10%?
   The total expenses are now $4,860.28. You can afford to go to Europe now, although you will have to stick carefully to your budget.

9. Change the font size to **14** for cells **A4** to the end of the data, format and print your budget so that it appears similar to the illustration in Figure P3-4, then save and close the workbook

Trip Planning Budget   [Your Name]

Budget
Five-Week Trip to Europe

Expense	Unit	Unit Cost	Number	Total
Airfare from New York	Ticket	$ 342.00	1	$ 342.00
Hotels	Night	60.00	5	300.00
Campsites	Night	11.00	20	220.00
Youth Hostels	Night	28.50	10	285.00
Food	Day	40.00	15	600.00
Food: Camping	Day	25.00	20	500.00
Car Lease	Week	217.86	4	871.44
Gas	Liter	1.00	250	250.00
Sightseeing	Day	20.00	35	700.00
Shopping	Day	10.00	35	350.00

Expenses: Subtotal	$ 4,418.44
Contingency: 10%	441.84
Total Expenses	$ 4,860.28

Independent Challenges

INDEPENDENT CHALLENGE 1

Create your own personal budget for the next six months, then ask a series of "What if?" questions to help you make decisions regarding how you will spend your money. Fill in the boxes below with the required information, then set up your budget in an Excel worksheet, and perform the calculations required to answer a variety of "What if?" questions.

1. Determine your sources of income. You may receive money from a paycheck, from investment dividends, or from a student loan. Each income source requires a label and a row on your budget worksheet. In the box below list the income labels you will require:

> **Income labels:**
>
> 1. ....
> 2. ....
> 3. ....
> 4. ....
> 5. ....

2. Determine your expenses. At the very least you will probably need to list your rent, food, utilities, and phone. You may also need to list transportation costs such as car payments, gas, insurance, and bus fares. In addition include labels for entertainment, incidentals, and savings. In the box below list the expense labels you have identified:

> **Expense labels:**
>
> 1. ....   6. ....
> 2. ....   7. ....
> 3. ....   8. ....
> 4. ....   9. ....
> 5. ....   10. ....

3. Even a personal budget should be created for a specific purpose. For example you may wish to save for a vacation or to buy a car, or even just to live within a set income. Identify the goal of your budget in the box below:

> **Budget Goal:** ....
> ....

4. Set up your budget in Excel as follows:
   a. Enter and enhance a title for your budget in cell A1.
   b. Enter the current date (use the Today function).
   c. Enter the Income and Expense labels in column A.
   d. Determine the time frame of your budget (e.g., monthly, weekly, annual), then enter the appropriate labels starting in column B.
   e. Enter the values required for your income and expenses. Adjust expenses according to the time of year. For example, your utilities costs will probably be less in the summer than in the winter, while your entertainment and holiday expenses may rise in the summer.
   f. Calculate your total income and expenses.

g. Ask yourself at least ten "What if?" questions, and then make the calculations required to answer them. Here are some sample "What if?" questions:

- What if I move in March to a new apartment where my rent is 30% more than the current rent?
- What if I eat out in restaurants only twice a month?
- What if I take the bus or subway to work twice a week?
- What if I join a fitness club with monthly dues?
- What if I buy a car with payments of $250/month? Remember to factor in costs for insurance and gas.
- What if I start taking violin lessons?

Try to formulate questions that will help you to plan your finances to achieve the goals you have set.

h. Save your worksheet as "Personal Budget."
i. Format and print a copy of your budget.

INDEPENDENT CHALLENGE 2

Create a planning budget to help you determine your expenses for a vacation of your choice. The following tasks will help get you started.

1. Before you create the worksheet in Excel, answer the questions listed below:
   a. Where do you plan to go for your vacation?
   b. What is your proposed budget?
   c. How long is your planned vacation?
   d. What kind of activities do you plan to do on your vacation (e.g., sightseeing, guided tours, horseback riding, skiing, etc.)?
2. Set up your worksheet with labels for transportation costs (airfare, car rental, train fares, etc.), accommodations, food, sightseeing, shopping, and any other expense categories appropriate to the kind of vacation you plan to take.
3. Include a contingency amount for emergency expenses that is 10% to 15% of your total expenses.
4. Try to make your budget as realistic as possible. You can choose to base your budget on a vacation you have already taken or on a vacation you hope to take.
5. Save your vacation planning budget as "My Vacation Plan," then format and print a copy.

INDEPENDENT CHALLENGE 3

You have decided to purchase a computer system that costs $3,100 plus 8% sales tax. The computer system includes a laser printer, a modem, and all the software you require. You have to choose between buying the computer with the aid of a bank loan (11% annual interest) or leasing it at 20% interest per month for 36 months.

1. Create a worksheet that will help you to determine which option you should choose. Base your worksheet on the Car Loan Amortization you created in Project 2.
2. Take into account the probable resale value of your computer at the end of three years, given the continually changing computer market. Calculate the straight line depreciation at 25% per year for 3 years.
3. Copy the worksheet into Sheet2 of the worksheet you created for Project 2, then study the personal budget you created in Sheet1 to determine the payment options you can afford. Include formulas that link the two worksheets. For example if you enter =Sheet2!B6 in cell A10 of Sheet 1, the value in cell B6 of Sheet 2 will appear. If you change the value in cell B6 of Sheet2, the value in cell A10 of Sheet1 will also change.
4. Try to reduce some of your expenses in your personal budget so you can afford to purchase the computer.
5. Save your modified personal budget and the worksheet containing your Computer Purchase Plan as "Computer Purchasing Plan," then print a copy of both sheets.

INDEPENDENT CHALLENGE 4

Create the worksheet in Figure IC-1, then perform the calculations required to answer the questions provided.

FIGURE IC-1: **Personal budgeting**

	A	B	C	D	E	F	G	H
1		January						
2	**Income**							
3	Pay Check	2,397.35						
4	Investment Dividends							
5	**Total Income**							
6								
7	**Expenses**							
8	Rent	600.00						
9	Food	400.00						
10	Phone	60.00						
11	Utilities	110.00						
12	Car Payment	350.00						
13	Gas	80.00						
14	Car insurance	100.00						
15	**Total Expenses**							
16								
17	**Total Savings**							
18								
19								
20								

Sheet1 / Sheet2 / Sheet3 /

Ready

NUM

Start | X Microsoft Excel - Com...   1:47 PM

1. Use the AutoFill function to fill in the months from February to June.
2. Copy the values for January across to June.
3. Add a column labeled "Totals," then calculate the row totals and display all the values in the Comma Style.
4. Calculate the Monthly and Total Income and the Monthly and Total Expenses. Your total income is 14,384.10, your total expenses are 10,200.00, and your total savings are 4,184.10.
5. You will need to think carefully about the calculations required. For some questions you will need to insert new rows.

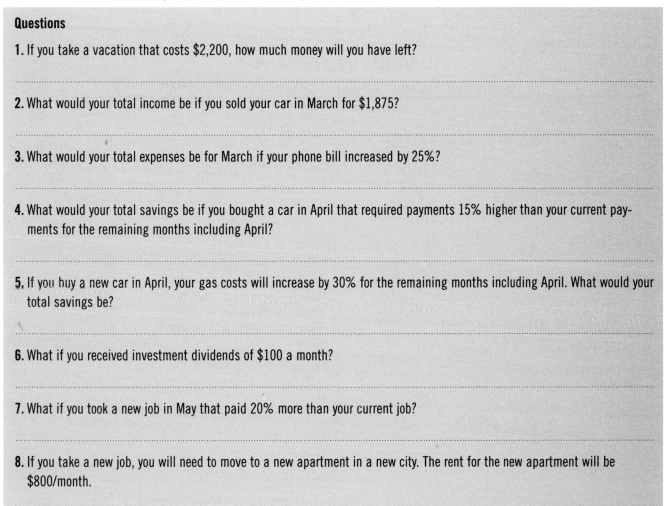

Questions

1. If you take a vacation that costs $2,200, how much money will you have left?

....

2. What would your total income be if you sold your car in March for $1,875?

....

3. What would your total expenses be for March if your phone bill increased by 25%?

....

4. What would your total savings be if you bought a car in April that required payments 15% higher than your current payments for the remaining months including April?

....

5. If you buy a new car in April, your gas costs will increase by 30% for the remaining months including April. What would your total savings be?

....

6. What if you received investment dividends of $100 a month?

....

7. What if you took a new job in May that paid 20% more than your current job?

....

8. If you take a new job, you will need to move to a new apartment in a new city. The rent for the new apartment will be $800/month.

....

6. When you have completed the questions above, add a title to the budget, format it attractively, save it as "Budget Practice," then print a copy.

Visual Workshop

Create the six-month budget as shown in Figure VW-1 for Web Wonders, a new company that provides Internet users with quick and easy access to the World Wide Web. Save the budget as "Web Wonders Budget" on your disk, then answer the following questions. Excel 5 Users: Save as WEB.XLS.

FIGURE VW-1: Web Wonders budget

	A	B	C	D	E	F	G	H
1				Web Wonders				
2				Proposed Six-Month Budget: July to September 1999				
3				[Current Date]				
4								
5		July	August	September	October	November	December	Totals
6	REVENUE							
7	Internet Subscriptions							
8	Homepage Server Space							
9	Total Revenue							
10								
11	EXPENSES							
12	Salaries	4500	4500	4500	7000	7000	4500	
13	Rent	1500	1500	1500	3500	3500	3500	
14	Equipment Leases	1000	1000	1500	2500	2500	2500	
15	Advertising	150	250	350	1200	1800	3500	
16	Operating Costs	350	350	350	780	780	780	
17	Total Expenses							
18								
19	PROFIT							
20								

Sheet1 / Sheet2 / Sheet3 /

Ready | NUM

Start | Microsoft Excel - We... | 1:57 PM

1. In July you estimate that 1000 Internet subscribers will join Web Wonders at a cost of $30 per subscriber. You project that the subscription revenue generated in July will increase by 5% in August, 10% in September, then 20% for each of the remaining months. Calculate all increases based on July revenue. What is the total revenue in cell H9?

2. In July you estimate that 50 subscribers will purchase space on the server for their homepages at a cost of $100 each. This revenue should increase by 30% each month to December. (Enter =B8*1.3 in cell C8, then copy the formula to cell G8.) What is the total revenue in cell H9?

3. Triple the October Salaries and Advertising expenses for November and December. What is the total Salaries expense? What is the total Advertising expense?

4. Quadruple the October equipment lease for November and December. What is the total Equipment Lease expense?

5. What is the total projected profit in cell H19?

6. Save the worksheet again, then preview and print it.

Microsoft
► Excel
Projects

Workbook Linking

In This Unit You Will Create:

PROJECT 1 ► **Simple Payroll**

PROJECT 2 ► **Record of Earnings**

PROJECT 3 ► **Travel Expense Reports**

You can enter a value in one worksheet, then enter just the sheet name and cell address of the value in up to 16 other worksheets in the same workbook. When you change the value in the first worksheet, all the values with the same cell address will also change—regardless of which worksheet contains them. This ability to link worksheets enables you to keep track of complex transactions such as payroll records and expenses. For example, you can enter the time sheet for all the employees of a company in one worksheet, the payroll record in another worksheet, and the payroll register that lists the deductions and amounts paid in yet another worksheet. Once you have set up these worksheets, you can simply change the hours in the time sheet—the amounts entered in the payroll record and payroll register are then updated automatically. You can also link worksheets in one workbook with worksheets in other workbooks to create links between two or more files. ► In this unit, you will create a variety of linked worksheets and workbooks to produce a simple payroll, a record of earnings, and a travel expense report.

Simple Payroll for The Marina Café

You run a small neighborhood restaurant called the Marina Café near the beach in Crescent City, California. Three employees work from 16 to 40 hours a week. Now that you have Microsoft Excel installed on your computer, you've decided to set up several worksheets in one workbook to contain the weekly payroll records that you will use to update the monthly payroll register. Three activities are required to complete the payroll for the Marina Café:

Project Activities

Set Up the Payroll Records

You will first create a payroll record for the week of August 2 to August 8, 1998, and then copy this record to three new worksheets for the remaining three weeks in August. The payroll record contains the hours that each employee worked. Figure P1-1 displays the weekly payroll record for August 2 to August 8, 1998.

Set Up the Payroll Register

You calculate each employee's net pay in a payroll register. The net pay is the amount that the employee actually receives in a paycheck after taxes and other deductions are subtracted. Figure P1-2 displays the payroll register completed at the end of August 1998 for the three employees of the Marina Café. This payroll register displays all the hours entered in the four payroll records completed during the month of August. In addition, the payroll register displays each employee's earnings and deductions. The largest deduction is for Federal Tax, followed by smaller deductions for Social Security, State Tax, and Medicare. Some payroll registers will also display additional deductions for parking, union dues, and pension funds. As shown in Figure P1-2, the employees at the Marina Café pay only the required deductions.

Calculate Monthly Wages

Once you have set up the payroll register, you will link it with the payroll records so that every time you make a change to a payroll record, the totals in the payroll register will be updated. You will then print the completed payroll register for the month of August so that it appears as shown in Figure P1-2.

FIGURE P1-1: **Payroll record for August 2 to August 8, 1998**

	A	B	C	D	E	F	G	H	I
1	**The Marina Café**								
2	**Weekly Payroll**								
3	**Week of August 2 to August 8, 1998**								
4									
5		**Marla MacDuff**	**Juliet Arias**	**Gregory Saunders**					
6	**Sun**	8	0	0					
7	**Mon**	8	4	4					
8	**Tue**	8	0	4					
9	**Wed**	8	8	0					
10	**Thu**	0	8	4					
11	**Fri**	8	8	0					
12	**Sat**	0	4	4					
13									
14	**Total Hours**	40	32	16					
15									

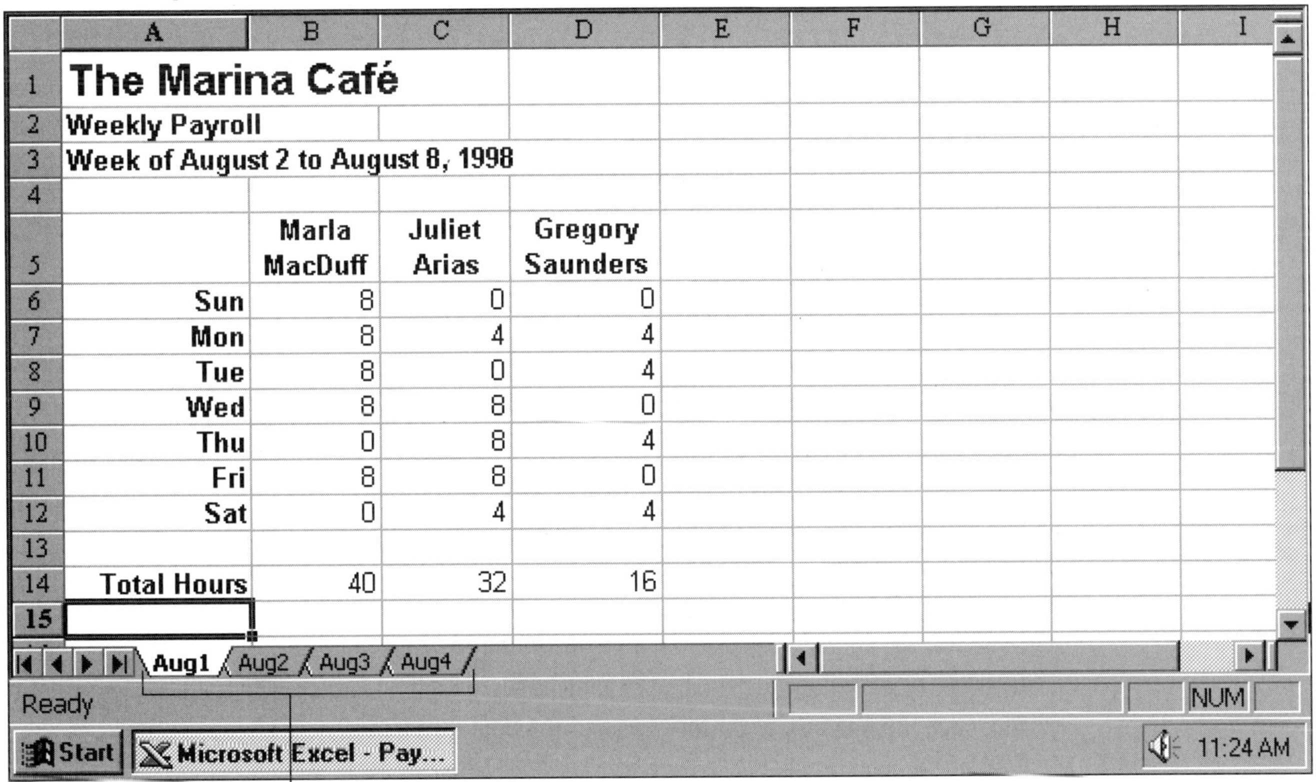

Tabs: **Aug1** / Aug2 / Aug3 / Aug4

Ready   NUM

Start   Microsoft Excel - Pay...   11:24 AM

Sheet tabs named for each week in August

FIGURE P1-2: **Completed payroll register for August 1998**

August Payroll Register   [Your Name]

The Marina Café
Monthly Payroll

Employee Data			Rate	Earnings	Deductions					Net Pay	
Name	**Tax-able**	**Allow-ances**			**Federal Tax**	**Social Security (6.3%)**	**Medicare (1.35%)**	**State Tax**	**Total Deductions**		
Marla MacDuff	M	4	$ 8.25	$ 1,196.25	$ 110.75	$ 75.36	$ 16.15	$ 24.50	$ 220.76	$ 969.49	124
Juliet Arias	S	2	$ 7.50	$ 918.75	$ 92.45	$ 57.88	$ 12.40	$ 19.75	$ 182.48	$ 736.27	125
Gregory Saunders	S	3	$ 7.00	$ 504.00	$ 48.50	$ 31.75	$ 6.80	$ 14.50	$ 101.56	$ 402.44	126

Total net pay for each employee

activity:

Set Up the Payroll Records

You need to enter and enhance the labels for one payroll record, enter the hours that each employee worked each day, and then calculate the total hours worked. You will then copy the payroll record into three new worksheets so that you have four records—one for each week in August—and then adjust the hours worked by each employee in each week.

steps:

1 Open a blank Excel worksheet, enter and enhance the labels in cells **A1** to **A3** as shown in Figure P1-3, then save the workbook as **Payroll Records for the Marina Cafe** to the disk where you plan to store all the files for this book

2 Click cell **B5**, type **Marla MacDuff**, press **[Tab]**, type **Juliet Arias**, press **[Tab]**, type **Gregory Saunders**, press **[Enter]**, select cells **B5** to **D5**, click the **right mouse button**, click **Format Cells**, click the **Alignment tab**, select **Center** in both the **Horizontal and Vertical** sections, click the **Wrap Text check** box to select it, click **OK**, click the **Bold button** **B**, then slightly increase the size of column **D** so that Gregory Saunders' complete name appears on two lines
   Next, enter the days of the week from Sunday to Saturday in cells A6 to A12.

3 Click cell **A6**, type **Sun**, drag the corner handle down to cell **A12**, then with cells **A6** to **A12** still selected, click the **Align Right button** and the **Bold button**
   The days of the week from Sunday to Saturday appear! Next, enter the hours that each employee worked from Sunday, August 2 to Saturday, August 8.

4 Click cell **B6**, enter the values in cells **B6** to **D12** as shown in Figure P1-3, select cells **B6** to **D14**, then click the **AutoSum button** **Σ**

5 Enter and enhance **Total Hours** in cell **A14** as shown in Figure P1-3, then widen column A
   Next, name the sheet tabs for each of the four payroll records required.

6 Double-click the **Sheet1 tab**, type **Aug1**, press **[Enter]**, right-click the **Sheet2 tab**, click **Insert**, click **OK** to insert a new worksheet, then name the sheet tabs **Aug2**, **Aug3**, and **Aug4** as shown in Figure P1-3

7 Click the **Aug1 tab**, select cells **A1** to **D14**, click the **Copy button** , click the **Aug2 tab**, click the **Paste button** , click the **Aug3 tab**, click the **Paste button**, then paste the record into the **Aug4** sheet
   Next, modify the hours that the employees worked in each week.

8 As shown in the table below, change only the hours for each employee on the days and weeks specified (do not change any other hours), change the dates in cell **A3** in each worksheet as indicated, and widen columns **A** and **D** as needed in each sheet

	Marla MacDuff	Juliet Arias	Gregory Saunders
AUG2 **August 9 to August 15**	5 hours on Monday	7 hours on Friday	6 hours on Tuesday
AUG3 **August 16 to August 22**	0 hours on Wednesday	7.5 hours on Friday	8 hours on Saturday
AUG4 **August 23 to August 29**	4 hours on Tuesday	4 hours on Thursday	6 hours on Saturday

9 Check the hourly totals for each payroll record against Figures P1-4, P1-5, and P1-6, then save the workbook
   Next, go on to create the payroll register for the month of August.

FIGURE P1-3: Completed payroll record for August 2

16 pt.

	A	B	C	D	E	F	G	H	I
1	**The Marina Café**								
2	Weekly Payroll								
3	Week of August 2 to August 8, 1998								
4									
5		Marla MacDuff	Juliet Arias	Gregory Saunders					
6	Sun	8	0	0					
7	Mon	8	4	4					
8	Tue	8	0	4					
9	Wed	8	8	0					
10	Thu	0	8	4					
11	Fri	8	8	0					
12	Sat	0	4	4					
13									
14	Total Hours	40	32	16					
15									

Label right-aligned and bolded

Aug1 / Aug2 / Aug3 / Aug4

Ready   NUM

Start Microsoft Excel - Pay...   11:32 AM

Sheet tabs named

FIGURE P1-4: Payroll record in the Aug2 sheet

	A	B	C	D	E	F	G	H	I
1	**The Marina Café**								
2	Weekly Payroll								
3	Week of August 9 to August 22, 1998								
4									
5		Marla MacDuff	Juliet Arias	Gregory Saunders					
6	Sun	8	0	0					
7	Mon	5	4	4					
8	Tue	8	0	6					
9	Wed	8	8	0					
10	Thu	0	8	4					
11	Fri	8	7	0					
12	Sat	0	4	4					
13									
14	Total Hours	37	31	18					
15									

Aug1 \ Aug2 / Aug3 \ Aug

Ready

Start Microsoft Excel - Pay...

FIGURE P1-5: Payroll record in the Aug3 sheet

	A	B	C	D	E	F	G	H
1	**The Marina Café**							
2	Weekly Payroll							
3	Week of August 16 to August 22, 1998							
4								
5		Marla MacDuff	Juliet Arias	Gregory Saunders				
6	Sun	8	0	0				
7	Mon	8	4	4				
8	Tue	8	0	4				
9	Wed	0	8	0				
10	Thu	0	8	4				
11	Fri	8	7.5	0				
12	Sat	0	4	8				
13								
14	Total Hours	32	31.5	20				
15								

Aug1 / Aug2 \ Aug3 \ Aug

Ready

Start Microsoft Excel - Pay...

FIGURE P1-6: Payroll record in the Aug4 sheet

	A	B	C	D	E	F	G	H
1	**The Marina Café**							
2	Weekly Payroll							
3	Week of August 23 to August 29, 1998							
4								
5		Marla MacDuff	Juliet Arias	Gregory Saunders				
6	Sun	8	0	0				
7	Mon	8	4	4				
8	Tue	4	0	4				
9	Wed	8	8	0				
10	Thu	0	4	4				
11	Fri	8	8	0				
12	Sat	0	4	6				
13								
14	Total Hours	36	28	18				
15								

Aug1 / Aug2 / Aug3 \ Aug4

Ready   NUM

Start Microsoft Excel - Pay...   11:33 AM

Verify your total hours for each week

activity:

Set Up the Payroll Register

You will create a form for the monthly payroll register in a new workbook and then enter the cell and file addresses of the total hours that appear in the four worksheets in the Payroll Records workbook. First, you will open a new workbook and then copy the heading labels from the Aug1 sheet in the Payroll Records workbook into cells A1 to A3 of the new workbook.

steps:

1 Click the **Aug 1 tab**, click the **New button** to display a new blank worksheet, click **Window** on the menu bar, click **Payroll Records for the Marina Cafe**, select cells **A1** to **A2**, click the **Copy button**, click **Window**, click **Book2**, click cell **A1**, click the **Paste button**, enter **Monthly Payroll** in cell **A2**, then save the new workbook as **Payroll Register for the Marina Cafe**

Next, set up the labels for row 5.

2 Click cell **A5**, type **Employee Data**, press **[Enter]**, select cells **A5** to **C5**, click the **Merge and Center button** 🖳, click cell **D5**, type and center **Rate**, click cell **E5**, type and center **Earnings**, type and center **Deductions** and **Net Pay** as shown in the printed version in Figure P1-7, select cells **A5** to **L5**, click the **Bold button**, click the **Borders list arrow**, then click the **All Borders button** ⊞

3 As shown in Figure P1-7, enter the labels for **row 6**, select cells **A6** to **L6**, select **Wrap Text** from the **Alignment** dialog box (**Format, Cells, Alignment**), bold and center the labels, modify the column widths, select cells **A6** to **L9**, then add inside and outside border lines

4 As shown in Figure P1-7, enter the names of the three employees in cells **A7** to **A9**, then enter the Taxable codes in cells **B7** to **B9**, the Allowances in cells **C7** to **C9**, and the hourly rate of pay (formatted in the Currency style) in cells **D7** to **D9**

Next, enter a formula in the "Earnings" column for Marla MacDuff that adds the total hours that Marla worked in each of the four weeks and then multiplies this amount by her hourly rate of pay. To enter this formula, you will switch frequently between the Payroll Records and Payroll Register workbooks, so you first need to display the two workbooks side-by-side on your screen.

5 Click **Window** on the menu bar, click **Arrange**, click the **Vertical radio button**, then click **OK**

6 Click the **Payroll Register**, click cell **E7**, type an **equals sign (=)**, type an open parenthesis, click the **Aug1 tab** in the **Payroll Records** worksheet, click cell **B14**, type a **plus sign (+)**, click the **Aug2 tab** in the Payroll Records worksheet, click cell **B14**, type a **plus sign (+)**, repeat the process to enter cell **B14** from the **Aug3** and **Aug4** worksheets, then type a closed parenthesis

7 Click at the end of the formula in the Formula bar, type ***D7**, then press **[Enter]**

You should see $1,196.25 in cell E7. Now that you've taken the time to enter the formula components for Marla, you can maximize the Payroll Register workbook, then copy and modify the formula for Juliet and Gregory.

8 Click **Window** on the menu bar, click **Arrange**, click the **Windows of active workbook check box**, click **OK**, click cell **E7**, drag the corner handle down to cell **E9**, apply the Currency style, then widen the column, if necessary

Excel has entered cell B14 in all the formulas. You need to modify the cell addresses for the earnings owed to Juliet and Gregory.

9 Click cell **E8**, click the formula in the Formula bar, delete the first **B** in the formula, type a **C**, replace the remaining three **B**'s with **C**'s as shown in Figure P1-8, click cell **E9**, then replace the **B**'s with **D**'s

Compare the values in cells E7 to E9 with the values displayed in Figure P1-9. Next, go on to calculate each employee's deductions and net pay.

Hint

Type a hyphen as shown for "Taxable" and "Allowances" and then adjust the column widths so that the labels wrap after the hyphens.

FIGURE P1-7: Payroll register in progress

	A	B	C	D	E	F	G	H	I	J	K	L
1	**The Marina Café**											
2	Monthly Payroll											
3												
4												
5	Employee Data			Rate	Earnings			Deductions			Net Pay	
6	Name	Tax-able	Allow-ances			Federal Tax	Social Security (6.3%)	Medicare (1.35%)	State Tax	Total Deductions		
7	Marla MacDuff	M	4	$ 8.25								
8	Juliet Arias	S	2	$ 7.50								
9	Gregory Saunders	S	3	$ 7.00								

Center cells B7 to C9

FIGURE P1-8: Modified formula for cell E8

Cell addresses changed from $B$14 to $C$14

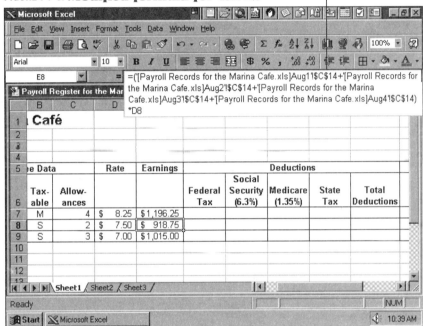

FIGURE P1-9: Earnings calculated in cells E7 to E9

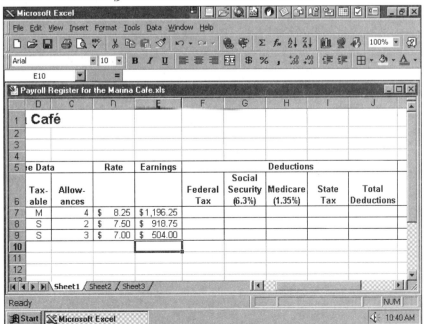

SIMPLE PAYROLL FOR THE MARINA CAFÉ

activity:

Calculate Monthly Wages

In order to calculate the monthly wages due to each employee, you need to calculate the deductions and then subtract the total deductions from the total earnings. The resulting values represent each employee's net pay.

steps:

1 As shown in Figure P1-10, enter the deductions for Federal Tax and State Tax in the appropriate cells in columns **F** and **I**, then display the values in the Currency style
Next, calculate the deductions for Social Security and Medicare.

2 Click cell **G7**, enter the formula: **=E7*.063**, press **[Enter]**, copy the formula to cells **G8** and **G9**, click cell **H7**, enter the formula that calculates **1.35%** of each employee's earnings, then copy the formula to cells **H8** and **H9**
Next, calculate the total deductions and then each employee's net pay.

3 Select cells **F7** to **J7**, click the **AutoSum button**, copy the formula to cells **J8** and **J9**, click cell **K7**, subtract the Total Deductions from the Earnings, then copy the formula to cells **K8** and **K9**
Compare the totals in cells K7, K8, and K9 to the values displayed in Figure P1-10. Next, format the payroll register for printing.

4 Enter the check numbers in cells **L7** to **L9** as shown in Figure P1-10, click the **Print Preview button** , click **Setup**, click the **Page tab**, click the **Landscape radio button**, then click the **Fit to: radio button**

5 Click the **Margins tab**, click the **Horizontally** and **Vertically check boxes** to select them, click the **Header/Footer tab**, click **Custom Header**, type **August Payroll Register** in the left box, type your name in the right box, click **OK**, then click **OK**
Next, increase the height of rows 7, 8, and 9 so that the payroll register takes up more vertical space on the page.

6 Click **Close** to exit the Print Preview screen, select rows **7**, **8**, and **9** in the worksheet frame, click **Format** on the menu bar, click **Row**, click **Height**, type **25**, then click **OK**

7 Center cell **A1** across cells **A1** to **L1**, center cell **A2** across cells **A2** to **L2**, increase the font size of cell **A1** to **24 point**, then insert a blank row above cell **A4** so that more space appears between the titles and the register form

8 Check the Print Preview screen, print a copy of the completed payroll register, then save and close both workbooks

Hint

To insert a blank row, right-click the row number (4), then click Insert.

FIGURE P1-10: Completed payroll register for the Marina Café

August Payroll Register [Your Name]

The Marina Café
Monthly Payroll

Employee Data			Rate	Earnings	Deductions					Net Pay
Name	Tax-able	Allow-ances			Federal Tax	Social Security (6.3%)	Medicare (1.35%)	State Tax	Total Deductions	
Marla MacDuff	M	4	$ 8.25	$ 1,196.25	$ 110.75	$ 75.36	$ 16.15	$ 24.50	S 226.76	S 969.49	124
Juliet Arias	S	2	$ 7.50	$ 918.75	$ 92.45	$ 57.88	$ 12.40	$ 19.75	$ 182.48	$ 736.27	125
Gregory Saunders	S	3	$ 7.00	$ 504.00	$ 48.50	$ 31.75	$ 6.80	$ 14.50	$ 101.56	$ 402.44	126

PROJECT **2**

OVERVIEW

Record of Earnings for a Freelance Photographer

As a freelance photographer, you earn money in two principal ways: from contract work for which you are paid an hourly rate and for commissions on the sale of your photographs. For the past month, you've kept careful records of your earnings. Now you want to transfer these records to two worksheets in Excel and then link the worksheet with a workbook that contains a record of your total earnings from January 1 to January 31, 1998. To complete your record of earnings, you will **Calculate Hourly Earnings**, **Calculate Sales Commissions**, and then **Calculate the Total Earnings**.

activity:

Calculate Hourly Earnings

You will first enter the times you worked over 15 days in January and then calculate the total hours worked each day and your total earnings.

steps:

1 Open a blank Excel workbook, enter and enhance only the **labels** in cells **A1** and **A2** and **A4** to **F4** and widen the columns as shown in Figure P2-1, then save the workbook as **January Earning Records from Freelance Photography Work**

Next, enter the "From" and "To" times.

2 Click cell **A5**, type **Jan 5**, press [Tab] to display 5-Jan in cell A5, type **8:30** in cell **B5**, press [Tab], type **14:30** in cell **C5**, press [Tab] twice, type **17.50**, then click cell **A6**

3 Enter the remaining dates, times, and pay rates as shown in Figure P2-1 (to save time, you can copy and modify the data), then format the pay rates in column **E** in the Currency style

Note that you must *enter the times as displayed. You use the 24-hour format so that you can easily calculate the total hours worked each day. Next, enter the formula in cell D4 that will calculate the total hours worked on January 5.*

Hint

The formula you entered subtracts the "From" time (14:30 in cell C5) from the "To" time (8:30 in cell B5) and then multiplies the result by 24 in order to *convert* the time format to a "real" number.

4 Click cell **D5**, enter the formula: **=(C5-B5)*24**, then press [Enter]

Next, calculate the total pay earned on January 5.

5 Click cell **F5**, enter the formula: **=D5*E5**, then press [Enter]

6 Copy the formula in cell **D5** down to cell **D14**, then copy the formula in cell **F5** down to cell **F14**

7 Select cells **F5** to **F15**, click the **AutoSum button**, widen the column, then add the right-aligned label to cell **E15** as shown in Figure P2-2

Time To

✓ **Save**

8 Double-click the **Sheet1** tab, type **Hourly**, then press [Enter]

Next, go on to use the IF function to determine your earnings on sales commissions.

FIGURE P2-1: Labels and times entered

18 pt.

12 pt.

To fill cells A1 to F1, select them, click the Fill Color button list arrow, then select a gray fill

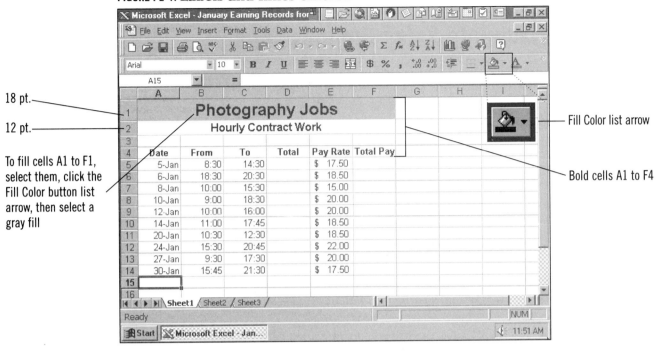

Fill Color list arrow

Bold cells A1 to F4

FIGURE P2-2: Hourly contract worksheet completed

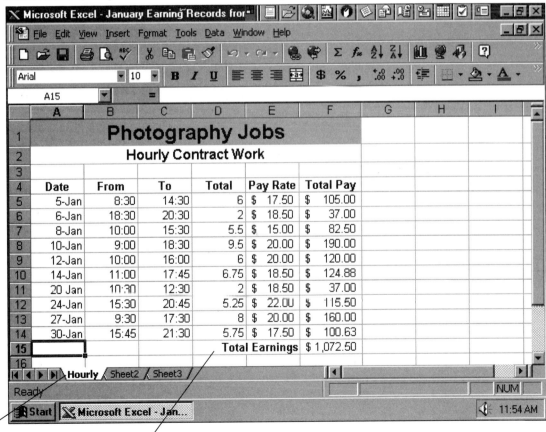

Sheet 1 tab renamed

Bold and right-align

RECORD OF EARNINGS FOR A FREELANCE PHOTOGRAPHER

activity:

Calculate Sales Commissions

In addition to your hourly contract work, you work on a commission-only basis for a local photography company. This company pays you a certain percentage on every photograph that you take when the photograph is then sold to a client. Your commissions are calculated based on the total amount of each sale. If the sale is greater than or equal to $500, you make a 20% commission, and if the sale is less than $500, you make a 15% commission. You will first enter all the January sales of your photographs and then use the IF function to calculate the commissions you will earn.

steps:

1 Double-click the **Sheet2 tab**, type **Sales**, then press **[Enter]**

2 Set up the Sales worksheet so that it appears as shown in Figure P2-3
Next, use the Paste Function to calculate your commission on each sale.

3 Click cell **C5**, click the **Paste Function button** f_x, select **Logical** from the Function category list, select **IF** from the Function name list, then click **OK**
The IF Function dialog box appears. Note that the logical test is that the value in cell B5 must be greater than or equal to (>=) $500. If the value in cell B5 is greater than or equal to $500, Excel performs the calculation you enter in the Value_if_true box. If the value in cell B5 is less than $500, Excel performs the calculation you enter in the Value_if_false box.

4 Type **B5>=500**, press **[Tab]** to move to the box next to **Value_if_true**, type **B5*.2**, press **[Tab]** to move to the box next to **Value_if_false**, then type **B5*.15**
The IF Function dialog box appears as shown in Figure P2-4. Next, complete the function.

5 Click **OK**
The sales commission entered in cell C5 is 37.5675. This amount is 15% of the value in cell B5 because the value in cell B5 is less than $500.

6 Copy the formula in **C5** down to cell **C12**

7 Enhance cells **C5** to **C12** with the Currency style
Check the values entered in cells C5 to C12 against Figure P2-5. Next, calculate the total amount of money you made from sales commissions in January.

Time To √ Save

8 Select cells **C5** to **C14**, click the **AutoSum button**, then enter and enhance the label in cell **B14** as shown in Figure P2-5
Your total earnings on sales commissions in January are $623.46. Next, go on to open a new workbook in which you will enter the cell addresses of your total earnings on contract work and commissions.

FIGURE P2-3: Sales worksheet setup

18 pt. Bold

12 pt. Bold

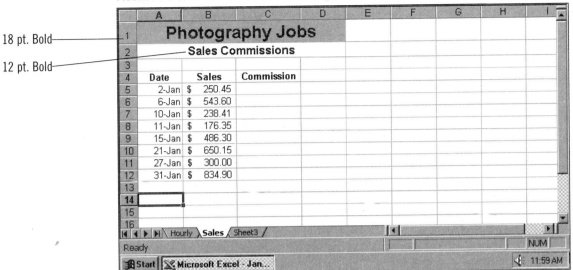

FIGURE P2-4: IF Function dialog box

Logical_test	B5>=500	= FALSE
Value_if_true	B5*.2	= 50.09
Value_if_false	B5*.15	= 37.5675

= 37.5675

Returns one value if a condition you specify evaluates to TRUE and another value if it evaluates to FALSE.

Value_if_false is the value that is returned if Logical_test is FALSE. If omitted, FALSE is returned.

Formula result =37.5675   OK   Cancel

FIGURE P2-5: Completed sales worksheet

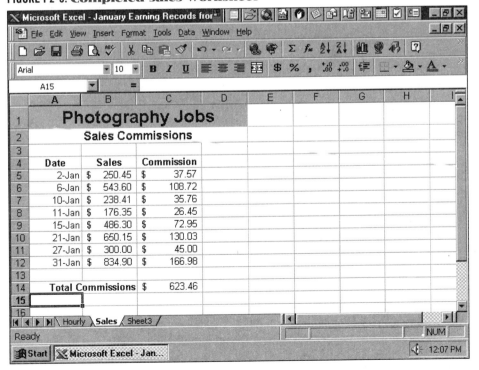

RECORD OF EARNINGS FOR A FREELANCE PHOTOGRAPHER

activity:

Calculate the Total Earnings

You will calculate your total earnings for the month of January in a new workbook and then calculate the percentage of your earnings that comes from each of the two sources (contract work and commissions).

steps:

1 Click the **New Workbook button**, set up the worksheet as shown in Figure P2-6, then save the workbook as **Total January Earnings**

Next, arrange your screen so the two workbooks appear side-by-side, then enter the cell address of your total earnings from contract work.

2 Click **Window**, click **Arrange**, click the **Vertical radio button**, click **OK**, click cell **A5** in the Total January Earnings workbook, type an **equals sign (=)**, click the Records workbook, click the **Hourly tab**, click cell **F15**, then press **[Enter]**

Your total hourly earnings of $1,072.50 appear in cell A5 in the Total January Earnings workbook. Next, enter your total earnings on sales commissions.

3 Click cell **B5**, type an **=**, then enter the cell address of the total commission sales earnings from the **Sales** sheet in the Records workbook

Your total sales earnings of $623.46 appear in cell B5 in the Total January Earnings workbook. Next, calculate your total earnings.

Hint

Widen column C if necessary.

4 Maximize the Total January Earnings workbook, select cells **A5** to **C5**, then click the **AutoSum button**

You made a total of $1,695.96 in January! Next, calculate the percentage of your earnings that came from hourly contract work and from commission sales.

5 Click cell **A7**, enter the formula: **=A5/C5*100%**, press **[Enter]**, click cell **A7**, click the **Percent Style button** %, click cell **B7**, calculate the percentage of your earnings from sales commissions, then display the result in the Percent style

63% of your January earnings came from hourly contract work and 37% came from sales commissions. Next, format the worksheet attractively so that it appears as shown in Figure P2-7.

6 Switch to **75% view**, click cell **A3**, click **Insert** on the menu bar, click **Columns**, click the **1** on the worksheet frame to select all of row 1, click the **right mouse button**, click **Insert**, then repeat the process to insert two more rows

Next, draw a rounded text box around the worksheet data.

7 Click the **Drawing button** 🖉, click **AutoShapes**, click **Basic Shapes**, select the **Rounded Rectangle shape**, draw a rounded rectangle around cells **B4** to **D10** as shown in Figure P2-7, click **Format** on the menu bar, click **AutoShape**, click the **Colors and Lines tab**, click the **Color list arrow** in the Fill section, click **No Fill**, click the **Style list arrow**, click **3 pt**, click **OK**, then click away from the rectangle to deselect it

Next, insert the picture.

Trouble

You may be prompted to insert the Office 97 CD into your computer. If you do not have access to the Office 97 CD, see your instructor for further directions or omit insertion of the picture.

8 Click **Insert** on the menu bar, click **Picture**, click **Clip Art**, click the **Pictures tab**, click **Nature**, select the **Ocean,Sunset,PhotoDisc** picture, click **Insert**, click **Close**, size and position the picture under the worksheet data so that it appears as shown in Figure P2-7, then close the Picture toolbar

9 Click the **Print Preview button**, click **Setup**, click the **Page tab**, increase the Adjust to size to 110, click the **Margins tab**, center the worksheet horizontally and vertically, click the **Header/Footer tab**, enter the header text as shown in Figure P2-7, print a copy of the completed worksheet, then save and close both workbooks

FIGURE P2-6: Worksheet setup

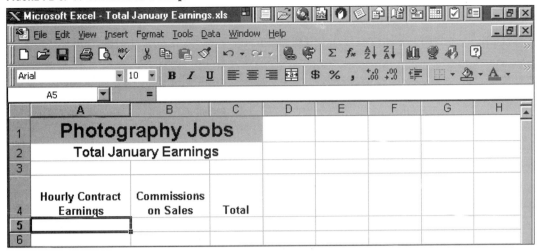

FIGURE P2-7: Completed worksheet

January Earnings   [Your Name]

Photography Jobs

Total January Earnings

Hourly Contract Earnings	Commissions on Sales	Total
$ 1,072.50	$ 623.46	$ 1,695.96
63%	37%	

OVERVIEW

Travel Expense Report for Feature Plus Online

The three sales representatives at Feature Plus Online, a company that develops home pages for corporate clients, have each submitted their travel expenses for the month of March. You have decided to use Excel to record these expenses and then prepare an expense report that summarizes the travel expenses incurred in March. To create the travel expense report, you will **Create the Expense Statements** and then **Prepare the Expense Report**.

activity

Create the Expense Statements

You will create an expense statement form in Sheet1 of a new workbook and then copy the form into sheets 2 and 3. Figure P3-1 shows the completed expense form.

steps

1 Open a new workbook, then refer to Figure P3-1 to enter and enhance all the labels
Next, hide the gridlines and add border lines.

2 Click **Tools** on the menu bar, click **Options**, click the **View tab**, click the **Gridlines check box** to deselect it, click **OK**, add border lines as shown in Figure P3-1, then save the worksheet as **Expense Statements for Feature Plus Online**
Next, enter only the formulas required for the expense report. You will enter the values specific to each employee in the next activity.

3 Click cell **H12**, enter the formula: =SUM (B12:G12), press [Enter], copy the formula down to cell **H25**, click cell **B26**, enter the formula: =SUM(B12:B25), press [Enter], then copy the formula across to cell **G26**

4 Click cell **H27**, enter the formula =SUM (H12:H25), press [Enter], click cell **H29**, enter the formula: =H27-H28, press [Enter], then select cells **B12 to H29** and click the **Currency Style button**

5 Select rows **6, 7, and 8**, click **Row Height**, type **20**, click **OK**, select cells **B11 to H29**, click the **right mouse button**, click **Format**, click **Column**, click **Width**, type **12**, click **OK**, then insert the label in cell **A30** as shown in Figure P3-1

6 Name the sheet tabs as follows: Sheet1 tab: **Wong**, Sheet2 tab: **Guenero**, Sheet3 tab: **Evans**

7 Select cells **A1 to H30** in the Wong sheet, copy it to the Guenero and Evans sheets, use your mouse to increase the width of column **A** in the two sheets, then increase the width of columns **B to H** to **12** and increase the height of rows **6 to 8 to 20** so that the structure of both sheets appears as shown in Figure P3-1
Next, go on to enter the expenses that each employee incurred.

FIGURE P3-1: Completed expense statement form

Impact font, 26 pt., Italics

Impact font, Italics

Change the height of rows 6 to 8 to 20

22 pt.

Set the width of columns B to H at 12

Note that the current mileage reimbursement rate is $.25 per mile.

Feature Plus Online

Suite 500 - 1803 West Main Street, San Francisco, CA 94171

Expense Statement

Employee Name: _____

Position: _____

From: _____   To: _____

Date	Accom.	Transport.	Fuel	Meals	Entertain.	Other	TOTAL
$ -	$ -	$ -	$ -	$ -	$ -	$ -	
					Subtotal	$ -	
					Subtract Advances	$ -	
					TOTAL	$ -	

TRAVEL EXPENSE REPORT FOR FEATURE PLUS ONLINE

activity

Prepare the Expense Report

First, you need to enter the expenses incurred by Grace Wong, Juan Guenero, and Marilyn Evans, and then you will prepare an expense report in Sheet4.

steps

1 Click the **Wong tab**, then enter the variable information and the expenses for Grace Wong as shown below:

Grace Wong, Sales Representative, incurred her expenses March 2 to March 5, 1998. On March 2, Grace flew to Dallas @ $194.00 + 8% tax, spent $42.50 on meals, and drove 12 miles. From March 2 through 4, she stayed at the Dallas Hilton Hotel @ $97.50/night + 9% tax. From March 3 through 4, she rented a car in Dallas @ $32.50/day + $4.30/day for insurance. On March 3, she drove 25 miles and spent $85 on meals and $72 on a theater ticket. On March 4, she drove 35 miles, spent $105 on meals and $12 on other expenses. On March 5, she drove 12 miles and spent $13 on other expenses. Note that you need to calculate some of the expenses and that the mileage reimbursement is $.25/mile. The total in cell H29 should be $952.45.

2 Click the **Guenero tab**, then refer to Figure P3-2 to enter the information and expenses for Juan Guenero
Check that Juan's total expenses (less his advance) are $624.92.

3 Click the **Evans tab**, then refer to Figure P3-2 to enter the information and expenses for Marilyn Evans
Check that Marilyn's total expenses are $530.36.

4 Click **Insert**, click **Worksheet**, name the new sheet **Report**, copy cells **A1** to **A4** from the **Wong** sheet to the **Report** sheet, click **Format** on the menu bar, click **Cells**, click the **Alignment tab**, click the **Horizontal** list arrow, click **Center Across Selection**, click **OK**, then change "Expense Statement" to "March Expense Report"

5 Enter the names of the three employees in cells **A8** to **A10**, widen **column A**, right-align the names, then enter the expense labels ("Accom" to "Total") in cells **B7** to **H7** as shown in Figure P3-3

6 Click cell **B8**, enter the cell address: **=Wong!B26**, press **[Enter]**, then copy the address across to cell **G8**

7 Click cell **B9**, enter the cell address: **=Guenero!B26**, copy it across to cell **G9**, click cell **B10**, enter the cell address: **=Evans!B26**, then copy it across to cell **G10**

8 Select cells **B8** to **H10**, click the **AutoSum button**, calculate the total advances in cell H12, then format the cells in the Currency style
To calculate the advances, click cell H12, then enter the formula: =Guenero!H28+Evans!H28.

Time To
✓ Save
✓ Close

9 Add and format the required labels for cells **G11** to **G13**, calculate the Subtotal and Total March Expenses, click **Insert** on the menu bar, click **Picture**, click **Clip Art**, click the **Clip Art tab**, click **Entertainment**, select the **Entertainment Furniture Chairs Directors Megaphones** picture, size and position the picture as shown in Figure P3-3, then format the report so that your printed copy appears as shown in Figure P3-3
Note that you need to increase the height of rows 7 to 13 to 20 and increase the top margin to about 3" (click the Margins tab in the Setup dialog box, then enter 3 for the top margin). The total March expenses should be $2,107.73. To remove the border from the picture, right-click the picture, click Format Picture, click the Colors and Lines tab, click the Color list arrow in the Line section, then click No Line.

FIGURE P3-2: Expense data

Juan Guenero, Sales Representative, incurred his expenses from March 5 to March 11, 1998 and has already been advanced $200. On March 5, Juan drove 28 miles and spent $55 on meals. On March 9, he flew to Chicago @ $224.00 + 8% tax, spent $72 on meals, and drove 18 miles. From March 9 to 10, he stayed at the Lakeside Hotel @ $125/night + 11% tax. On March 10, he spent $88 on meals, and $42.50 on other expenses. On March 11, he drove 18 miles and spent $32 on meals.

Marilyn Evans, Sales Representative, incurred her expenses from March 8 to March 16, 1998, and has already been advanced $150. On March 8, Marilyn drove 30 miles, flew to Seattle @ $90 + 9% tax, stayed overnight at the Baker Mountain Inn @ $80 + 7% tax, and spent $52 on meals. On March 9, she took a ferry ride @ $60; drove 30 miles, spent $45 on meals, and $22 on other expenses. On March 15, she drove 30 miles, flew to Phoenix @ $110 + 9% tax, stayed overnight at the Phoenix Best Western Motel @ $72 + 8% tax, and spent $40 on meals. On March 16, she drove 30 miles, spent $35 on meals, and $15 on other expenses.

FIGURE P3-3 Completed Travel Expense report

March Expense Report   [Your Name]

Feature Plus Online
Suite 500 - 1803 West Main Street, San Francisco, CA 94171

March Expense Report

	Accom.	Transport	Fuel	Meals	Entertain.	Other	Total
Grace Wong	$ 318.83	$ 283.12	$ 21.00	$ 232.50	$ 72.00	$ 25.00	$ 952.45
Juan Guenero	$ 277.50	$ 241.92	$ 16.00	$ 247.00	$ -	$ 42.50	$ 824.92
Marilyn Evans	$ 163.36	$ 278.00	$ 30.00	$ 172.00	$ -	$ 37.00	$ 680.36
					Subtotal		$ 2,457.73
					Less Advances	$	350.00
					Total March Expenses		$ 2,107.73

Independent Challenges

INDEPENDENT CHALLENGE 1

Set up the payroll records and a payroll register to record the hours worked by four employees of a company of your choice. Your employees all work for an hourly rate, which varies from a low of $8.00 an hour to a high of $12.50 an hour.

1. Determine a name for your company and the type of business it conducts. Examples include a retail operation such as a book store or clothing store, a service-based business such as a landscaping and gardening operation, or a small motel. Write the name of your company and a short description of its business in the box below:

   Company Name: ....

   Description of Business: ....

   ....

2. Select names for each of your four employees and determine an hourly rate for each employee. Write the names and hourly rates in the box below:

	Name	Hourly Rate
Employee 1		
Employee 2		
Employee 3		
Employee 4		

3. Select a month that the payroll will cover. Check a calendar to determine the correct dates for the days of the week, then start the payroll records on the first Sunday of the month.
4. Set up the payroll record for the first week of the month you have selected. Adapt the payroll record you created in Project 1 to include your company name, the dates you have chosen, and the names of your employees.
5. Enter the hours that each employee worked in the payroll record and then calculate their total hours for the week.
6. Name the first four sheet tabs with the name of the month and the week number (for example, March1, March2, etc.).
7. Copy the payroll record in Sheet1 to the remaining three sheets.
8. Modify the hours in the sheets for weeks 2 to 4. Presume that your employees do not work the exact same hours in each of the four weeks.
9. Save the payroll records workbook as Payroll Records for [Company Name].
10. Display a new blank workbook, copy selected labels from the Payroll Records workbook to save typing time and then set up the payroll register so that it appears similar to the payroll register you created for Project 1. If you wish, you can open the Payroll Register you created for Project 1, delete the variable data and then enter the data required for your payroll register.
11. Save the payroll register workbook as Payroll Register for [Company Name].
12. Arrange your screen so that the two workbooks appear side-by-side.
13. In the appropriate cell in the payroll register, enter the formula required to calculate the total earnings that your first employee earned for the month. Remember that you will need to type an equals (=) sign in the payroll register cell, click the cell address in the payroll records workbook that contains the total hours worked by the first employee in the first week, type a plus (+) sign, click the cell address in the payroll records workbook that contains the total hours worked by the first employee in the second week, and so on, until the total hours for all four weeks are included in the formula. You then need to multiply the total hours worked by the first employee's rate of pay.
14. Copy the formula entered for the first employee to calculate the total earnings for the remaining three employees and then modify the required cell addresses.

15. Enter deductions for federal and state taxes in the payroll register and then calculate the deductions required for each employee. You determine which deductions to include. For example, you can include deductions for Medicare, parking, company pension plan, etc.

16. Calculate the net pay earned by each employee.

17. Format the payroll register for printing in landscape orientation, print a copy, then save and close both workbooks.

INDEPENDENT CHALLENGE 2

You work for yourself and need to keep track of your monthly earnings. Create a record of earnings from at least two sources for one month and then calculate the percentage of your income that comes from each source.

1. First, determine the type of work you do and the kind of payments you will receive. For example, you could be an actor who earns an hourly rate for acting in commercials, a daily rate for play rehearsals, and a percentage of box-office receipts for acting in productions. Alternatively, you could be a freelance travel agent who earns a commission on every trip booked and an hourly rate for part-time work in the office of a national travel agency.

2. Designate at least one income source from hourly work and one income source from commissions that depend on sales volume.

3. Create a worksheet for each of the income sources you have identified.

4. For the hourly income, enter the starting and ending times you worked on at least 10 days during the month and then calculate your total income from hourly work.

5. For the commissions income, use the IF Function to calculate your commissions, depending on the volume of sales. For example, you could earn 25% of all sales over $600 and 15% on all sales that are equal to or less than $600. Calculate your total income from commissions.

6. Calculate any remaining income from other sources such as daily contract work, lump sum payments, etc.

7. Create a sheet called "Analysis," enter the total income from each source into the Analysis sheet, then calculate your total monthly earnings.

8. Calculate the percentage of income you make from each income source.

9. Format the worksheet attractively (add a picture from the ClipArt Gallery, if you wish), then save it as Record of Earnings for a [Name of Profession].

10. Print a copy of your record of earnings and then save and close the workbook.

INDEPENDENT CHALLENGE 3

You work for a company that requires you to travel frequently. Create expense records for three consecutive months and then prepare an expense report that totals all the expenses you incurred in each category, along with your total expenses for the three months.

1. Set up Sheet1 with labels for the date and each expense category. Categories include: accommodations, transportation, mileage (determine the mileage rate your company will pay, e.g., $.15/mile or $.12/kilometer), meals, entertainment, and miscellaneous (or other) expenses. If you wish, adapt the expense statements you created for Project 3.

2. Copy your expense sheet to the next two sheets and then name the sheet tabs (e.g., March, April, May).

3. Fill in your expenses for each month. Don't forget to include taxes in your calculations and to enter realistic expenses. For example, a flight from New York to Los Angeles should cost more than a flight from Montreal to Toronto. Assume that you drive your own car to the airport each time you fly from your home town and will therefore include the mileage calculation.

4. Save the expense statements as My Travel Expense Statements.

5. Open a blank Excel workbook and set up an attractive Expense Report for the three months. Include the name of the company for which you work and an appropriate picture from the ClipArt Gallery. Save the new workbook as My Travel Expense Report.

6. Arrange the two workbooks side-by-side on your screen and enter the formulas to calculate the total expenses in each category for each month into the Expense Report workbook.

7. Format the expense report and print a copy.

8. Return to the expense statements workbook and revise it so that it displays the expenses for three more months. Change the names of the sheet tabs and modify the expenses to reflect your travel activities.

9. Return to the expense report workbook, modify the title for the additional three months, note the new totals and then print a copy.

10. Save and close both workbooks.

INDEPENDENT CHALLENGE 4

You will create a payroll register from the payroll records provided for four employees of Quest Tours, a company that conducts wilderness adventure tours. Each of the employees is a tour guide in the company and is paid according to how many days per month they work.

1. Create the payroll record shown in Figure IC-1.

FIGURE IC-1: **Payroll record for June 1 to 30, 1998**

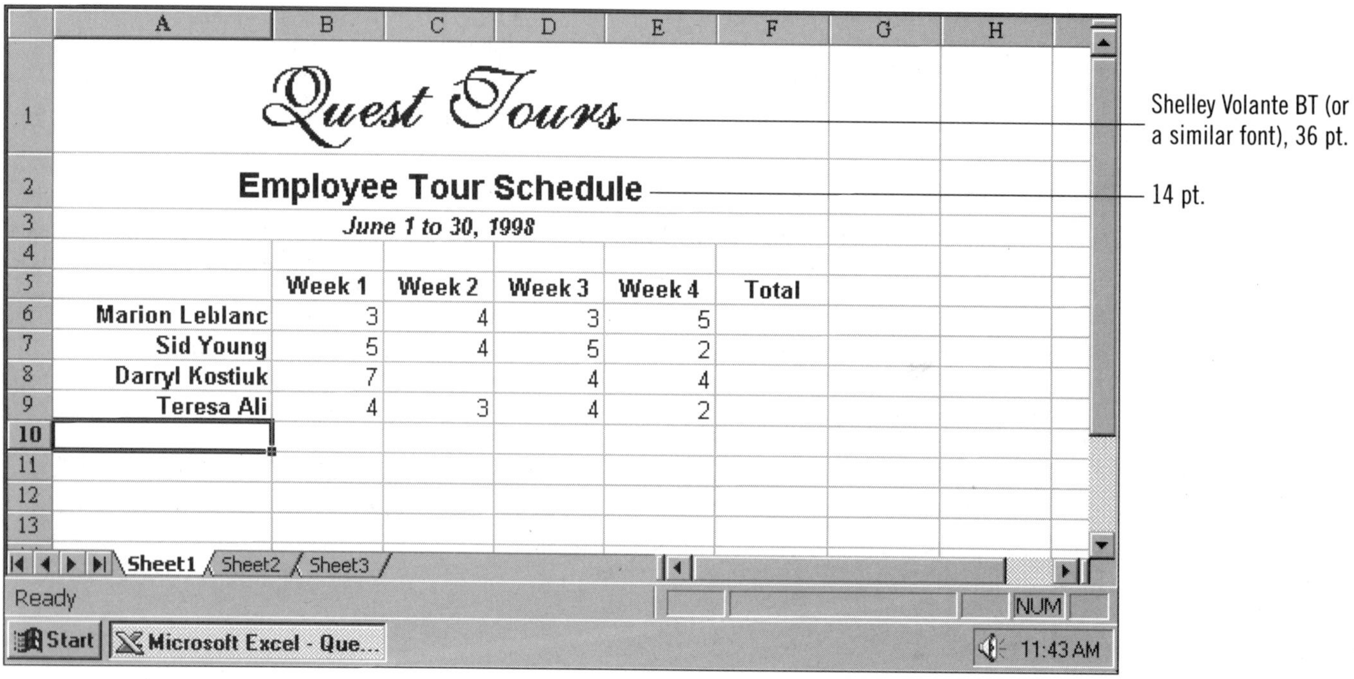

Shelley Volante BT (or a similar font), 36 pt.

14 pt.

	A	B	C	D	E	F
5		Week 1	Week 2	Week 3	Week 4	Total
6	Marion Leblanc	3	4	3	5	
7	Sid Young	5	4	5	2	
8	Darryl Kostiuk	7		4	4	
9	Teresa Ali	4	3	4	2	

2. Calculate the total days worked by each employee and enter the results in the Total column.

3. Name the Sheet1 tab "Records" and the Sheet2 tab "Register."

4. Display Sheet2, then set it up so that it appears as shown in Figure IC-2.

FIGURE IC-2: **Payroll register**

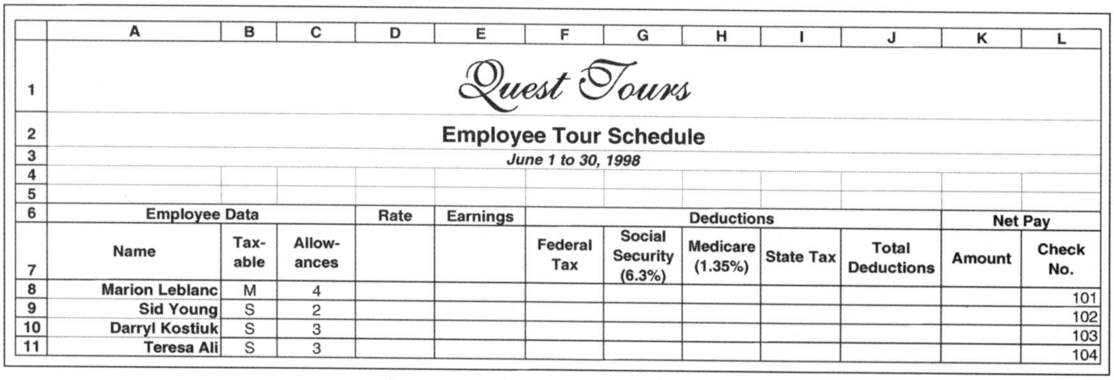

	A	B	C	D	E	F	G	H	I	J	K	L
6	Employee Data			Rate	Earnings	Deductions					Net Pay	
7	Name	Tax-able	Allow-ances			Federal Tax	Social Security (6.3%)	Medicare (1.35%)	State Tax	Total Deductions	Amount	Check No.
8	Marion Leblanc	M	4									101
9	Sid Young	S	2									102
10	Darryl Kostiuk	S	3									103
11	Teresa Ali	S	3									104

5. Use the IF Function, as described below, to determine the pay scale at which each employee will be paid. This scale depends on the total number of days each employee worked. If an employee worked 15 or fewer days in June, he or she will be paid a daily rate of $150. If an employee worked more than 15 days in June, he or she will be paid a daily rate of $180.

   a. Click cell D8 in the Register sheet.

   b. Click the Paste Function button, select IF from the Logical category, then click OK.

   c. In the logical_test box, enter Records!F6<=15.

   d. In the value_if_true box, enter $150.

   e In the value_if_false box, enter $180.

   f. Click OK, then copy the formula down to cell D11. All the employees except Sid Young will make $150 per day for the tours they conducted in June.

6. Click cell E8 in the Register sheet, then calculate the total pay for Marion Leblanc. Remember that the total days that Marion works appear in Records!F6 and her pay rate appears in cell D8.

7. Copy the formula in cell E8 down to cell E11.

8. Calculate Federal Tax as 14% of the total earnings and State Tax as 8% of the total earnings, then calculate the deductions for Social Security (6.3%) and Medicare (1.35%).

9. Copy the deduction calculations for the remaining four employees.

10. Calculate the total net pay earned by each employee.

11. Check the values in cells K8 to K11 against the following results:

Cell	Net Pay
K8	$ 1,582.88
K9	$ 2,026.08
K10	$ 1,582.88
K11	$ 1,371.83

12. Save the workbook as Payroll for Quest Tours.

13. Format the Register sheet to print in landscape orientation and centered horizontally on one page. Add a custom header that contains the company name and your name.

14. Print a copy of the Register sheet, then save and close the workbook.

Visual Workshop

As a gymnastics instructor, Julia Scott works for an hourly rate, depending on how many hours per week she works. You need to calculate the total hours she worked in each week in February 1998 and then format and print her record of earnings. Insert two new worksheets, name the sheet tabs, then create the time sheet shown in Figure VW-1.

FIGURE VW-1: Week1 sheet

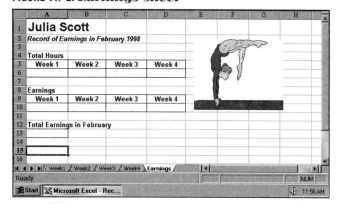

Copy the time sheet to the Week2, Week3, and Week4 sheets and modify the dates as follows: February 10 to 14, February 17 to 21, and February 24 to 28. Based on the information provided below, use the 24-hour format to enter the hours worked each day and then calculate the total hours worked in each of the four weeks. Remember that the formula to calculate total hours subtracts the "From" time from the "To" time and then multiplies the result by 24.

	Monday	Tuesday	Wednesday	Thursday	Friday
Week 1	9 a.m. to 5 p.m.		9:30 a.m. to 2 p.m.	10 a.m. to 4 p.m.	3 p.m. to 11 p.m.
Week 2	10 a.m. to 3 p.m.	3 p.m. to 8 p.m.	5 p.m. to midnight		8 a.m. to 3 p.m.
Week 3	9 a.m. to 6 p.m.	9 a.m. to 2 p.m.		8:30 a.m. to 1 p.m.	11 a.m. to 9 p.m.
Week 4	8 a.m. to 11 a.m.	2 p.m. to 11 p.m.	11 a.m. to 6 p.m.	4 p.m. to 11 p.m.	

Set up the Earnings sheet as shown in Figure VW-2 (you will find the picture in the Sports & Leisure ClipArt category), then calculate Julia Scott's total earnings for February based on the following scale: $40/hour for 25 or fewer hours in a single week and $40 + 12% of $40 for more than 25 hours in a single week.

FIGURE VW-2: Earnings sheet

Save the workbook as Record of Earnings for Julia Scott, format and print a copy of the Earnings sheet, then save and close the workbook.

Microsoft
►Excel
Projects

Charting

In This Unit You Will Create:

► **Course Grades Analysis**

► **Regional Sales Analysis**

► **Spending Analysis**

You create charts in Excel when you wish to present data in a clear and easy-to-understand format. In addition to the commonly used pie and column chart formats, you can choose to display data in an area chart, a line chart, a scatter chart, or a radar chart. You can even display geographical data in a map chart that will shade specified geographical areas such as the United States according to the data ranges displayed in the legend. The key to using charts effectively lies in developing a relevant analysis of the data entered in a worksheet. ► In this unit, you will use Pivot tables, IF functions, and sorting functions to analyze worksheet data and then present it in a variety of chart formats.

PROJECT 1

Course Grades Analysis for Marketing 200

As the instructor of Marketing 200, a college-level course in which 20 students are enrolled, you have used an Excel worksheet to record all the scores earned by the students throughout the term. Now you need to calculate a final grade for each student, and then create a variety of charts that will help you analyze how well your students, have performed. Three activities are required to produce a Course Grades Analysis for Marketing 200.

Project Activities

Set up the Worksheet

Your first task is to set up the worksheet that contains all the grades earned throughout the term. Each grade is assigned one of three categories: Assignments (A), Quizzes (Q), and Exams (E). As shown in Figure P1-1, the students completed three assignments, three quizzes, and two exams. After you have set up the worksheet, you will use the Sort feature to display the student names in alphabetical order.

Calculate Totals and Grades

You need to *weight* the grades earned by the students according to type. Assignments are worth 50% of the total grade; quizzes are worth 15%; and exams are worth 35%. For example, cell J4 in the sample worksheet, shown in Figure P1-1, displays the score that Kelly Knutson earned for assignments. To calculate this score, you will divide the total of the three scores Kelly earned on assignments (57) by the total points possible (80), and then multiply by 50 to give her a *weighted* score of 35.63 for assignments. You will use the same process to calculate Kelly's weighted score for Quizzes (9.92) and Exams (25.96). Finally, you will total the three scores for Assignments, Quizzes, and Exams to determine a score out of 100 (71.51). You create a lookup table that lists the grades earned according to the total score. Figure P1-2 displays the lookup table created for Project 1. Once you create the lookup table, you enter a formula in the grade column that instructs Excel to check the value entered in cell M4, match it to the lookup table, and then enter the appropriate grade. With a total score of 71.51, Kelly earned a C. After you calculate the grades for the first student listed on the worksheet, you will copy the formulas down to the last student.

Create a Pivot Table and Pie Chart

Once you have determined the final grade that each student earned, you will create a Pivot table that *counts* the number of times each grade (e.g., "A," "B," etc.) appears in the worksheet. You will then use the data contained in the Pivot table to create a pie chart that graphically displays the grade breakdown. The pie chart you will produce appears in Figure P1-3.

FIGURE P1-1: Course Grades worksheet

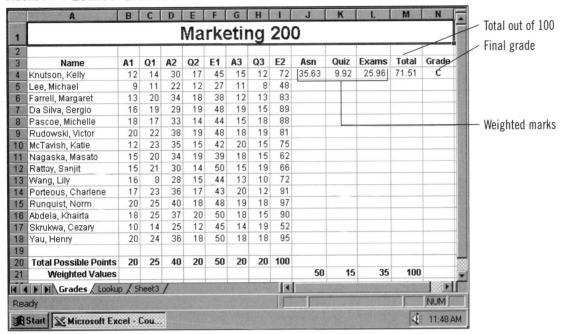

	A	B	C	D	E	F	G	H	I	J	K	L	M	N
1	Marketing 200													
2														
3	Name	A1	Q1	A2	Q2	E1	A3	Q3	E2	Asn	Quiz	Exams	Total	Grade
4	Knutson, Kelly	12	14	30	17	45	15	12	72	35.63	9.92	25.96	71.51	C
5	Lee, Michael	9	11	22	12	27	11	8	48					
6	Farrell, Margaret	13	20	34	18	38	12	13	83					
7	Da Silva, Sergio	16	19	29	19	48	19	15	89					
8	Pascoe, Michelle	18	17	33	14	44	15	18	88					
9	Rudowski, Victor	20	22	38	19	48	18	19	81					
10	McTavish, Katie	12	23	35	15	42	20	15	75					
11	Nagaska, Masato	15	20	34	19	39	18	15	62					
12	Rattay, Sanjit	15	21	30	14	50	15	19	66					
13	Wang, Lily	16	8	28	15	44	13	10	72					
14	Porteous, Charlene	17	23	36	17	43	20	12	91					
15	Runquist, Norm	20	25	40	18	48	19	18	97					
16	Abdela, Khairta	18	25	37	20	50	18	15	90					
17	Skrukwa, Cezary	10	14	25	12	45	14	19	52					
18	Yau, Henry	20	24	36	18	50	18	18	95					
19														
20	Total Possible Points	20	25	40	20	50	20	20	100					
21	Weighted Values									50	15	35	100	

Grades / Lookup / Sheet3

Ready — NUM

Start — Microsoft Excel - Cou... — 11:48 AM

Total out of 100
Final grade
Weighted marks

FIGURE P1-2: Lookup table

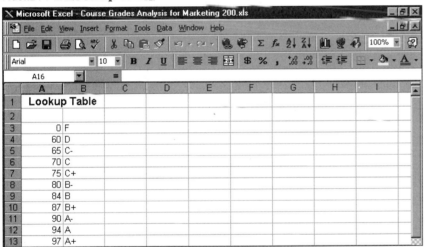

	A	B
1	Lookup Table	
2		
3	0	F
4	60	D
5	65	C-
6	70	C
7	75	C+
8	80	B-
9	84	B
10	87	B+
11	90	A-
12	94	A
13	97	A+

FIGURE P1-3: Breakdown of Final Grades pie chart

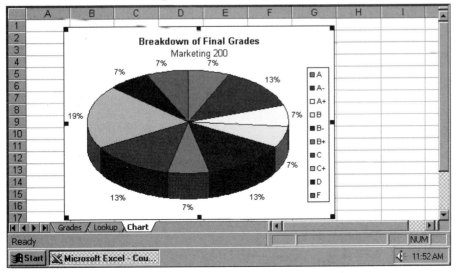

activity:

Set up the Worksheet

You need to enter and enhance the labels for the worksheet, and then enter the scores that each student earned on the assignments, quizzes, and exams.

steps:

1. Open a blank Excel workbook, type **Marketing 200** in cell **A1**, press **[Enter]**, select cells **A1** to **N1**, click the **Merge and Center button** [⊞] on the Formatting toolbar, click the **Bold button** [**B**] on the Formatting toolbar, then increase the font size to **20 point**

2. Save the workbook as **Course Grades Analysis for Marketing 200** to the disk where you plan to store all the files for this book

3. Click cell **A3**, type **Name**, press **[Tab]**, then enter the labels in cells **B3** to **N3** as shown in Figure P1-4
   Next, adjust the column widths.

4. Select cells **B3** to **I3**, click **Format** on the menu bar, click **Column**, click **Width**, type **4**, then click **OK**

5. Select cells **J3** to **N3**, then change the column width to **6**

6. Click cell **A4**, type **Knutson, Kelly**, press **[Tab]**, increase the width of column **A** so the entire name fits, then enter the remaining values and labels for the worksheet as shown in Figure P1-4
   Next, use the Sort Ascending feature to display the student names in alphabetical order.

7. Select cells **A4** to **N18**, click **Data** on the menu bar, click **Sort**, then click **OK** to accept an ascending sort by Name
   The first student in the list is now Abdela, Khairta, as shown in Figure P1-5.

8. As shown in Figure P1-5, bold and center the labels in cells **A3** to **N3**, bold the labels in cells **A20** to **M21**, right align the labels in cell **A20** and **A21**, then save the workbook
   Next, go on to calculate the grade each student earned in Marketing 200.

FIGURE P1-4: Labels and values for Course Grades worksheet

	A	B	C	D	E	F	G	H	I	J	K	L	M	N
1					Marketing 200									
2														
3	Name	A1	Q1	A2	Q2	E1	A3	Q3	E2	Asn	Quiz	Exams	Total	Grade
4	Knutson, Kelly	12	14	30	17	45	15	12	72					
5	Lee, Michael	9	11	22	12	27	11	8	48					
6	Farrell, Margaret	13	20	34	18	38	12	13	83					
7	Da Silva, Sergio	16	19	29	19	48	19	15	89					
8	Pascoe, Michelle	18	17	33	14	44	15	18	88					
9	Rudowski, Victor	20	22	38	19	48	18	19	81					
10	McTavish, Katie	12	23	35	15	42	20	15	75					
11	Nagaska, Masato	15	20	34	19	39	18	15	62					
12	Rattay, Sanjit	15	21	30	14	50	15	19	66					
13	Wang, Lily	16	8	28	15	44	13	10	72					
14	Porteous, Charlene	17	23	36	17	43	20	12	91					
15	Runquist, Norm	20	25	40	18	48	19	18	97					
16	Abdela, Khairta	18	25	37	20	50	18	15	90					
17	Skrukwa, Cezary	10	14	25	12	45	14	19	52					
18	Yau, Henry	20	24	36	18	50	18	18	95					
19														
20	Total Possible Points	20	25	40	20	50	20	20	100					
21	Weighted Values									50	15	35	100	
22														

Sheet1 / Sheet2 / Sheet3

Ready — NUM — Start — Microsoft Excel - Cou... — 12:10 PM

FIGURE P1-5: Course Grades worksheet sorted and enhanced

	A	B	C	D	E	F	G	H	I	J	K	L	M	N
1					Marketing 200									
2														
3	Name	A1	Q1	A2	Q2	E1	A3	Q3	E2	Asn	Quiz	Exams	Total	Grade
4	Abdela, Khairta	18	25	37	20	50	18	15	90					
5	Da Silva, Sergio	16	19	29	19	48	19	15	89					
6	Farrell, Margaret	13	20	34	18	38	12	13	83					
7	Knutson, Kelly	12	14	30	17	45	15	12	72					
8	Lee, Michael	9	11	22	12	27	11	8	48					
9	McTavish, Katie	12	23	35	15	42	20	15	75					
10	Nagaska, Masato	15	20	34	19	39	18	15	62					
11	Pascoe, Michelle	18	17	33	14	44	15	18	88					
12	Porteous, Charlene	17	23	36	17	43	20	12	91					
13	Rattay, Sanjit	15	21	30	14	50	15	19	66					
14	Rudowski, Victor	20	22	38	19	48	18	19	81					
15	Runquist, Norm	20	25	40	18	48	19	18	97					
16	Skrukwa, Cezary	10	14	25	12	45	14	19	52					
17	Wang, Lily	16	8	28	15	44	13	10	72					
18	Yau, Henry	20	24	36	18	50	18	18	95					
19														
20	Total Possible Points	20	25	40	20	50	20	20	100					
21	Weighted Values									50	15	35	100	
22														

Sheet1 / Sheet2 / Sheet3

Ready — NUM — Start — Microsoft Excel - Cou... — 12:12 PM

activity:

Calculate Totals and Grades

You will first enter totals for each of the three grade categories (Assignments, Quizzes, and Exams), calculate the total grade out of 100, and then use a Lookup table that will return the letter grade earned by each student.

steps:

1. Click cell **J4**, type **=(B4+D4+G4)/(B20+D20+G20)*J21**, click **B20** in the formula, press **[F4]**, click **D20**, press **[F4]**, click **G20**, press **[F4]**, click **J21**, then press **[F4]**

   You used the [F4] command to insert the dollar signs ($) because you want to make the values in cells B20, D20, and G20 absolute. When you copy the formula for the rest of the students, you want each formula to divide the total assignment score by the values in rows 20 and 21.

2. Press **[Enter]**, copy the formula down to cell **J18**, then click the **Comma Style button** ![comma] on the Formatting toolbar

   Khairta Abdela earned a score of 45.63 out of a possible total of 50 on assignments. Check that Sergio Da Silva earned 40.00 points. Next, calculate Khairta's score for Quizzes.

3. Click cell **K4**, enter the formula: **=(C4+E4+H4)/(C20+E20+H20)*K21**, make the relevant cells absolute, press **[Enter]**, copy the formula down to cell **K18**, click the **Comma Style button**, click cell **L4**, enter the formula that calculates the weighted score for exams, copy the formula down to cell **L18**, then click the **Comma Style button**

   Remember to divide the total exam score by the correct absolute values in rows 20 and 21, and then multiply the result by 35. Khairta earned 13.85 for quizzes and 32.67 for exams. Next, calculate the total score out of 100 that each student earned.

4. Click cell **M4**, type an equals sign (**=**), type **Asn+Quiz+Exams**, press **[Enter]**, copy the formula down to cell **M18**, then click the **Decrease Decimal button** ![decrease decimal] on the Formatting toolbar so that no decimal places appear after the values in cells M4 to M18

   Next, create a lookup table that Excel will refer to in order to enter the correct letter grade earned by each student, depending upon the total score entered in column M.

5. Double-click the **Sheet1 tab**, type **Grades**, press **[Enter]**, double-click the **Sheet2 tab**, type **Lookup**, press **[Enter]**, then set up the worksheet so that it appears as shown in Figure P1-6

   Next, enter the lookup formula required in cell M4 to calculate the letter grade earned by Khairta Abdela.

6. Click the **Grades tab**, click cell **N4**, click the **Paste Function button** ![paste function] on the Standard toolbar, select **Lookup & Reference** from the list of function categories, click **LOOKUP**, then click **OK**

7. Click **lookup_value, array**, click **OK**, type **M4**, then press **[Tab]**

   You've entered the cell address of the value that the lookup table will find. This value represents Khairta's total score out of 100 for the course. You want the lookup formula to find this value in the lookup table and then enter the required grade in cell N4. Next, designate the range of cells (the array) that contains the lookup table.

8. Click the **Lookup tab**, drag the Lookup dialog box to the right, select cells **A2** to **B12**, click **A2** in the dialog box, press **[F4]**, click **B12**, press **[F4]**, then compare the **Lookup** dialog box to Figure P1-7

   Next, complete the formula.

9. Click **OK**, copy the formula in cell **N4** down to cell **N18**, click the **Center button** ![center], then save the workbook

   Compare the grades listed in column N to Figure P1-8. Next, go on to create a pie chart that displays the breakdown of grades.

Hint

Click No to remove the Office Assistant.

FIGURE P1-6: Lookup table

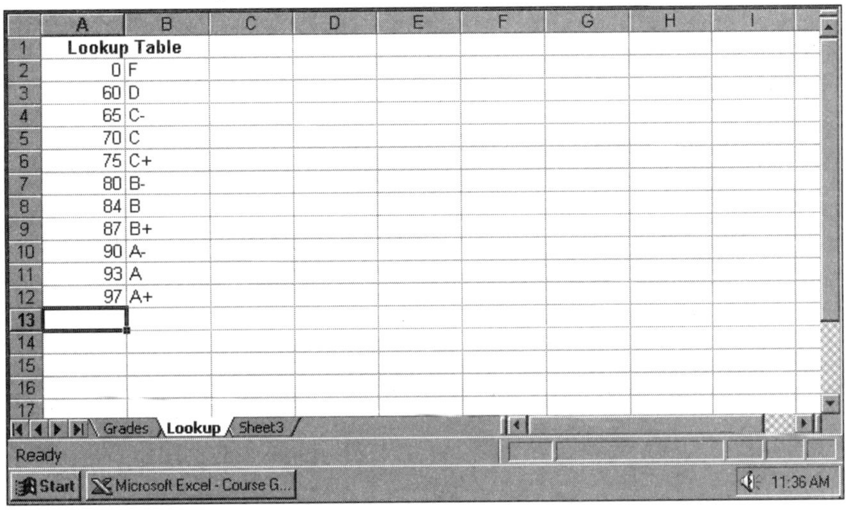

	A	B
1	Lookup Table	
2	0	F
3	60	D
4	65	C-
5	70	C
6	75	C+
7	80	B-
8	84	B
9	87	B+
10	90	A-
11	93	A
12	97	A+

Grades / Lookup / Sheet3

Ready

Start | Microsoft Excel - Course G... | 11:36 AM

FIGURE P1-7: Lookup dialog box

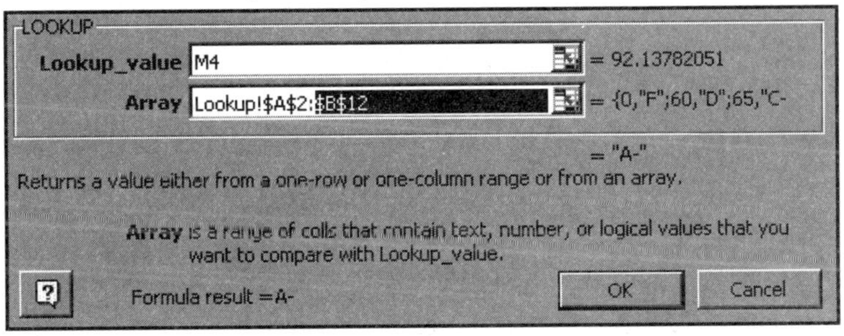

LOOKUP

Lookup_value M4 = 92.13782051

Array Lookup!$A$2:$B$12 = {0,"F";60,"D";65,"C-

= "A-"

Returns a value either from a one-row or one-column range or from an array.

Array is a range of cells that contain text, number, or logical values that you want to compare with Lookup_value.

Formula result =A-

OK   Cancel

FIGURE P1-8: Worksheet complete with letter grades

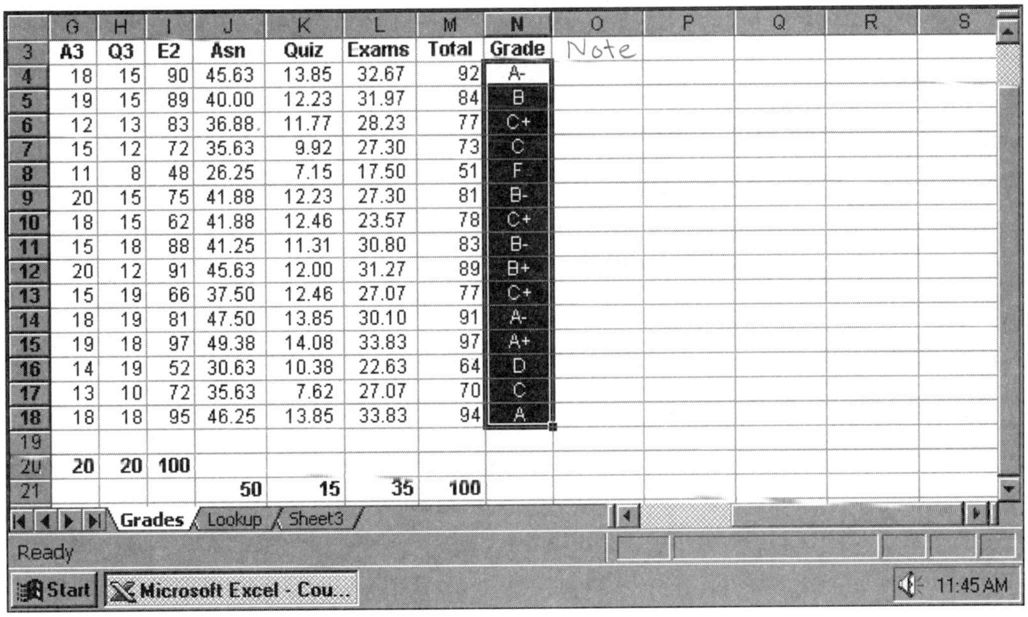

	G	H	I	J	K	L	M	N
3	A3	Q3	E2	Asn	Quiz	Exams	Total	Grade
4	18	15	90	45.63	13.85	32.67	92	A-
5	19	15	89	40.00	12.23	31.97	84	B
6	12	13	83	36.88	11.77	28.23	77	C+
7	15	12	72	35.63	9.92	27.30	73	C
8	11	8	48	26.25	7.15	17.50	51	F
9	20	15	75	41.88	12.23	27.30	81	B-
10	18	15	62	41.88	12.46	23.57	78	C+
11	15	18	88	41.25	11.31	30.80	83	B-
12	20	12	91	45.63	12.00	31.27	89	B+
13	15	19	66	37.50	12.46	27.07	77	C+
14	18	19	81	47.50	13.85	30.10	91	A-
15	19	18	97	49.38	14.08	33.83	97	A+
16	14	19	52	30.63	10.38	22.63	64	D
17	13	10	72	35.63	7.62	27.07	70	C
18	18	18	95	46.25	13.85	33.83	94	A
19								
20	20	20	100					
21				50	15	35	100	

Grades / Lookup / Sheet3

Ready

Start | Microsoft Excel - Cou... | 11:45 AM

Clues to Use

Using LOOKUP

A lookup table contains a list of ranges and values. The LOOKUP function searches the ranges in the lookup table, finds the range that includes the value (e.g., 92 in a range that begins with 90 when the next range up begins at 93), then enters the value for that range (e.g., "A-").

Excel 97

PROJECT 1

activity:

Create a Pivot Table and Pie Chart

Before you can create a pie chart that will display the breakdown of student grades, you need to create a Pivot table that will *count* the number of times that each letter grade appears in column N.

steps:

1. Select cells **N3** to **N18**, click **Data** on the menu bar, click **PivotTable Report**, click **Next**, then click **Next**

The PivotTable Wizard Step 3 of 4 dialog box appears. You need to tell Excel to create a table that will display the number of times each letter grade appears in cells N4 to N18.

2. Click **Grade**, drag it into the space next to **COLUMN**, click **Grade** again, then drag it above **DATA** as shown in Figure P1-9

3. Click **Next**, then click **Finish** to display the Pivot table in a new worksheet

The Pivot table appears in cell A1 of a new sheet as shown in Figure P1-10. Now you have the data you need to create a pie chart.

4. Select cells **B2** to **K3**, click the **Chart Wizard button** 📖 on the Standard toolbar, click **Pie**, click the **middle pie** in the top row, click **Next**, click **Next**, click the box under the **Chart title**, type **Breakdown of Final Grades**, click the **Data Labels tab**, click the **Show percent radio button**, then click **Finish**

Next, adjust the "tilt" of the pie chart.

5. Right-click the pie chart, click **3-D View…**, type **30** in the **Elevation box**, then click **OK**

Next, add a subtitle to the pie chart.

6. Click **Breakdown of Final Grades**, click after **Grades**, press [Enter], type **Marketing 200**, select **Marketing 200**, then click the **Bold button** **B** on the Formatting toolbar to remove the bold formatting

7. Click away from the pie chart, click the **Zoom Control list arrow**, click **75%**, then drag the **bottom right sizing handle** to increase the size of the pie chart so that it fills the screen

Next, copy the pie chart to the Grades sheet and format the sheet for printing.

8. Right-click the pie chart, click **Copy**, click the **Grades tab**, right-click cell **B24**, click **Paste**, then position the pie chart so that it appears centered under the labels in rows 20 and 21

9. Bold the letter grades in column N, click the **Print Preview button** 🔍 on the Standard toolbar, click **Setup**, click the **Page tab**, click the **Fit to: radio button**, click the **Margins tab**, click **Horizontally** and **Vertically**, click the **Header/Footer tab**, create a custom header that appears as shown in Figure P1-11, click **OK**, then print, save, and close the workbook

Compare your printed worksheet to Figure P1-11.

FIGURE P1-9: PivotTable Step 3 of 4 dialog box

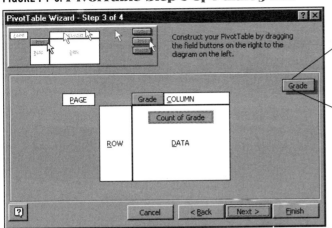

Click Grade and drag it next to COLUMN

Click Grade and drag it above DATA

FIGURE P1-10: Completed Pivot table in Sheet3

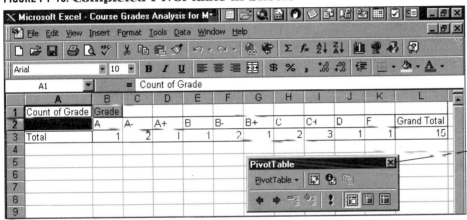

Click here to hide the Pivot table toolbar

FIGURE P1-11: Completed Course Grades Analysis

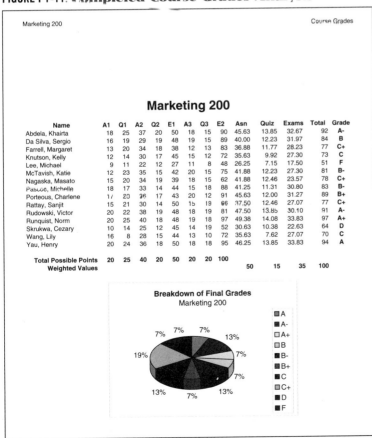

Regional Sales Analysis for Data Time Books

As the Assistant Marketing Manager for Data Time Books, you have been asked to analyze the company sales in 10 states. You will then present your analysis in the form of two charts—a map chart and a line chart. To create the Regional Sales Analysis, you will **Enter and Analyze the Sales Data**, **Create a Map Chart**, and then **Create a Line Chart and Format the Analysis**.

activity:

Enter and Analyze the Sales Data

First, you need to create a worksheet that displays the quarterly sales for each of 10 states. You will then sort the states in alphabetical order.

steps:

1. Open a blank Excel workbook, type the first three labels displayed in Figure P2-1 (**Data Time Books** to **January 1 to December 31, 1998**), select cells **A1** to **G3**, click **Format** on the menu bar, click **Cells**, click the **Alignment tab**, click the **Horizontal list arrow**, click **Center Across Selection**, then click **OK**

2. Enhance cell **A1** with a font size of **18 point** and **Bold**, enhance cell **A2** with a font size of **12 point**, enhance cell **A3** with **Italics**, then save the workbook as **Regional Sales Analysis for Data Time Books**
   Next, select the Comma style for the values you will enter in cells B6 to E15. Selecting a number format before entering the values simplifies the task.

3. Select cells **B6** to **F15**, click the **Comma Style button** [,] on the Formatting toolbar, then click the **Decrease Decimal button twice**

4. Click cell **A5**, enter and enhance the labels and values for cells **A5** to **E15**, then widen column A as shown in Figure P2-1
   Next, calculate the total annual sales for each state.

5. Click cell **F5**, type **Total**, center it and enhance it with **Bold**, click cell **F6**, click the **AutoSum button**, press **[Enter]**, then copy the formula down to cell **F15**

6. Select cells **A6** to **F15**, click the **Sort Ascending button** [↓] on the Standard toolbar, compare your worksheet to Figure P2-2, then save the workbook
   Next, go on to rank the total sales and then create a map chart.

FIGURE P2-1: Worksheet labels and values

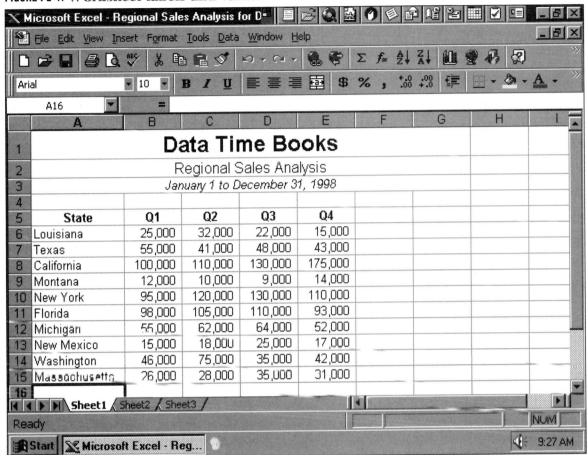

State	Q1	Q2	Q3	Q4
Louisiana	25,000	32,000	22,000	15,000
Texas	55,000	41,000	48,000	43,000
California	100,000	110,000	130,000	175,000
Montana	12,000	10,000	9,000	14,000
New York	95,000	120,000	130,000	110,000
Florida	98,000	105,000	110,000	93,000
Michigan	55,000	62,000	64,000	52,000
New Mexico	15,000	18,000	25,000	17,000
Washington	46,000	75,000	35,000	42,000
Massachusetts	26,000	28,000	35,000	31,000

FIGURE P2-2: Regional Sales worksheet complete

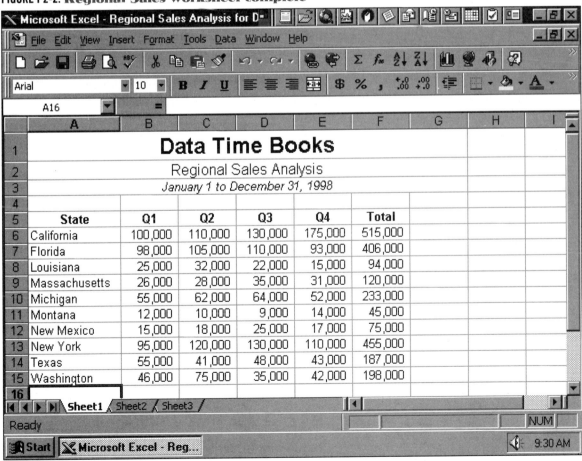

State	Q1	Q2	Q3	Q4	Total
California	100,000	110,000	130,000	175,000	515,000
Florida	98,000	105,000	110,000	93,000	406,000
Louisiana	25,000	32,000	22,000	15,000	94,000
Massachusetts	26,000	28,000	35,000	31,000	120,000
Michigan	55,000	62,000	64,000	52,000	233,000
Montana	12,000	10,000	9,000	14,000	45,000
New Mexico	15,000	18,000	25,000	17,000	75,000
New York	95,000	120,000	130,000	110,000	455,000
Texas	55,000	41,000	48,000	43,000	187,000
Washington	46,000	75,000	35,000	42,000	198,000

REGIONAL SALES ANALYSIS FOR DATA TIME BOOKS

activity:

Create a Map Chart

To create the map chart, you first need to enter an IF formula that will *rank* the annual sales in each state according to the following classification: High, Medium, and Low. You will then copy the states and ranking columns to Sheet2 and create a map chart of the United States that shades each of the 10 states according to its category.

steps:

Hint

Make sure you enter the correct number of zeroes for 300000 and 100000 (five zeroes each).

1. Click cell **G5**, type **Rank**, center it and enhance it with **Bold**, click cell **G6**, click the **Paste Function button**, select **Logical**, select **IF**, then click **OK**

   You need to enter a nested IF formula in cell G6 that instructs Excel to enter "High" if the total sales are greater than 300,000; "Medium" if the total sales are greater than 100,000; and "Low" if the total sales are less than or equal to 100,000.

2. Type **F6>300000**, press **[Tab]**, type **High**, press **[Tab]**, click the **IF** button on the formula bar, type **F6>100000**, press **[Tab]**, type **Medium**, press **[Tab]**, type **Low**, click **OK**, then copy the formula in cell **G6** down to cell **G15**

3. Select cells **A5** to **A15**, press and hold the **[Ctrl]** key, select cells **G5** to **G15**, release the **[Ctrl]** key, click the **Copy button** on the Standard toolbar, click the **Sheet2 tab**, then click the **Paste button** on the Standard toolbar

4. With cells **A1** to **B11** still selected, click the **Map button** on the Standard toolbar, draw a box for the map from cell **C2** to **H16**, click **United States in North America**, then click **OK**

   In a few seconds, the US map will appear on the screen along with the Data Map Control dialog box. To modify the map so that the states are shaded according to rank, you need to replace Count of State in the bottom section of the Data Map Control dialog box with Rank.

5. Move the mouse over **Count of State** in the bottom section of the Data Map Control dialog box until the appears as shown in Figure P2-3, click the , then drag it up to **Count of State** in the top section of the Data Map Control dialog box

   The handle turns into a recycle bin as you drag Count of State up.

Hint

You may need to drag the Data Map Control dialog box out of the way.

6. Move the mouse over **Rank** in the top section of the Data Map Control dialog box, click the , then drag it down to the bottom section of the Data Map Control dialog box

   The states appear in three different colors, according to rank. Next, modify the map legend title.

7. Double-click the map legend in the lower right corner of the map, type **Regional Sales**, press **[Tab]** **twice** to move to the **Subtitle box**, press **[Delete]**, then click **OK**

   Next, modify the map so that only the US states appear.

8. Right-click the map, click **Features**, click the appropriate check boxes to remove the following elements: **Canada, Canada Lakes**, and **Mexico**, then click **OK**

Time To
✓ **Save**

9. Move the Data Map Control dialog box away from the map, click the legend, drag it to the left side of the map as shown in Figure P2-4, double-click the box containing **North America**, drag the mouse across **North America** to select it, type **United States**, click away from the title, click it again, increase the size of the box and drag it up so that the extra map element is hidden as shown in Figure P2-5, then click away from the map to exit the Data Map Control dialog box

   Your map chart is complete. Next, go on to create a line chart and then format the regional sales analysis for printing.

FIGURE P2-3: Moving Count of State in the Data Map Control dialog box

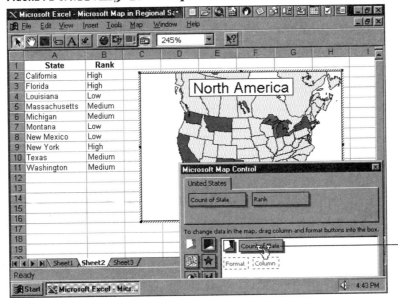

Click Count of State and drag it up

FIGURE P2-4: Legend repositioned

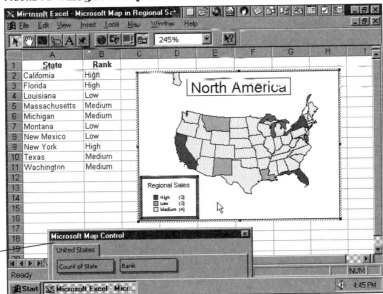

You can move the Data Map Control dialog box anywhere on the screen

FIGURE P2-5: Chart title modified and repositioned

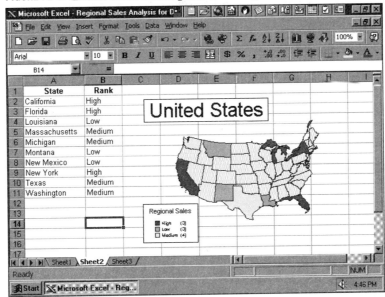

activity:

Create a Line Chart and Format the Analysis

You will create a line chart that shows each state's regional sales in all four quarters, and then format an attractive regional sales analysis in Sheet4. The completed analysis appears in Figure P2-6. First, add a new worksheet, then name the worksheet tabs.

steps:

1. Click **Insert** on the menu bar, click **Worksheet**, double-click the **Sheet1** tab, type **Sales**, press **[Enter]**, double-click the **Sheet2** tab, type **Map**, press **[Enter]**, double-click the **Sheet3** tab, type **Line**, press **[Enter]**, double-click the **Sheet4** tab, type **Analysis**, then press **[Enter]**

2. Click the **Line** tab, click the **ChartWizard** button, click **Line**, click **Next**, click the **Sales** tab, select cells **A5** to **E15**, click the **Rows** radio button, click **Next**, click the **Titles** tab if necessary, click the **Chart Title** box, type **1998 Regional Sales Progression**, then click **Finish**

3. Increase the chart size so that it fills the screen, right-click the **legend**, click **Format Legend**, click **Font**, select a font size of **9**, click **OK**, right-click a blank area of the gray chart area, click **Format Plot Area**, click the **None** radio button in the **Area** section, then click **OK**

4. Click the **Sales** tab, select cells **A1** to **G3**, click the **Copy** button, click the **Analysis** tab, then click the **Paste button**

5. Click cell **A5**, click the **Drawing** button 🔧 on the Standard toolbar to display the Drawing toolbar, click the **Text Box** button 📧 on the Drawing toolbar, draw a box from cell **A5** to **G10**, then type the text in the box as shown in Figure P2-6

6. Click the **Map** tab, click the map chart to select it, click the **Copy** button, click the **Analysis** tab, click cell **B12**, then click the **Paste button**

7. Click cell **A29** (or a cell below the map chart), create a text box as shown in Figure P2-6, then copy the line chart below the text box

8. Adjust the positioning of the boxes and charts so that they appear centered in relation to each other, then click the **Print Preview** button 🔍 on the Standard toolbar

9. Click the **Setup** button, click the **Page** tab, click the **Fit to:** radio button, click the **Margins** tab, click the **Horizontally** and **Vertically** check boxes, insert a **Custom Header** as shown in Figure P2-6, print a copy of the worksheet, then save and close the workbook

Excel 97

1998 Regional Sales Analysis   [Your Name]

Data Time Books
Regional Sales Analysis
January 1 to December 31, 1998

From January to December, 1998, Data Time Books realized total sales of $2,328,000. The map chart illustrated below displays the breakdown of sales by state according to three categories: High sales (over $300,000), Medium sales ($100,000 to $300,000), and Low sales (below $100,000).

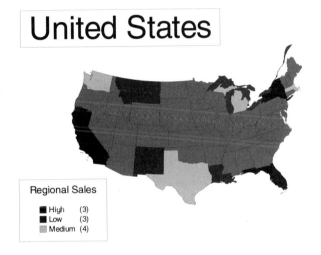

United States

Regional Sales

- ■ High   (3)
- ■ Low   (3)
- ▨ Medium (4)

In all but one state (California), sales have not increased to planned levels. Sales in Florida and New York, in particular, have decreased to unacceptable levels. The line chart illustrated below displays the quarterly sales progression for Data Time Books. In 1999, our marketing plan will be revised to ensure a steady progression of sales in all states.

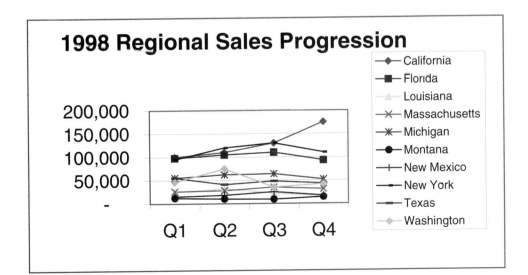

1998 Regional Sales Progression

- ◆ California
- ■ Florida
- ▲ Louisiana
- ✕ Massachusetts
- ✱ Michigan
- ● Montana
- ┼ New Mexico
- ━ New York
- ━ Texas
- ◆ Washington

200,000
150,000
100,000
50,000
-

Q1   Q2   Q3   Q4

Spending Analysis for Greg Barr

Since graduating from college two years earlier, Greg Barr has been working as a computer technician for a net salary of $1,680 per month. Unfortunately, he's having trouble making ends meet while paying off his student loan and maintaining his own apartment. To help organize his personal finances, he has decided to analyze his spending habits to determine where he can cut back on expenses. For three months, he has kept careful track of his expenses. Now he's ready to use Excel to analyze his financial position. To create a spending analysis for Greg Barr, you will **Create an Income and Expenses Worksheet** and then **Prepare a Spending Analysis**.

activity:

Create an Income and Expenses Worksheet

steps:

1. Open a blank Excel workbook, enter and enhance the labels and values as shown in the printout in Figure P3-1, then save the worksheet as **Spending Analysis for Greg Barr**
Remember to use time-saving techniques to enter repetitive information. For example, you can type "March" in cell B4, then drag the corner handle to cell D4 to enter the two months from March to May. You can also copy across all the expenses that are the same each month. Next, calculate Greg's total income and expenses.

2. Select cells **B6** to **E7**, click the **AutoSum button**, select cells **B10** to **E20**, then click the **AutoSum button**

3. Click cell **C22**, enter the formula: **=B23**, press [**Enter**], then copy the formula across to cell **D22**
Next, calculate the surplus, including the balance forward from the previous month.

4. Click cell **B23**, type **=B7-B20**, press [**Enter**], click cell **C23**, type **=C7-C20+C22**, press [**Enter**], then copy the formula to cell **D23**
Next, calculate the total surplus.

5. Click cell **E23**, type **=E7-E20**, then press [**Enter**]
As shown in the printout in Figure P3-2, Greg's total income in cell E7 is 5,040.00 and his total expenses in cell E20 are 5,445.00. At the end of three months, his surplus in cell E23 is (405.00), a negative number. Greg needs to find a way to save money! Next, go on to create charts that will help Greg determine where he should cut expenses.

6. Name the **Sheet1 tab** "Income & Expenses" and name the **Sheet2 tab** "Analysis," then save the workbook

FIGURE P3-1: **Printout of worksheet setup**

	A	B	C	D	E	
1	**Greg Barr**					— 20 pt., Bold
2	**Personal Spending Analysis**					— 14 pt., Bold
3						
4		**March**	**April**	**May**	**Total**	
5	**Income**					
6	Pay Check (net)	1,680.00	1,680.00	1,680.00		
7	**Total Income**					
8						
9	**Expenses**					
10	Rent	450.00	450.00	450.00		
11	Food	350.00	350.00	350.00		
12	Phone	75.00	55.00	62.00		
13	Utilities	55.00	55.00	55.00		
14	Car Insurance	75.00	75.00	75.00		
15	Gas	80.00	75.00	120.00		
16	Entertainment	200.00	250.00	250.00		
17	Miscellaneous	300.00	250.00	250.00		
18	Student Loan Payment	200.00	200.00	200.00		
19	Bank Charges & Interest	27.00	27.00	34.00		
20	**Total Expenses**					
21						
22	**Balance Forward**					
23	**Surplus**					

FIGURE P3-2: **Printout of worksheet calculations complete**

	A	B	C	D	E
1	**Greg Barr**				
2	**Personal Spending Analysis**				
3					
4		**March**	**April**	**May**	**Total**
5	**Income**				
6	Pay Check (net)	1,680.00	1,680.00	1,680.00	5,040.00
7	**Total Income**	1,680.00	1,680.00	1,680.00	5,040.00
8					
9	**Expenses**				
10	Rent	450.00	450.00	450.00	1,350.00
11	Food	350.00	350.00	350.00	1,050.00
12	Phone	75.00	55.00	62.00	192.00
13	Utilities	55.00	55.00	55.00	165.00
14	Car Insuranoo	75.00	75.00	75.00	225.00
15	Gas	80.00	75.00	120.00	275.00
16	Entertainment	200.00	250.00	250.00	700.00
17	Miscellaneous	300.00	250.00	250.00	800.00
18	Student Loan Payment	200.00	200.00	200.00	600.00
19	Bank Charges & Interest	27.00	27.00	34.00	88.00
20	**Total Expenses**	1,812.00	1,787.00	1,846.00	5,445.00
21					
22	**Balance Forward**		(132.00)	(239.00)	
23	**Surplus**	(132.00)	(239.00)	(405.00)	(405.00)

activity:

Prepare a Spending Analysis

You will create two charts: a pie chart that shows the breakdown of Greg's expenses by type (e.g., Rent, Food, etc.) and a pyramid chart that compares Greg's monthly income with his monthly expenses. You will then modify the worksheet to display Greg's projected income and expenses for June, July, and August.

steps:

1. Click the **Analysis** tab, click the **Chart Wizard button** on the Standard toolbar, click **Pie**, click **Next**, click the **Collapse Dialog Box button** to collapse the Chart Wizard Step 2 of 4 dialog box, click the **Income & Expenses** tab, select cells **A10** to **A19**, type a comma, select cells **E10** to **E19**, click the **Restore Dialog Box button** to display the dialog box, click **Next**, name the chart **Expenses Breakdown**, click the **Data Labels** tab, click the **Show Percent** radio button, then click **Finish**

2. Increase the chart size so that it fills the screen, right-click the chart legend, click **Format Legend**, click the **Font tab**, select a font size of **8**, click **OK**, right-click a data label, click **Format Data Labels**, then change the font size of the data labels to **8**

   Next, create a pyramid chart that compares Greg's monthly income to his monthly expenses.

3. Click below the pie chart, click the **Chart Wizard button**, click **Pyramid** (you will need to scroll down), click **Next**, collapse the dialog box, click the **Income & Expenses** tab, select cells **B4** to **D4**, type a comma, select cells **B7** to **D7**, type a comma, select cells **B20** to **D20**, restore the dialog box, click **Next**, name the chart **Income and Expenses Comparison**, then click **Finish**

   You want "Income" and "Expenses" to appear as legend entries instead of Series 1 and Series 2.

4. Right-click one of the blue pyramids, click **Source Data**, click the **Series tab**, click the **Name box**, type **Income**, click **Series 2**, click **Name box**, type **Expenses**, then click **OK**

5. Double-click the numbers on the Y-Axis, click the **Number tab**, reduce the number of decimal places to **0**, click the **Symbol list arrow**, click **$**, click the **Scale tab**, double-click the value next to **Maximum**, type **2500**, click **OK**, increase the chart size and position it so that it appears similar to Figure P3-3, then click away from the chart to deselect it

   Greg can see that he spends 28% of his income on entertainment and miscellaneous expenses. He decides to cut back on these expenses in the next three months. To see the effects of these cutbacks on the two charts while still retaining a copy of his original worksheet, Greg will first make a copy of the worksheet in the Income and Expenses sheet.

6. Click the **Income & Expenses** tab, select cells **A4** to **E23**, click the **Copy button** on the Standard toolbar, click cell **A27**, then click the **Paste button** on the Standard toolbar

   Next, modify the income and expenses to display Greg's projections for June, July, and August.

7. Change the labels in cells **B4** to **D4** to **June**, **July**, and **August**, change the Entertainment expense to **150** for all three months, change the **Miscellaneous** expense to **200** for all three months, then click the **Analysis** tab to see the effect of your changes on the charts

   The pyramids representing income and expenses are nearly the same height. Greg realizes that he will save interest payments now that he is no longer overdrawn on his bank account at the end of each month.

Time To

✓ **Save**

✓ **Close**

8. Change the Bank Charges & Interest expense to **15** for all three months, display the **Analysis** sheet, modify the size and position of the charts and add the three text boxes as shown in Figure P3-3, display the Print Preview screen, format the sheet so that it is horizontally and vertically centered on one page, add a custom header, then print a copy and compare your finished worksheet to Figure P3-3

   You may wish to switch to 75% view in order to position the charts and then add the text boxes.

FIGURE P3-3: Completed Personal Spending Analysis

Greg Barr's Personal Spending Analysis   [Your Name]

Greg Barr
Personal Spending Analysis
Goal for June, July, and August 1998

By reducing my Entertainment and Miscellaneous expenses from 28% of my total expenses to 24%, I can reduce my interest charges, thereby saving $43 on interest charges and $350 on Entertainment and Miscellaneous expenses over three months.

Expenses Breakdown

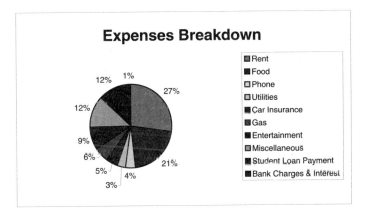

If I can make the required reductions in my expenses, my income will exceed my expenses by $88.00 at the end of three months.

Income and Expenses Comparison

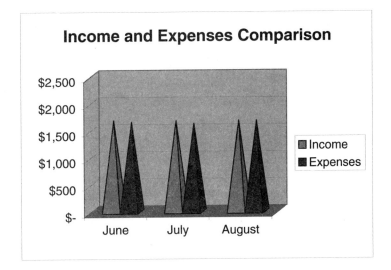

Independent Challenges

INDEPENDENT CHALLENGE 1

You have been working all term as a teaching assistant for a course of your choice. The instructor you work for has given you the grade sheet she has kept "by hand" and has asked you to transfer it to Excel and then calculate the students' grades. Complete the steps below to create a course grades analysis for a course of your choice.

1. Determine the name of the course and write it in the box below:

Course Name: ....

2. Determine the grade categories and the percentage of scores allocated to each category. For example, you could allocate 40% of the total grades to Assignments, 30% to Exams, and 30% to oral presentations. Allocate at least four grade categories and make sure the percentages you assign add up to 100%. Enter the grade categories and percentages in the box below:

Category	Name (e.g., Assignments)	Percentage
1.		
2.		
3.		

3. Set up a worksheet with the name of the course, a list of at least 20 students, and labels for the various assignments, exams, quizzes, etc. You determine the number of items in each of the three grade categories you have selected.
4. Determine the total scores possible for each item in each score category and enter the totals a row below the list of names. To check the setup of your Course Grades Analysis, refer to the Course Grades Analysis you created for Project 1.
5. Enter the points for each student. Make sure you refer to the totals you entered to ensure that each score you enter for each student is equal to or less than the total points possible.
6. Calculate the total points for each score category, divide the total points by the total of the possible points, then multiply the result by the percentage you assigned to the mark category. The formula required is: Sum of Student's Points/Sum of Total Points* Percentage. For example, if the Assignment points are entered in cells C4, D4, and F4, the total possible points are entered in cells C25, D25, and F25, and the percentage of Assignments is 40%, the formula required is: =(C4+D4+F4)/($C$25+$D$25+$F$25)*40.
7. Calculate the total points out of 100 earned by the first student on your list.
8. Copy the formulas you used to calculate the first student's weighted score in each category for the remaining students.
9. Sort the list of students alphabetically by last name.
10. Create a Lookup table that lists the letter grades and ranges.
11. Enter the LOOKUP formula in the appropriate cell, then copy it down for the remaining students.
12. Create a Pivot table in Sheet2 that counts the number of times each letter grade appears.
13. Create a pie chart in Sheet1 from the data in the Pivot table to show the breakdown of scores by letter grade.
14. Save the workbook as Course Grades Analysis for [Course Name], format Sheet1 attractively, print a copy, then save and close the workbook.

INDEPENDENT CHALLENGE 2

Create a regional sales analysis that contains two charts for a company of your choice as instructed in the steps below.

1. Select one of the geographical areas included in Excel's list of maps. To check the maps available, click the Map button in Excel, then draw a box for the map. A dialog box that lists all the maps available will appear. Scroll through the list to find the map you want, then close the dialog box.

2. Determine a name for your company and the location for your regional sales analysis.

3. Set up your worksheet so that it contains the name of your company, the dates covered by the sales analysis, and the list of states, countries, provinces, etc., in the geographical area you have selected. For example, if you chose Canada, you would list five or six of the provinces. Make sure you spell the area names correctly and use a standard format. For example, you need to enter "United Kingdom" instead of "England" if you wish to include the United Kingdom in the World Countries map. If you wish to list states in the United States, use the standard postal abbreviation (e.g., CA, NY, AZ, etc.) or spell out the state names.

4. Enter sales data for each of four quarters for each geographical area listed in your worksheet, calculate the total annual sales for each area, then sort the areas in alphabetical order.

5. Use the IF Function to rank the total annual sales for each area according to a set scale (for example, "High," "Medium," "Low," "Excellent," "Fair," and "Poor," or even "Over $1,000,000," "$500,000 to $999,999," and "Under $500,000").

6. Copy the IF formula to the remaining areas, then select the list of areas and the list of ranks and copy them to Sheet2.

7. Create a map chart from the list of areas and ranks. If a dialog box warns you that Excel cannot identify the geographical regions, check the list of regions to ensure they conform to a standard format. You may need to experiment with different formats until you find a list of regions that Excel will accept.

8. Move the Count of [State] box to the upper section of the Data Map Control dialog box and the Rank box to the lower section.

9. Double-click the legend, then enter a title and subtitle for your map

10. Right-click the map, select Features, then select or deselect any features that you do not wish to display. You will need to experiment until your map displays the data in a clear and easy-to-understand format.

11. Create a line chart in Sheet3 that displays the quarterly sales for each region, then modify the line chart so that it displays the data attractively.

12. Insert a new worksheet, copy the map chart and the line chart into the new sheet, then add text boxes to explain the charts.

13. Save your worksheet as "Regional Sales Analysis for [Company Name]", format it attractively for printing, print a copy, then save and close the workbook.

INDEPENDENT CHALLENGE 3

Create a record of your own income and expenses for the past three months. Your goal is to determine how you spend your money and to find ways in which you can economize on certain expenses.

1. Set up your worksheet so that the income you receive appears first, followed by the list of your expenses for three months. Name the worksheet Income & Expenses.

2. Calculate your total monthly income and expenses, and then your total income and expenses for three months.

3. Name Sheet2 Analysis, then create a pie chart in the Analysis sheet that shows the breakdown of your total expenses.

4. Create a pyramid, cone, or cylinder chart below the pie chart that compares your monthly income with your monthly expenses. Note that you will need to include three sets of cells in this chart: the month labels, the values representing the total income for each month, and the values representing the total expenses for each month. Modify the chart so that the legend displays "Income" and "Expenses."

5. Copy the charts into a new worksheet, then copy the income and expenses for the current three months to a blank area of Sheet1.

6. Modify the original income and expenses to reflect projected changes in your spending habits over the next three months. Try to determine where you could save money. For example, you could try to reduce your car expenses by walking to work or school or your entertainment expenses by eating out less often. The changes you make will reflect your own priorities.

7. Change the month labels to the three months following the current months.

8. Add a heading to Sheet2 that contains your name and "Personal Spending Analysis", then add text boxes to explain the changes you plan to make to your spending habits.

9. Save the workbook as My Personal Expenses, format it attractively for printing on one page, print a copy, then save and close the workbook.

INDEPENDENT CHALLENGE 4

As a sales manager at Worldwide Travel, Inc., you have been asked to prepare an analysis of the tours sold to Canadian destinations in 1997. This analysis will include both a map chart and a line chart.

1. Open a blank Excel workbook, set it up so that it appears as shown in Figure 1C-1, insert a new worksheet, name the sheet tabs, then save the workbook as Canadian Sales Analysis for Worldwide Tours.

FIGURE IC-1: Tour Sales worksheet

	A	B	C	D	E
1	**Worldwide Travel, Inc.**				
2	Canadian Tours				
3	January 1 to December 31, 1997				
4					
5	**Province**	**Summer Tours**	**Winter Tours**	**Total**	**Rank**
6	Quebec	15	20		
7	Nova Scotia	5	2		
8	Manitoba	2	1		
9	Saskatchewan	2	1		
10	Ontario	25	10		
11	Yukon	10	5		
12	British Columbia	40	30		
13	Alberta	35	25		

Sheet tabs: Sales / Map / Column / Analysis

2. Calculate the total sales for each province in column D, click cell E6, then use the IF Function to create an IF formula that enters "Over 55 Tours," if the total number of tours in cell D6 is greater than 55, "30 to 55 Tours," if the total number of tours is greater than or equal to 30, and "Less than 30 Tours" if neither condition applies.
3. Copy the formula in cell E6 for the remaining provinces, widen the column, then sort the provinces alphabetically so that Alberta appears first.
4. Select cells A5 to A13 and cells E5 to E13 (use the [Ctrl] key), copy them to the map sheet, then create a map chart of Canada. Note that you will need to change "Yukon" to "Yukon Territory."
5. Move the "Count of Province" box to the upper section of the Data Map Control dialog box, then move the "Rank" box to the lower section of the Data Map Control dialog box.
6. Change the legend title to "Canadian Tours," then delete the subtitle.
7. Right-click the chart, click features, click Canada, click the custom option button, click the Fill Color list arrow, click the white box, then click OK.
8. Modify the chart title, move the chart legend, then increase the chart size so that it fills the screen.
9. Create a 3-D bar chart in the Column sheet from cells A5 to C13 in the Sales sheet, then modify the chart so that it appears as shown in Figure 1C-2. You need to increase the chart size so that it fills the screen, reduce the font size of the legend, X-Axis, and Y-Axis, then increase the size of the chart grid.
10. Copy the map chart and the column chart into the Analysis sheet.
11. As shown in Figure IC-2, add text boxes (display the text in 12 point), format the sheet for printing in landscape orientation, print a copy, then save and close the workbook.

FIGURE IC-2: Completed Canadian Tours Analysis

Canadian Tours in 1997

[Your Name]

Worldwide Tours, Inc.
Canadian Tours
January 1 to December 31, 1997

From January to December, 1997, Worldwide Tours, Inc., sold a total of 228 tours to Canadian destinations. The map chart illustrated below displays the total number of tours by province according to the three categories displayed in the chart legend. Only British Columbia and Alberta attracted more than 55 tours. Tours to these provinces should be advertised more aggressively to capitalize on their current popularity. Fewer than 30 tours were sold to the Yukon, Saskatchewan, Manitoba, and Nova Scotia. A marketing campaign should be launched to encourage sales to these provinces. Both Quebec and Ontario attracted fewer tours than projected in 1997. These provinces will be advertised more aggressively in 1998.

In all but one province (Quebec), summer tours proved more popular than winter tours. Skiing holidays to British Columbia and Alberta, in particular, should be promoted in 1998 to bolster the already high interest shown in these provinces by our clients.

Worldwide Travel, Inc.

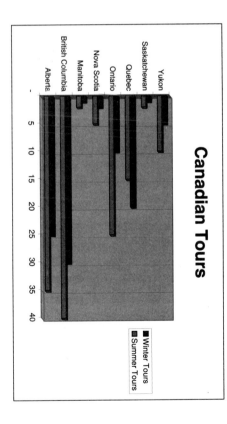

Canadian Tours
- 30 to 55 Tours (2)
- Less than 30 Tours (4)
- Over 55 Tours (2)

Canadian Tours

Alberta
British Columbia
Manitoba
Nova Scotia
Ontario
Quebec
Saskatchewan
Yukon

- 5 10 15 20 25 30 35 40

- ■ Winter Tours
- ■ Summer Tours

Visual Workshop

You have just completed a survey of the leisure activities most preferred by your classmates in Marketing 200. Now you want to create a chart to visually display the results of your survey. Create the worksheet shown in Figure VW-1, then create a Pivot table in Sheet2 that counts the number of times each activity appears in column B of Sheet1. Note that you will need to drag the Activity box next to Column and above Data in the PivotTable Step 3 of 4 dialog box. Once you have created the Pivot table, create the pie chart shown in Figure VW-2. You will need to show labels and percents, clear the legend, adjust the elevation of the 3-D view to 40, move and enlarge the title, add a subtitle, increase the size of the pie chart, and reduce the font size of the data labels. Save your workbook as Leisure Activities Preferred by Marketing 200 Classmates, format and print a copy of Sheet2, then save and close the workbook.

FIGURE VW-1: Worksheet setup

	A	B	C	D	E	F	G	H	I
1	Student #	Activity							
2	1	Sports							
3	2	Music							
4	3	Sports							
5	4	Dancing							
6	5	Music							
7	6	Art							
8	7	Travel							
9	8	Sports							
10	9	Sports							
11	10	Travel							
12	11	Art							
13	12	Travel							
14	13	Sports							
15	14	Sports							
16	15	Art							
17									

Sheet1 / Sheet2 / Sheet3

Ready — NUM

Start | Microsoft Excel - Leis... — 12:24 PM

FIGURE VW-2: Completed pie chart

	A	B	C	D	E	F	G	H	I
1	Count of Activity	Activity							
2		Art	Dancing	Music	Sports	Travel	Grand Total		
3	Total	3	1	2	6	3	15		
4									

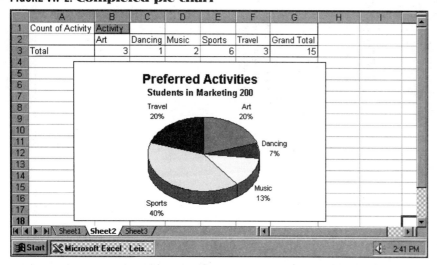

Preferred Activities
Students in Marketing 200

Travel 20%
Art 20%
Dancing 7%
Music 13%
Sports 40%

Sheet1 \ Sheet2 / Sheet3

Start | Microsoft Excel - Leis... — 2:41 PM

Microsoft
► Excel
Projects

Financial Analysis

In This Unit You Will Create:

PROJECT 1 ► **Savings Plan**

PROJECT 2 ► **Investment Analysis**

PROJECT 3 ► **Mortgage Options**

You can use the many financial functions in Excel to analyze investment opportunities and predict financial gains or losses. For example, you can use Excel to predict how much $10 invested at an 8% annual interest rate will be worth in 20 years, or what the monthly mortgage payment will be on a $200,000 house that you purchase with a 10% down payment. You also can determine how big a loan you can get if you can afford a monthly payment of $200 or how much money you need to save now in order to have a good retirement income. ► In this unit, you will use Excel's financial functions, charts, and drawing tools to create worksheets that analyze and solve specific financial problems.

PROJECT 1

OVERVIEW

Savings Plan for Donna Burgess

Donna Burgess has just graduated from college and started her first full-time job. She is 25 years old and would like to retire when she is 55 so that she can spend several years traveling around the world. Donna needs to determine how much money she needs to invest each month in order to have enough money to fund her dreams when she is 55. Four activities are required to set up a savings plan for Donna.

Project Activities

Set Up the Savings Data

Before you can formulate a savings plan for Donna, you need to set up a worksheet that contains information about her age, the age at which she plans to stop working, and financial information regarding the amount of money she plans to invest and the interest rates she can expect. Figure P1-1 displays the completed savings plan you will create for Donna. The data used to calculate the savings plan appear in the top-left portion of the page below the text box heading.

Calculate Total Savings

You will use the Table function to calculate the total savings that Donna can expect from a monthly investment of $100, $200, or $300 at each of the three interest rates: 7%, 8%, and 9%. The Table function uses the Future Value function to calculate how much money each monthly payment at each interest rate will be worth in 30 years. The Calculation of Total Savings table in Figure P1-1 displays the total savings Donna can expect from each option. For example, she will save a total of $298,071.89 if she invests $200 a month at an 8% interest rate for 30 years.

Calculate Savings Income

Once you have determined Donna's total savings, you will use the Table function again to calculate the monthly income Donna can expect to make from her investments when she stops working. The Calculation of Investment Income table in Figure P1-1 uses the PMT function to calculate the monthly income Donna can expect, depending on how much she invests each month for the next 30 years. For example, if Donna invests $200 a month at 8% interest for 30 years, she will have a monthly income of $2,493.19 for a further 20 years.

Format and Print the Savings Plan

Finally, you will create a line chart and a column chart to graphically compare Donna's investment options as shown in Figure P1-1. You will then format all the elements of the savings plan so that they appear as shown in Figure P1-1, and use the drawing tools to draw arrows to the chart elements that represent Donna's most realistic savings option.

FIGURE P1-1: Completed Savings Plan for Donna Burgess

Savings Plan

[Your Name]

Donna Burgess
Savings Plan

Current Age		25	
Age to stop working		55	
Years to receive savings income		20	
Monthly contributions			
	Plan 1	$	100.00
	Plan 2	$	200.00
	Plan 3	$	300.00
Expected interest rates			
	Plan 1		7%
	Plan 2		8%
	Plan 3		9%

Calculation of Total Savings

Interest	7%			8%			9%		
Payment	$ 100.00		$ 100.00	$ 200.00		$ 200.00	$ 300.00		$ 330.00
	$ 121,997.10		$ 121,997.10	$ 243,994.20		$ 365,991.30			
		0.07	$ 149,035.94		0.08	$ 298,071.89		$ 447,137.83	
		0.09	$ 183,074.35			$ 366,148.70		$ 549,223.04	

Best Option → $ 298,071.89

Calculation of Savings Income
At 8% Interest

	$ 100.00	$ 200.00	$ 300.00	**Monthly Income**
7%	$1,020.43	$2,040.87	$3,061.30	
8%	$1,246.60	$2,493.19	$3,739.79	
9%	$1,531.31	$3,062.61	$4,593.92	

$ 2,493.19

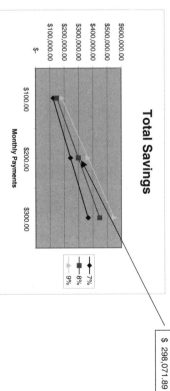

Total Savings

Savings Income

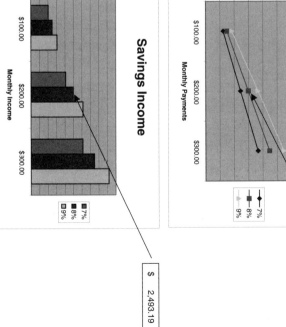

SAVINGS PLAN FOR DONNA BURGESS

activity:

Set Up the Savings Data

You need to enter the data that Donna will use as the basis of her savings plan. This data includes her current age (25), the age at which she plans to stop working (55), the number of years she plans to receive income from her investments (20), three monthly savings options ($100, $200, and $300), and three interest rate options (7%, 8%, and 9%).

steps:

1. Open a blank Excel workbook, click the **Drawing button** 🔧 on the Standard toolbar to display the Drawing toolbar, click the **Text Box button** 📰 on the Drawing toolbar, then draw a text box as shown in Figure P1-2

2. Type **Donna Burgess**, press [**Enter**], type **Savings Plan**, enhance "Donna Burgess" with **18 point** and **Bold** and "Savings Plan" with **14 point** and **Italics**, then select both lines of text and click the **Center button** ≡ on the Standard toolbar

3. Click the outside border of the text box, click the **Shadow button** 🔲 on the Drawing toolbar, click Shadow style 5 as shown in Figure P1-2, click away from the text box to deselect it, then save the workbook as **Savings Plan for Donna Burgess** to the disk where you plan to store all the files for this book

   Next, enter the data required for Donna's savings plan.

4. Click cell **A8**, enter the labels in cells **A8** to **A16** as shown in Figure P1-3, then widen Column A

5. Click cell **C8**, enter the values in cells **C8** to **C10**, click cell **B12**, type **Plan 1**, press [**Tab**], type **100**, enter the labels and values for cells **B13** to **C14** as shown in Figure P1-3, then select cells **C12** to **C14** and click the **Currency Style button** 💲 on the Formatting toolbar

6. Select cells **B12** to **B14**, click the **Copy button** 📑 on the Standard toolbar, click cell **B17**, then click the **Paste button** 📋 on the Standard toolbar

7. Click cell **C17**, type **.07**, press [**Enter**], type **.08**, press [**Enter**], type **.09**, then press [**Enter**]

8. Select cells **C17** to **C19**, then click the **Percent Style button** % on the Formatting toolbar, then save the workbook

   Compare your worksheet to Figure P1-3. Next, go on to set up a 2-variable table that will calculate how much money Donna Burgess will make on each of the three monthly contributions at each of the three interest rates.

FIGURE P1-2: **Completed text box**

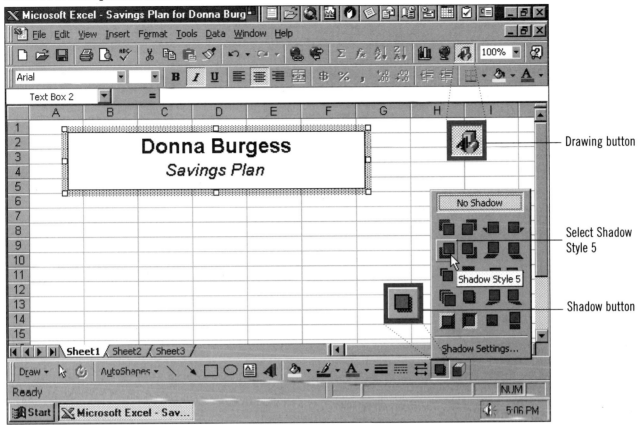

Donna Burgess
Savings Plan

Drawing button

No Shadow

Select Shadow Style 5

Shadow Style 5

Shadow button

Shadow Settings...

FIGURE P1-3: **Worksheet setup complete**

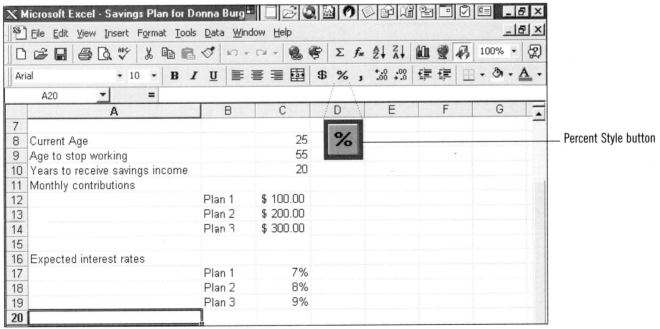

	A	B	C	D	E	F	G
7							
8	Current Age		25				
9	Age to stop working		55				
10	Years to receive savings income		20				
11	Monthly contributions						
12		Plan 1	$ 100.00				
13		Plan 2	$ 200.00				
14		Plan 3	$ 300.00				
15							
16	Expected interest rates						
17		Plan 1	7%				
18		Plan 2	8%				
19		Plan 3	9%				
20							

Percent Style button

activity:

Calculate Total Savings

Donna needs to know how much money she can hope to make on each of the three monthly contributions at each of the three interest rates. To determine this information, you will set up a 2-variable table that uses the Future Value (FV) function to calculate Donna's total savings over 30 years for each option.

steps:

1. Click cell **B21**, type **Calculation of Total Savings**, press [Enter], enhance cell B21 with **Bold** and a font size of **14 point**, then select cells **B21** to **F21** and click the **Merge and Center button** 🔳 on the Formatting toolbar

2. Click cell **B23**, type **Interest**, press [Tab], type **.07**, press [Enter], click cell **C23**, click the **Percent Style button** 🔲 on the Formatting toolbar, click cell **B24**, type **Payment**, press [Tab], type **100**, press [Enter], then enhance cell **C24** with the Currency style

   Next, assign range names to the values in cells C23 and C24 in order to simplify formulas.

3. Click cell **C23**, click **C23** in the Name box on the formula bar, type **Interest**, press [Enter], click cell **C24**, click the Name box, type **Payment**, then press [Enter]

   Now, when you want to refer to cells C23 or C24 in a formula, you can enter "Interest" or "Payment."

4. Enter and enhance the values in cells **C27** to **C29** and **D26** to **F26** as shown in Figure P1-4

   Remember to display the values in cells C27 to C29 in the Percent style and the values in cells D26 to F26 in the Currency style. Next, you need to enter a formula to calculate the Future Value (FV) of each monthly contribution ($100, $200, or $300) at each of the three annual interest rates (7%, 8%, and 9%).

5. Click cell **C26**, click the **Paste Function button** 🔲 on the Standard toolbar, select **Financial** from the list of **Function categories**, select **FV** from the list of **Function names**, then click **OK**

   The Rate you will enter is the annual interest rate (7%) in cell C23 (now called "Interest") divided by 12 (to determine the monthly interest). The Nper is the number of years Donna will make contributions (30) multiplied by 12 (to determine the total number of months). The Pmt is the value ($100) in cell C24 (now called "Payment").

6. Type **Interest/12**, press [Tab], type **30*12**, press [Tab], type **-Payment**, then compare the FV Function dialog box to Figure P1-5

   Note that you enter the Pmt amount as a negative number because it represents an outflow of funds.

7. Click **OK**

   As you can see, $121,997.10 appears in cell C26. This value represents the total amount of money that Donna will have in 30 years if she invests $100 per month at 7% interest for 30 years. Next, use the Table function to calculate the total amount of money that Donna will have for each of the three monthly investment amounts at each of the three interest rates.

8. Select cells **C26** to **F29**, click **Data** on the menu bar, click **Table**, type **Payment** in the box next to **Row input cell**, press [Tab], type **Interest** in the box next to **Column input cell**, then click **OK**

   Next, assign a range name to the table.

9. Select cells **D27** to **F29**, click the **Name box**, type **SavingsTable** (no space), press [Enter], click the **Currency Style button** 🔲 on the Formatting toolbar, then save the worksheet

   Cells B21 to F29 of your worksheet appear as shown in Figure P1-6. Now that you know how much Donna's investments will be worth in 30 years, depending on how much she saves per month at which interest rate, you can calculate the income she can expect to make when she stops working at age 55. Next, go on to create another 2-variable table that will use the Payment (PMT) function to determine Donna's monthly income after she stops working.

FIGURE P1-4: **Calculation of Total Savings table**

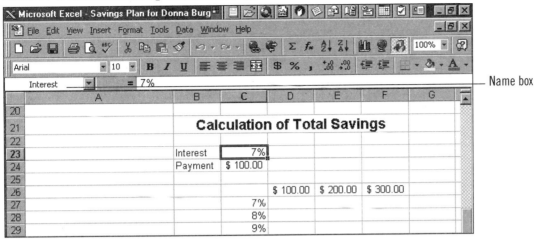

Name box

FIGURE P1-5: **FV Function dialog box**

FV

Rate	Interest/12
Nper	30*12
Pmt	-Payment
Pv	
Type	

= 0.005833333
= 360
= -100
= number
= number

= 121997.0996

Returns the future value of an investment based on periodic, constant payments and a constant interest rate.

Pmt is the payment made each period; it cannot change over the life of the annuity.

Formula result =121997.0996   OK   Cancel

FIGURE P1-6: **Calculation of Total Savings table complete**

	B	C	D	E	F	G	H	I
20								
21		Calculation of Total Savings						
22								
23	Interest	7%						
24	Payment	$ 100.00						
25								
26		$121,997.10	$ 100.00	$ 200.00	$ 300.00			
27		7%	$121,997.10	$243,994.20	$365,991.30			
28		8%	$149,035.94	$298,071.89	$447,107.83			
29		9%	$183,074.35	$366,148.70	$549,223.04			
30								
31								
32								
33								
34								
35								
36								

⏮ ◀ ▶ ▶⏭ \ Sheet1 / Sheet2 / Sheet3 /

▦ Start   ✕ Microsoft Excel - Sav...   ◑ 8:25 PM

Clues to Use

Data Tables

The Data Table function creates a data table based on input values and formulas that you define on a worksheet. You use data tables to perform a what-if analysis by changing certain constant values in your worksheet to see how values in other cells are affected.

SAVINGS PLAN FOR DONNA BURGESS

activity:

Calculate Savings Income

Now, Donna needs to know what monthly income she can expect at age 55 for each of her savings plan options. She predicts that she will invest her savings at a rate of 8% over the 20 years she expects to receive savings income.

steps:

1. Click cell **B31**, then enter and format the labels and values as shown in Figure P1-7

You already know that Donna will save $121,997.10 (the value in cell D27) if she invests $100 a month for 30 years at 7% interest. Now, you need to know how much Donna will make if she invests the amount in cell D27 at 8% interest for 20 years after she retires. You will use the Function Wizard to enter a PMT formula that calculates how much Donna will make per month on each investment amount entered in the table.

2. Click cell **D35**, click the **Paste Function button** 🔲 on the Standard toolbar, select **PMT**, then click **OK**

3. Complete the PMT Function Wizard so that it appears as shown in Figure P1-8, then click **OK**

Donna will make $1,020.43 per month for 20 years if she invests $100 per month at 7% interest after she reaches the age of 55. Next, copy the PMT formula in cell D35 to the remaining cells in the table.

4. Click cell **D35**, drag the corner handle to cell **F35**, then drag the corner handle down to cell **F37**

As you can see, Donna should try to invest $300 a month at 9% interest so that she can make $4,593.92 per month when she is 55. Next, create a line chart that displays Donna's calculations of her total investments.

5. Click cell **C39**, click the **ChartWizard button** 🔲 on the Standard toolbar, click **Line**, click **Next**, then type **=SavingsTable**

6. Click the **Series tab**, click the **Name box**, type **7%**, click **Series 2**, click the **Name box**, type **8%**, click **Series 3**, click the **Name box**, then type **9%**

7. Click the **Collapse button** to the right of the Category (X) Axis labels box, select cells **D26** to **F26**, click the **Restore button** to display the dialog box, click **Next**, enter **Total Savings** as the chart title, enter **Monthly Payments** as the Category (X) title, then click **Finish**

8. Move the chart down so that it begins at cell **C39**, then increase the chart size to fill the screen

9. Right-click the values in the Y-Axis, click **Format Axis**, click the **Font tab**, select a font size of **8 point**, click **OK**, right-click the legend, click **Format Legend**, click the **Font tab**, select a font size of **8 point**, click **OK**, change the font size to **8 point** for the X-Axis and "Monthly Payments," click the **Drawing button** 🔲 on the Standard toolbar to remove the Drawing toolbar, compare your line chart to Figure P1-9, then save the workbook

Next, go on to create a column chart and then format your worksheet for printing.

FIGURE P1-7: **Calculation of Savings Income table**

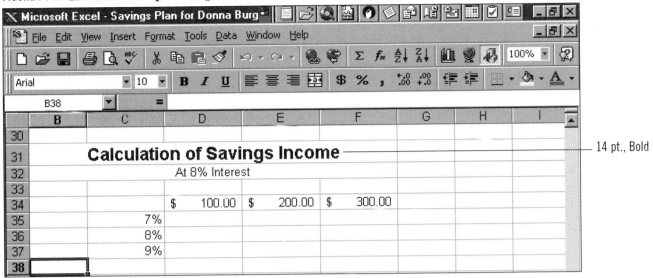

14 pt., Bold

FIGURE P1-8: **PMT Function dialog box**

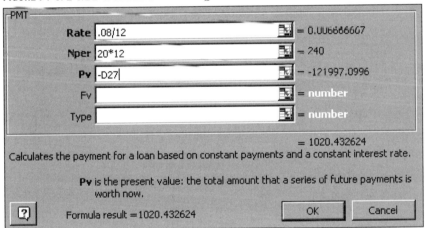

FIGURE P1-9: **Line chart complete**

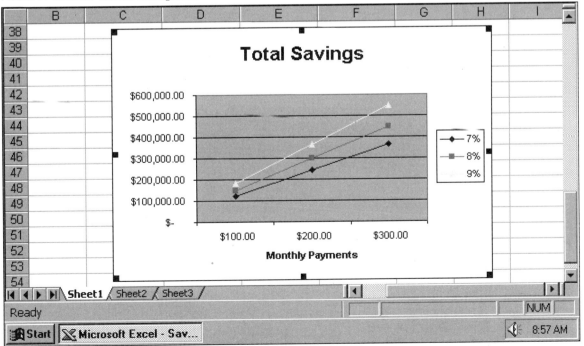

activity:

Format and Print the Savings Plan

You need to create a column chart that displays the monthly income Donna can expect to make when she is 55 years old for each of the three monthly contributions at each of the three interest rates. You will then use the drawing tools to highlight the option that Donna feels is most realistic.

steps:

1. Select cells **C34** to **F37**, click the **Name box**, type **SavingsIncome**, press [Enter], click away from the selected cells, click the **ChartWizard button** 📊 on the Standard toolbar, click **Next**, type **SavingsIncome**, click **Next**, enter **Savings Income** as the chart title, enter **Monthly Income** as the Category (X) Axis title, click **Finish**, then move the chart below the line chart, increase its size, and reduce the font size of the X-Axis, Y-Axis, Legend, and X-Axis title to **8 point**

    Donna decides that she will invest $200 a month in a savings plan that will yield an 8% annual interest. Next, draw an oval around this option in the Calculation of Total Savings table.

2. Click cell **E28**, click the **Drawing button** 🖎 on the Standard toolbar to display the Drawing toolbar, click the **Oval button** ⬭ on the Drawing toolbar, point the mouse to just above and to the left of cell **D28**, click and drag the mouse to draw an oval around the cell, right-click the oval, click **Format AutoShape**, click the **Color list arrow**, click **No Fill**, then click **OK**

    If necessary, you can adjust the size of the oval by dragging the sizing handles. Next, draw an arrow that points to cell E28.

3. Click the **Arrow button** ↘ on the Drawing toolbar, point the mouse to cell **F25**, then click and drag the mouse to draw an arrow that points to cell **E28** as shown in Figure P1-10

    Next, create a text box that explains the significance of cell E28.

4. Click the **Text Box button** 📄 on the Drawing toolbar, draw a text box as shown in Figure P1-10, type **Best Option** in the text box, center and bold the text, then, if necessary, adjust the size of the text box so that it appears as shown in Figure P1-10

5. As shown in Figure P1-10, draw an oval around cell **E36**, remove the fill, draw an arrow, draw a text box, then enter and enhance **Monthly Income** in the text box

6. Switch to **75% view**, move and resize the Line chart so that it begins in cell **H15** and extends to cell **N30**, move and resize the Column chart so that it begins in cell **H32** and extends to cell **N47**, click cell **E28**, click the **Copy button**, click cell **P15**, click the **Paste button**, increase the column width, delete the oval, click the **Rectangle button** ▢, draw a rectangle around cell **P15**, remove the fill, then adjust the size and position of the rectangle so that it appears as shown in Figure P1-10

7. As shown in Figure P1-10, draw an arrow pointing to the $200 mark on the line chart for the **8%** line, click cell **E36**, click the **Copy button**, click cell **P32**, click **Edit** on the menu bar, click **Paste Special**, click **Values**, click **OK**, click the **Currency Style button** $ on the Formatting toolbar, draw a rectangle around cell **P32**, remove its fill, then draw an arrow pointing to the middle column in the **$200** series on the column chart as shown in Figure P1-10

    Note that you use the Paste Special command because the formula in cell E36 includes a cell address. You need to copy only the value, not the formula it represents.

8. Center the text box (contains "Donna Burgess") as shown in Figure P1-10, click the **Print Preview button** 📄 on the Standard toolbar, click **Setup**, click the **Fit to radio button**, click the **Landscape radio button**, click the **Margins tab**, then click the **Horizontally** and **Vertically** check boxes

9. Click the **Header/Footer tab**, click **Custom Header**, enter **Savings Plan** in the **Left section**, enter your name in the **Right section**, print a copy of the worksheet, then save and close the workbook

FIGURE P1-10: Completed Savings Plan

Savings Plan

[Your Name]

Donna Burgess
Savings Plan

Current Age			25
Age to stop working			55
Years to receive savings income			20
Monthly contributions	Plan 1	$	100.00
	Plan 2	$	200.00
	Plan 3	$	300.00
Expected interest rates	Plan 1		7%
	Plan 2		8%
	Plan 3		9%

Calculation of Total Savings

		Interest	7%			8%			9%			Best Option
		Payment	$	100.00	$	200.00	$	300.00				
Plan 1	$ 121,997.10	0.07	$	100.00	$	200.00	$	300.00				
Plan 2	$	0.08	$ 121,997.10	$ 243,994.20	$ 365,991.30							
Plan 3	$	0.09	$ 149,035.94	$ 298,071.89	$ 447,107.83							
			$ 183,074.35	$ 366,148.70	$ 549,223.04							

$ 298,071.89

Calculation of Savings Income
At 8% Interest

	Monthly Income		
	$ 100.00	$ 200.00	$ 300.00
7%	$1,020.43	$2,040.87	$3,061.30
8%	$1,246.60	$2,493.19	$3,739.79
9%	$1,531.31	$3,062.61	$4,593.92

$ 2,493.19

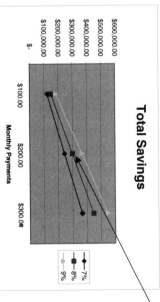

Total Savings

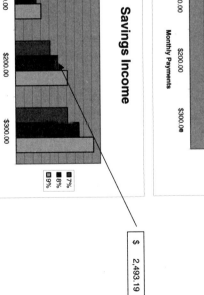

Savings Income

Investment Analysis

You have just inherited $15,000 and have decided to use Excel to analyze your investment options. To analyze investment options, you will **Determine the Future Value of a Present Amount** and then **Determine the Present Value of a Future Amount and Print the Investment Analysis.**

activity:

Determine the Future Value of a Present Amount

First, you decide to invest your $15,000 inheritance in a secure savings plan at a rate of 7.5% per year. You need to know how much your $15,000 will grow over the next 20 years. To calculate the future value of a present amount, you use the following formula: Future Value=Present Value*(1+interest rate)$^{\text{number of years}}$. To determine how much $15,000 is worth in 20 years, at a 7.5% rate the formula is as follows: Future Value = 15000*(1+.075)^20. The caret sign (^) is the symbol for exponential.

steps:

1. Open a blank Excel workbook, then enter the formula: **=15000*(1+.075)^20**

Note that the carat sign (^) is located above the "6" on your keyboard.

2. Press **[Enter]**, format cell **A1** with the Currency style, then save the workbook as **Investment Analysis Worksheet**

In 20 years, $15,000 will be worth $63,717.77 if you invest it at an annual interest rate of 7.5%. Next, calculate how much your $15,000 will be worth at the end of each five-year period for 30 years.

3. Click cell **B3**, type **5**, press **[Tab]**, type **10**, select cells **B3** to **C3**, then drag the handle to cell **G3** to fill the cells as shown in Figure P2-1.

4. Click cell **B4**, enter the formula: **=15000*(1+.075)^B3**, press **[Enter]**, then copy the formula across to cell **G4**

5. With cells **B4** to **G4** selected, click the **Currency Style button** $ on the Formatting toolbar

As you can see, your $15,000 grows by leaps and bounds over the 30 years. Next, create a line chart to graphically display this growth.

6. Select cells **B4** to **G4**, click the **ChartWizard button** on the Standard toolbar, click **Line**, click **Next**, click the **Series tab**, click the **Collapse button** to the right of the Category (X) Axis Labels dialog box, select cells **B3** to **G3**, click the **Restore button**, then click **Next**

7. Click the **Chart Title box**, type **$15,000 Invested at 7.5% for 30 Years**, click the **Legend tab**, click the **Show Legend check box** to deselect it, then click **Finish**

8. Move and size the chart so that it extends from cells **B5** to **G20**, change the font size of the Y-Axis to **8 point**, right-click the X-Axis, click **Format Axis**, change the font size to **8 point**, click the **Alignment tab**, click the **up arrow** to rotate the text by **20 degrees**, click **OK**, then save the workbook

The line chart appears as shown in Figure P2-2. Next, go on to calculate the Present Value of a Future Amount.

FIGURE P2-1: Labels for cells B3 to G3

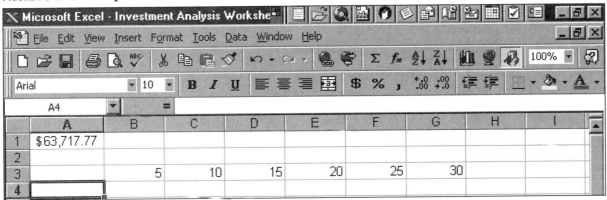

FIGURE P2-2: Completed line chart

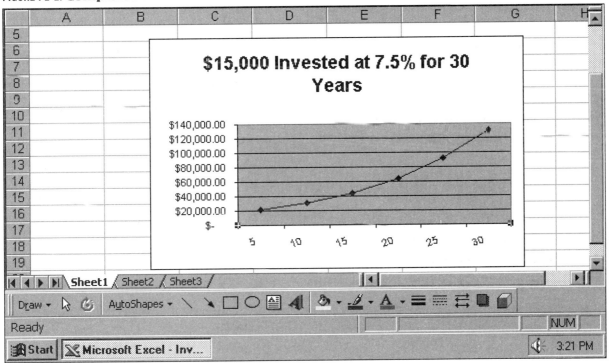

Clues to Use

Using Future Values

The Future Value formula calculates how much money will be worth in the future if you invest it now at a certain interest rate. This formula is: Future Value = Present Value*(1+interest rate)$^{number\ of\ years}$. The Present Value formula calculates how much money you need to invest now to have a certain amount in a specified period of time if you invest the money at a certain interest rate. The Present Value formula is: Present Value = Future Value/(1 + interest rate)$^{number\ of\ years}$.

activity:

Determine the Present Value of a Future Amount and Print the Investment Analysis

You would like to know how much money you need to save now in order to have $15,000 in 10 years if you invest the money at a 7% rate of return. To calculate the present value of a future amount, you use the following formula: Present Value=Future Value/(1+interest rate)$^{\text{number of years}}$. This formula differs from the formula used to calculate the future value of a present value in that the future value is *divided* by the interest rate instead of multiplied. To determine how much to invest now to have $15,000 in 10 years if you invest the amount at 7%, you modify this formula as follows: Present Value = 15000/(1+.07)^10.

steps:

1. Click cell **A22** below the line chart, then type the following text: How much money do I invest now to have $15,000 in 10 years if I invest at a 7% rate of return?

2. Click cell **A23**, type Answer:, right align and bold it, click cell **B23**, enter the formula: =15000/(1+.07)^10, press [Enter], click cell **B23**, then click the **Currency Style button** **$** on the Formatting toolbar

You need to invest $7,625.24 now at a 7% rate of return in order to have $15,000 in 10 years. Next, you decide to return to your calculations of the future value of $15,000 and increase your investment to $25,000 for the last 10 years of the investment period.

3. Click cell **E4**, then click at the end of the formula on the formula bar

4. Change **15000** to **25000**, press [Enter], copy the formula across to cell **G4**, and increase the width of column **F**, if necessary

The line chart now has a "bump" in it to show how your investment is affected when you increase your investment after 20 years. Next, change the line chart to an area chart.

5. Right-click a blank area of the line chart, click **Chart Type**, click **Area**, then click **OK**

Next, add a text box and arrow to the area chart to explain the "bump."

6. Click the **Text Box button** on the Drawing toolbar, draw a text box as shown in Figure P2-3, type Investment Increased on two lines, select the text, bold and center the text, change the font size to 8 point, click the **Line Style button** on the Drawing toolbar, click 1 pt, click the **Fill Color list arrow** on the Drawing toolbar, click the **White box**, click the **Arrow button**, then draw an arrow from the text box to where the area chart begins to incline sharply as shown in Figure P2-3

7. Modify the chart title so that it appears as shown in Figure P2-3, select the text, then change the font size to **12 point**

Next, answer a series of questions that require you to use the PV and FV formulas.

8. Click cell **A25**, then, as shown in Figure P2-4, enter the questions and enter and enhance Answer where indicated

Time To
✓ **Save**
✓ **Close**

9. Use the PV or FV formulas where required to enter the correct answers in cells **B26, B29, B32,** and **B35**, format the answers in the Currency style, format the worksheet to fit on one page, then print a copy

Check your answers in cells B26, B29, B32, and B35 against the table displayed in Figure P2-5. If your answers are incorrect, check your formulas and try again.

FIGURE P2-3: Completed area chart

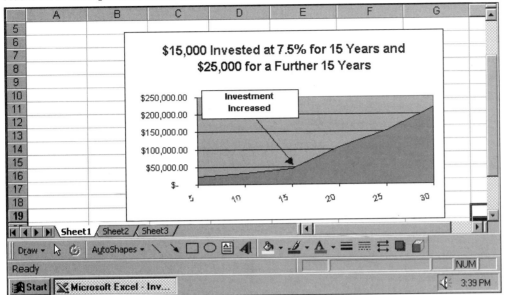

FIGURE P2-4: Future Value and Present Value questions

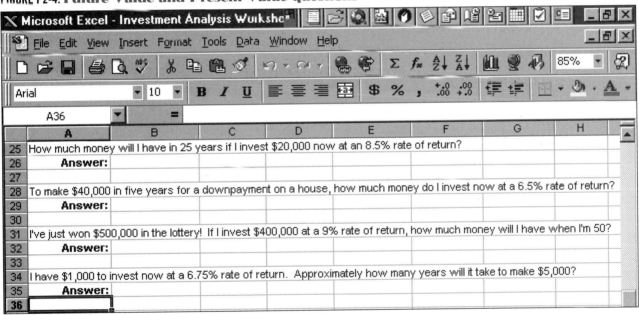

	A	B	C	D	E	F	G	H
25	How much money will I have in 25 years if I invest $20,000 now at an 8.5% rate of return?							
26	Answer:							
27								
28	To make $40,000 in five years for a downpayment on a house, how much money do I invest now at a 6.5% rate of return?							
29	Answer:							
30								
31	I've just won $500,000 in the lottery! If I invest $400,000 at a 9% rate of return, how much money will I have when I'm 50?							
32	Answer:							
33								
34	I have $1,000 to invest now at a 6.75% rate of return. Approximately how many years will it take to make $5,000?							
35	Answer:							
36								

FIGURE P2-5: Answers to questions

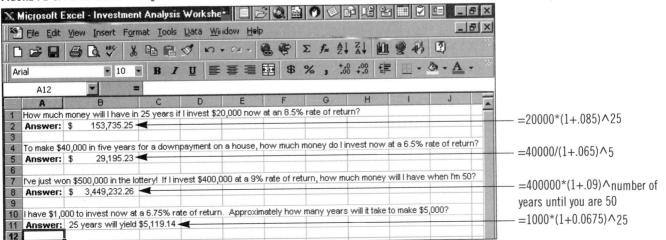

=20000*(1+.085)^25

=40000/(1+.065)^5

=400000*(1+.09)^number of years until you are 50

=1000*(1+0.0675)^25

	A	B	C	D	E	F	G	H	I	J
1	How much money will I have in 25 years if I invest $20,000 now at an 8.5% rate of return?									
2	Answer:	$ 153,735.25								
3										
4	To make $40,000 in five years for a downpayment on a house, how much money do I invest now at a 6.5% rate of return?									
5	Answer:	$ 29,195.23								
6										
7	I've just won $500,000 in the lottery! If I invest $400,000 at a 9% rate of return, how much money will I have when I'm 50?									
8	Answer:	$ 3,449,232.26								
9										
10	I have $1,000 to invest now at a 6.75% rate of return. Approximately how many years will it take to make $5,000?									
11	Answer:	25 years will yield $5,119.14								
12										

Mortgage Options for the Watson Family

The Watson family has decided to purchase a house for around $220,000. They have $40,000 saved for a down payment and can afford no more than a $1,150 per month mortgage payment. The Watsons need to know how large a mortgage they can afford, based on current interest rates, and presuming a repayment period of 30 years. To calculate the best mortgage option for the Watson family, you will **Create a 2-variable Table** and then **Create a Chart and Format the Worksheet.**

activity:

Create a 2-variable Table

To calculate the Watson's mortgage options, you will set up a 2-variable table that uses the PMT Function Wizard to calculate monthly mortgage payments for each of five mortgage amounts at each of five interest rates.

steps:

1. Open a blank Excel workbook, enter and enhance the labels and values as shown in Figure P3-1, then save the workbook as **Mortgage Options for the Watson Family**

2. Click cell **B8**, type **.06**, press [Enter], click cell **B8**, click the **Percent Style button**, click cell **B9**, type **.065**, press [Enter], click cell **B9**, click the **Percent Style button**, then click the **Increase Decimal button** [icon] on the Formatting toolbar once

3. Enter **7%** in cell **B10**, **7.5%** in cell **B11**, and **8%** in cell **B12**

4. Click cell **B4**, click the **Name box**, type **Interest**, press [Enter], then assign **HouseCost** as the range name for cell **B5**

    Next, use the PMT formula to calculate the payments required on a principal amount (e.g., $160,000) at a specific interest rate (e.g., 6%) for a specific term (e.g., 30 years). When you complete the PMT Function Wizard, you will divide the interest rate by 12 (for 12 months) and multiply the term by 12 to determine the total number of months.

5. Click cell **B7**, click the **Paste Function button** [icon] on the Standard toolbar, select the **Financial** category, if necessary, select **PMT**, then click **OK**

6. Complete the PMT Function Wizard dialog box so that it appears as shown in Figure P3-2, click **OK**, then format cell B7 in the Currency style

    Now you know that the Watsons will pay $959.28 a month for 30 years if they purchase a home for $200,000 with a $160,000 mortgage at a 6% interest rate. They can certainly afford a home for $200,000. Next, use the Table function to determine the payments required for the remaining options.

7. Select cells **B7** to **G12**, click **Data** on the menu bar, click **Table**, enter **HouseCost** for the **Row input cell**, enter **Interest** for the **Column input cell**, then click **OK**

8. Select cells **C8** to **G12**, click the **Currency Style button**, then compare your worksheet to Figure P3-3

    Next, go on to create a column chart that displays only the mortgage payments that the Watsons can afford.

Time To
✓ Save

FIGURE P3-1: Worksheet setup

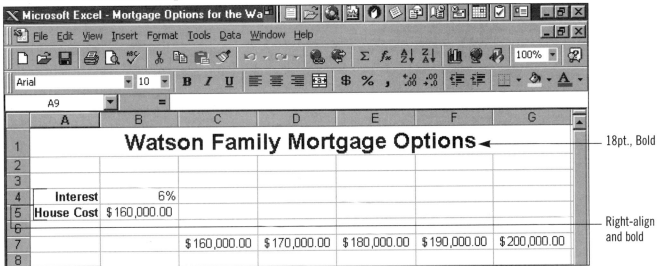

18pt., Bold

Right-align and bold

FIGURE P3-2: PMT Function Wizard dialog box

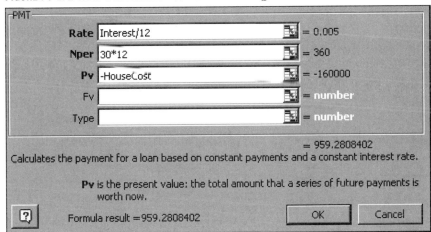

FIGURE P3-3: Completed table

	A	B	C	D	E	F	G
1		Watson Family Mortgage Options					
2							
3							
4	Interest	6%					
5	House Cost	$160,000.00					
6							
7		$959.28	$160,000.00	$170,000.00	$180,000.00	$190,000.00	$200,000.00
8		6%	$ 959.28	$ 1,019.24	$ 1,079.19	$ 1,139.15	$ 1,199.10
9		6.5%	$ 1,011.31	$ 1,074.52	$ 1,137.72	$ 1,200.93	$ 1,264.14
10		7%	$ 1,064.48	$ 1,131.01	$ 1,197.54	$ 1,264.07	$ 1,330.60
11		7.5%	$ 1,118.74	$ 1,188.66	$ 1,258.59	$ 1,328.51	$ 1,398.43
12		8%	$ 1,174.02	$ 1,247.40	$ 1,320.78	$ 1,394.15	$ 1,467.53
13							
14							
15							
16							

activity:

Create a Chart and Format the Worksheet

You will create a column chart that shows *only* the mortgage payments that the Watsons can afford; that is, no more than $1,150 per month. To create this chart, you will first create the chart from cells C8 to C11. These cells contain the four mortgage payments the Watsons can afford if they purchase a house with a $160,000 mortgage. You will then insert the payments that the Watsons can afford if they purchase a house with a $170,000 mortgage, a $180,000 mortgage, and so on.

steps:

1. Select cells **C8** to **C11**, click the **ChartWizard button** on the Standard toolbar, click **Next** to accept the Column chart, then click the **Series tab**, click the **Name box**, then type **$160,000**

2. Click **Add**, click the **Collapse button** to the right of the **Values box**, select cells **D8** to **D10**, click the **Expand button** to restore the dialog box, then name Series 2 **$170,000**

3. Click **Add**, click the **Collapse button** to the right of the **Values box**, select cells **E8** to **E9**, restore the dialog box, then name Series 3 **$180,000**

4. Click **Add**, collapse the dialog box, select cell **F8** as the value, restore the dialog box, then name Series 4 **$190,000**

5. Click the **Collapse button** to the right of the Category (X) axis labels box, select cells **B8** to **B11**, restore the dialog box, then click **Next**

6. Enter the **Affordable Mortgages** as the chart title, enter **Monthly Payment** as the Values (Y) axis title, click **Finish**, move and resize the chart so that it extends from cells **A16** to **G36**, then reduce the font size of the various text elements to **8 point** so that your chart appears similar to Figure P3-4
   Next, enhance the worksheet for printing.

7. Click cell **A1**, click the **Fill Color list arrow** on the Formatting toolbar, click the **black box**, click the **Font Color list arrow** on the Formatting toolbar, click the **white box**, select cells **C7** to **G7**, click the **Bold button**, then change the fill color to **gray**

8. Enhance the percentages in cells **B8** to **B12** with **Bold**, select cells **C7** to **G12**, click the **Borders list arrow** on the Formatting toolbar, then click the **All Borders button**

9. Click the **Print Preview button**, click **Setup**, center the worksheet horizontally, create a custom header that appears as shown in Figure P3-4, then print, save, and close the completed worksheet
   Your completed worksheet appears as shown in Figure P3-4.

Mortgage Options   [Your Name]

Watson Family Mortgage Options

Interest   6%
House Cost $ 160,000.00

$959.28	$ 160,000.00	$ 170,000.00	$ 180,000.00	$ 190,000.00	$ 200,000.00
6%	$ 959.28	$ 1,019.24	$ 1,079.19	$ 1,139.15	$ 1,199.10
6.5%	$ 1,011.31	$ 1,074.52	$ 1,137.72	$ 1,200.93	$ 1,264.14
7%	$ 1,064.48	$ 1,131.01	$ 1,197.54	$ 1,264.07	$ 1,330.60
7.5%	$ 1,118.74	$ 1,188.66	$ 1,258.59	$ 1,328.51	$ 1,398.43
8%	$ 1,174.02	$ 1,247.40	$ 1,320.78	$ 1,394.15	$ 1,467.53

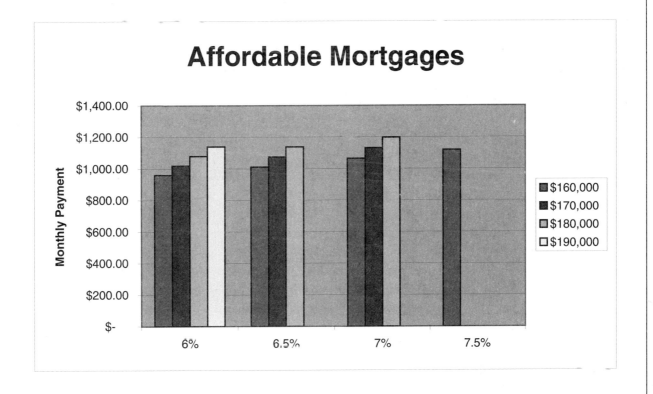

Independent Challenges

INDEPENDENT CHALLENGE 1

You are thinking about making monthly investments in a retirement savings plan. To help you decide how much you should invest in order to have a livable income when you retire, you will create your own retirement savings plan.

1. Complete the table below with your personal data and savings goals. Try to select monthly contributions that you can realistically afford. Check with your local bank to determine current interest rates for various savings plans. Interest rates vary from month to month, so try to select rates that reflect the current financial situation.

Description	Value
Current age	
Age at retirement	
Number of years to receive retirement income	
Monthly Contributions:	
Plan 1	
Plan 2	
Plan 3	
Expected interest rates:	
Rate 1	
Rate 2	
Rate 3	
Expected interest rate during retirement	

2. Enter and enhance "Savings Plan for [Your Name]" as the title of your worksheet, then enter the labels and data from the table into the worksheet. Refer to the worksheet you completed for Project 1 to determine formatting.
3. Set up a 2-variable table called "Calculation of Total Investments" to calculate what each monthly contribution at each of the three interest rates will be worth when you retire. To set up the table, you enter the three monthly contributions as column headings and the three interest rates as row headings, then enter the first contribution and first interest rate in two cells above the table as shown in Figure IC-1. Note that the labels and values will appear in different cells in your worksheet.

FIGURE IC-1: Setup for 2-variable table

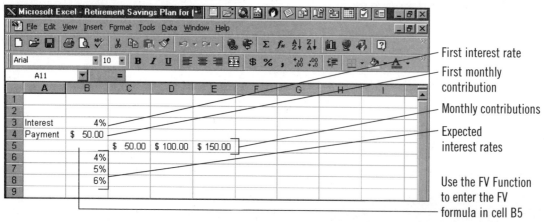

4. Assign range names to cells B3 and B4 (e.g., "Interest" and "Payment").

5. Use the FV Function to calculate the future value of the monthly contribution at the specified interest rate for the number of years until you retire. For the sample table shown above, the rate is cell A3 (4%) divided by 12 (Interest/12), the Nper is the number of years until you retire multiplied by 12, and the Pmt is cell B4 ($50) entered as a negative number (-Payment).

6. Select all the cells in the table, then use the Table function to calculate the total worth of all three monthly contributions at all three interest rates.

7. Set up a 2-variable table called "Calculation of Investment Income" to calculate the income you expect to receive when you retire, based on your monthly contributions. To set up the table, you enter the three monthly contributions as column headings and the three interest rates as row headings.

8. Click the first cell below the first monthly contribution and to the right of the first interest rate, then use the PMT function to calculate the monthly payments you can expect to receive from the total amount calculated for the first monthly contribution and first interest rate in the Calculation of Total Investments table. For the sample table shown in Figure IC-1, the rate is the interest rate you expect to receive on your investments when you retire (e.g., 7%) divided by 12, the Nper is the number of years you expect to receive investment income (e.g., 20) multiplied by 12, and the Pmt is the cell address of the total amount calculated for first monthly contribution and first interest rate in the Calculation of Total Investments table. Remember to enter this cell address as a negative (e.g., -C23).

9. Create a line chart to display the data in the Calculation of Total Investments table, then draw an ellipse and an arrow to highlight the investment option you feel is most realistic. Create a text box to explain your choice.

10. Create a column chart to display the data in the Calculation of Investment Income table, then draw an ellipse and an arrow to highlight the monthly income you expect to make, based on the investment option you have selected.

11. Save the worksheet as "My Investment Plan," format the worksheet so that all the elements appear attractively spaced in Print Preview, print a copy, then save and close the workbook.

INDEPENDENT CHALLENGE 2

You have just won $500,000 in the lottery! You can choose to accept the entire $500,000 right now or a monthly payment of $6,000 for 15 years. Which option should you choose?

1. First, you need to determine the future value of $500,000 in 15 years, presuming that you will invest the money at a 5% annual interest rate.

2. Click cell A1, then enter the Future Value formula required to calculate the worth of $500,000 in 15 years invested at 5%. The formula required is: =500000*(1+.05)^15.

3. Format the result in cell A1 in the Currency style. In 15 years, $500,000 will be worth $1,039,464.09 if you invest it at 5%.

4. Next, you need to use the Future Value Function to calculate how much $6,000 per month will be worth in 15 years if you invest it at 5% per year, compounded monthly.

5. Click cell A2, click the Paste Function button, select FV from the list of financial functions, then click OK.

6. Enter .05/12 as the rate, 12*15 as the Nper, and -6000 as the Pmt, then click OK.

7. Format the result in cell A2 in the Currency style. In 15 years, $6,000 per month will be worth $1,603,733.66 if you invest it at 5%. Perhaps you should consider taking the $6,000 a month payment instead of the $500,000!

8. You have decided to create a line chart that compares the growth of your money, depending on which option you choose ($500,000 now or $6,000 a month for 15 years). Set up your worksheet as follows:

   a. Enter "Lump Sum" in A6 and "Monthly Payment" in cell A7. Widen columns as necessary.

   b. Enter "1" in cell B5 and "2" in cell C5.

   c. Select cells B5 and C5, then drag the corner handle to cell P5 to enter numbers from 1 to 15. These numbers represent the years over which you will invest your winnings.

   d. Click cell A1, click the Copy button, click cell B6, then click the Paste button.

   e. Modify the formula in cell B6 to change the number of years (currently 15) to cell B5 so that the formula is: =500000*(1+0.05)^B5, then copy the formula across to cell P6.

f. Click cell A2, click the Copy button, click cell B7, then click the Paste button.

g. Modify the formula in cell B7 to change the number of years (currently 15) to cell B5 so that the formula is: =FV(0.05/12,12*B5,-6000), then copy the formula across to cell P6.

h. Select cells A5 to P7, then create and modify a line chart that includes a text box with the text: "Investment from monthly payments exceed lump sum investment after 8 years." Draw an arrow from the text box to the point on the chart where the monthly payments line intersects the lump sum line.

9. Save your worksheet as Lottery Investment Options, format the sheet attractively for printing, print a copy, then save and close the workbook.

INDEPENDENT CHALLENGE 3

To complete your education, you need to take out a student loan for $20,000. Before you take out the loan, you want to know how much you will pay each month to repay the loan, depending on how many years you need to pay off the full $20,000 plus interest. The loan is interest-free until you graduate, after which time you will pay an interest charge of 11% per annum. Follow the steps provided below to calculate your monthly payments and the total amount of the loan by the time you pay it off in 5 years, 10 years, or 15 years.

1. Enter "5" in cell B2, "10" in cell C2, "15" in cell D2, and 11% in cell A3.

2. Click cell B3, click the Paste Function button, select PMT from the list of financial functions, click OK, then enter .11/12 as the rate, B2*12 as the Nper, and -20000 as the pv.

3. Copy the formula in cell B3 across to cell D3, click cell B4, then calculate the total amount of the loan based on the value in cell B3. You will need to multiply the value in cell B3 by B2 by 12 (e.g., =B3*B2*12).

4. Display the value in cell B4 in the Currency style, then copy the formula across to cell D4 and widen the columns, if necessary. Now you know how much your $20,000 student loan will cost you to repay. If possible, you should try to repay it in 5 years at a monthly payment of $434.85.

5. Create a column chart to compare the three payment options.

6. Add a text box to explain which payment option you prefer.

7. Save the workbook as Student Loan Options, format the worksheet for printing, print a copy, then save and close the workbook.

INDEPENDENT CHALLENGE 4

For this challenge, you will use the various financial functions you have learned to solve a variety of problems. Set up a worksheet as shown in Figure IC-2, then solve the problems provided. Note that the problems are contained in text boxes. Save the worksheet as Financial Problem-Solving, format the sheet for printing, print a copy, then save and close the workbook.

FIGURE IC-2: Financial Problem-Solving worksheet

	A	B	C	D	E	F	G
1	**Financial Problem-Solving**						
2	[Your Name]						
3							
4	**Problem 1:**						
5	You decide to invest $350 every month for 25 years at a 6.5% per annum compounded						
6	monthly rate of return. Use the FV Function to calculate how much money you will have at the						
7	end of 25 years.						
8							
9	**Solution:**						
10							
11							
12	**Problem 2:**						
13	You want to have $30,000 in 15 years. How much money do you need to invest now at a 4%						
14	rate of return to have $30,000 in 15 years? Use the Present Value formula: Present Value =						
15	Future Value/(1+interest rate)^number of years.						
16							
17							
18	**Solution:**						
19							
20							
21	**Problem 3:**						
22							
23	You want to know the monthly payments on three loan amounts at four interest rates over 20						
24	years. The loan amounts are: $80,000, $90,000, and $100,000 and the interest rates are						
25	5.5%, 6%, 6.5%, 7%, and 7.5%. Set up a 2-variable table as shown below and then use the						
26	PMT Function to solve this problem.						
27							
28	**Solution:**						
29	5.5%						
30	$80,000						
31		$ 80,000.00	$ 90,000.00	$ 100,000.00			
32	5.5%						
33	6.0%						
34	6.5%						
35	7.0%						
36	7.5%						
37							
38	**Problem 4:**						
39							
40	You've decided to invest $8,000 at the beginning of each year for 6 years at a 6.5% rate of return.						
41	Use the FV formula to calculate the yearly growth of your investment and then create a line chart						
42	to display this growth. The FV formula is: Future Value=Present Value*(1+interest rate)^number of						
43	years.						
44							
45	**Solution:**						
46		1	2	3	4	5	6

Visual Workshop

You have just completed a long-term financial savings plan and now want to display the results in an area chart. Over the 15 years of your investment plan, you will invest $5,000 now in a savings plan that yields a 5% annual rate of return. In five years, you will invest a further $5,000 in the same plan, and then you will invest $5,000 more over the final three years. Set up your worksheet to calculate the growth of your money, then create the area chart displayed below. Save the workbook as Investment Analysis Area Chart, format the worksheet attractively, print a copy, then save and close the workbook.

FIGURE VW-1: Completed Area chart

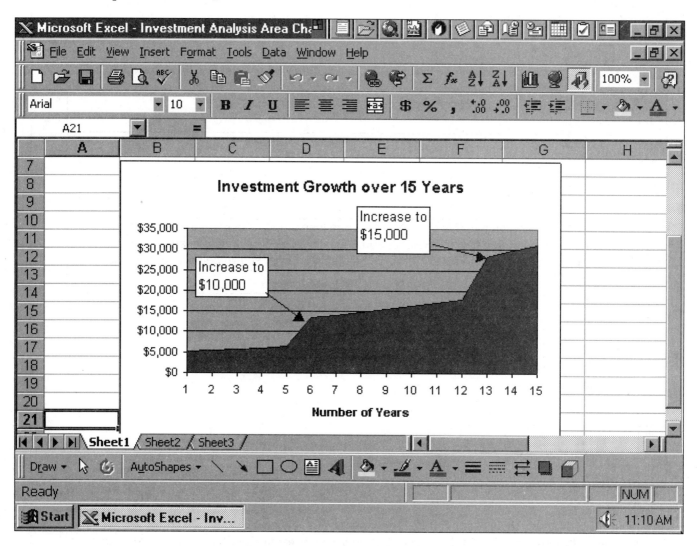

Microsoft
► Excel
Projects

Data Analysis

In This Unit You Will Create:

► **Inventory Report**

► **Customer Profile**

► **Research Report**

You create data lists in Excel to analyze information, make calculations, and create charts. For example, you can create a list that displays all the inventory currently in stock for a small retail operation and then use the PivotTable function to determine which items you need to reorder. You can also use other data functions such as Advanced AutoFilter to display all the items in a list that conform to multiple criteria. Suppose you have created a list of all the CDs in your collection. You set up a list with field names such as CD Title, Artist, Genre, and Date, and then enter the required information about each CD under the field names. You can then use the Advanced AutoFilter function to create a new list that displays only the CDs of Beatles' music from 1966 to 1969 or the CDs of rap music from 1992. ► In this unit, you will use the database functions of Excel to create and analyze information entered in list form.

OVERVIEW

Inventory Report for Premium Videos

Premium Videos is a mail-order video franchise that specializes in quality videos of movie classics from around the world. As the owner of the Premium Videos franchise in Portland, Oregon, you need to present an inventory report to the corporate headquarters in New York. This report will include an itemized inventory list, an analysis of your current stock levels, and a list of the videos you need to order. Four activities are required to create an **Inventory Report for Premium Videos**.

Project Activities

Create the Inventory List

Figure P1-1 displays the first 15 records in the inventory list. This list consists of fields and records. A field is the label used to designate the type of record listed, and at least one field should designate information unique to each record. In the inventory list, the Stock No. field assigns a unique number to each video title. Once you have created the inventory list, you will use Excel's database functions to answer the four questions listed in Figure P1-2.

Analyze Stock Levels

The first two questions in Figure P1-2 relate to the analysis of stock levels. To answer the first question, you will use the Subtotal function to organize the inventory list according to the country listed in the Country field (e.g., Germany, Italy, etc.) and then enter the total worth of the videos from each country. To answer the second question, you will create a PivotTable that counts the number of videos in stock from each country and then display the PivotTable data in a pie chart. Figure P1-3 displays the pie chart you will create.

Select Videos to Order

Questions 3 and 4 relate to the videos that you will order. You will first use the Advanced Filter function to list only those videos with stock levels of less than (<) 10 and then format this list for inclusion in your presentation. Your investors are particularly interested in sales of videos from Italy, Japan, and the United States. You will include a list in your presentation that displays only Italian, Japanese, and U.S. videos with stock levels higher than 10 and a total worth of more than $200.00. To create this list, you will create a complex criteria range that instructs Excel to list only the videos from Italy, Japan, and the United States that conform to two criteria: stock levels greater than (>)10 and a total worth of more than $200.00.

Format and Print the Inventory Report

Finally, you will bring all the elements you have developed into a two-page presentation. This presentation will include text boxes that explain the significance of the various elements to your investors.

FIGURE P1-1: First 15 records in the Premium Videos inventory list

X Microsoft Excel - Inventory Report for Premium

File Edit View Insert Format Tools Data Window Help

Arial   10   B I U

A1   = Stock Nu.

	A	B	C	D	E	F	G
1	Stock No.	Quantity	Title	Country	Unit Price	Total	
2	PV-140	15	Aguirre: The Wrath of God	Germany	$ 35.00	$525.00	
3	PV-141	10	Bicycle Thief, The	Italy	$ 25.00	$250.00	
4	PV-142	8	Casablanca	United States	$ 30.00	$240.00	
5	PV-143	13	Citizen Kane	United States	$ 28.00	$364.00	
6	PV-144	7	Cries and Whispers	Sweden	$ 25.00	$175.00	
7	PV-145	14	Das Boot	Germany	$ 25.00	$350.00	
8	PV-146	7	Dr. Bethune	Canada	$ 30.00	$210.00	
9	PV-147	2	Dr. Strangelove	Britain	$ 30.00	$ 60.00	
10	PV-148	5	Entre Nous	France	$ 25.00	$125.00	
11	PV-149	12	Fellini's Eight and a Half	Italy	$ 30.00	$360.00	
12	PV-150	9	Gallipoli	Australia	$ 20.00	$180.00	
13	PV-151	7	Garden of Finzi-Continis, The	Italy	$ 30.00	$210.00	
14	PV-152	8	Gone with the Wind	United States	$ 35.00	$280.00	
15	PV-153	10	Kind Hearts and Coronets	Britain	$ 20.00	$200.00	
16	PV-154	6	Mon Oncle Antoine	Canada	$ 20.00	$120.00	
17	PV-155	12	My Brilliant Career	Australia	$ 25.00	$300.00	

FIGURE P1-2: Inventory analysis questions

QUESTION	METHOD
1. What is the current stock worth for each country?	Create a Subtotals list
2. How many products are currently in stock from each country?	Create a PivotTable and Pie Chart
3. Which products do I need to order?	Create an Advanced Filter list
4. Which videos from Italy, Japan, and the United States have stock levels higher than 10 and totals of more than $200?	Create a Complex Criteria Range

FIGURE P1-3: Pie chart showing the breakdown of video titles by country

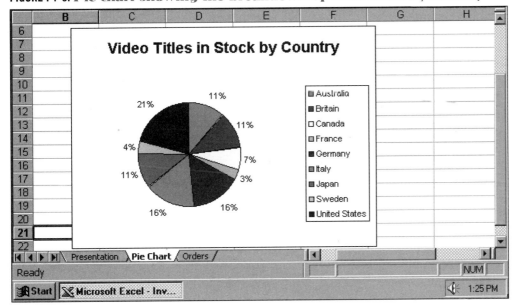

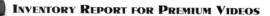

activity:

Create the Inventory List

You need to label the sheet tabs and then create the inventory list in the first worksheet.

steps:

1. Open a blank Excel workbook, double-click the **Sheet1 tab**, type **Presentation**, press **[Enter]**, double-click the **Sheet2 tab**, type **Pie Chart**, press **[Enter]**, then name the Sheet3 tab **Orders**

2. Click the **Presentation tab**, click the **Drawing button** on the Standard toolbar to display the Drawing toolbar, if necessary, click the **Text Box button** on the Drawing toolbar, then draw a text box from cell **A1** to cell **E5** as shown in Figure P1-4

3. Type **Premium Videos**, press **[Enter]**, type **Inventory Report**, then enhance **Premium Videos** and **Inventory Report** as shown in Figure P1-4

4. Select both lines in the text box, then click the **Center button** on the Formatting toolbar

5. Click the **3-D button** on the Drawing toolbar, select **3-D Style 3** as shown in Figure P1-4, then click away from the text box to deselect it

6. Save the workbook as **Inventory Report for Premium Videos**

Next, enter the field names and records for the 20 video titles that Premium Videos currently stocks.

7. Click cell **A8**, enter the labels in cells **A8** to **F8** as shown in the *printout* in Figure P1-5, then bold and center the labels

8. Click cell **A9**, type **PV-140**, press **[Enter]**, type **PV-141** in cell **A10**, select cells **A9** and **A10**, then drag the corner handle of cell **A10** down to cell **A29** to enter the remaining stock numbers

9. As shown in Figure P1-5, enter and enhance the remaining data in cells **B9** to **E29**, calculate the totals required for column F, adjust the column widths so that all the data is clearly visible then save the workbook

Note the directions regarding cell formatting. Next, go on to create a Subtotals list.

FIGURE P1-4: Text box in progress

Drawing button

Britannic Bold and 20 pt.

Bold and 14 pt.

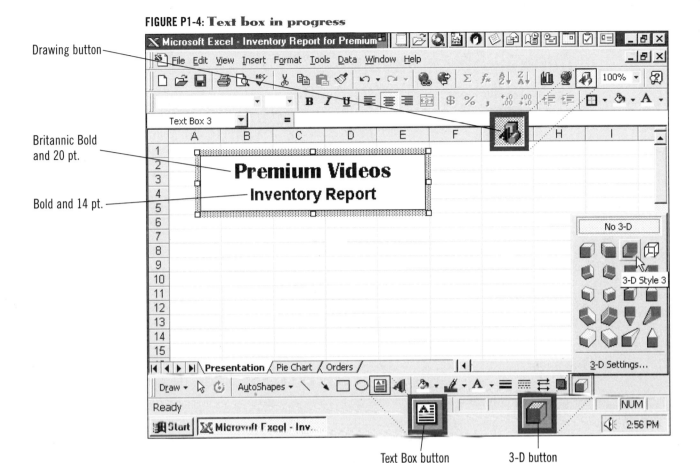

Text Box button

3-D button

FIGURE P1-5: Printout of inventory data for cells A8 to F29

	A	B	C	D	E	F
8	**Stock No.**	**Quantity**	**Title**	**Country**	**Unit Price**	**Total**
9	PV-140	15	*Aguirre: The Wrath of God*	Germany	$35.00	$525.00
10	PV-141	10	*Bicycle Thief, The*	Italy	$25.00	$250.00
11	PV-142	8	*Casablanca*	United States	$30.00	$240.00
12	PV-143	13	*Citizen Kane*	United States	$28.00	$364.00
13	PV-144	7	*Cries and Whispers*	Sweden	$25.00	$175.00
14	PV-145	14	*Das Boot*	Germany	$25.00	$350.00
15	PV-146	7	*Dr. Bethune*	Canada	$30.00	$210.00
16	PV-147	2	*Dr. Strangelove*	Britain	$30.00	$60.00
17	PV-148	5	*Entre Nous*	France	$25.00	$125.00
18	PV-149	12	*Fellini's Eight and a Half*	Italy	$30.00	$360.00
19	PV-150	9	*Gallipoli*	Australia	$20.00	$180.00
20	PV-151	7	*Garden of Finzi-Continis, The*	Italy	$30.00	$210.00
21	PV-152	8	*Gone with the Wind*	United States	$35.00	$280.00
22	PV-153	10	*Kind Hearts and Coronets*	Britain	$20.00	$200.00
23	PV-154	6	*Mon Oncle Antoine*	Canada	$20.00	$120.00
24	PV-155	12	*My Brilliant Career*	Australia	$25.00	$300.00
25	PV-156	9	*Night at the Opera*	United States	$20.00	$180.00
26	PV-157	3	*Rocky Horror Picture Show*	Britain	$30.00	$90.00
27	PV-158	6	*Scarlet Pimpernel, The*	Britain	$25.00	$150.00
28	PV-159	12	*Seven Samurai, The*	Japan	$35.00	$420.00
29	PV-160	8	*Woman in the Dunes*	Japan	$35.00	$280.00

Center values

Enhance with italics

Enhance with the Currency style

activity:

Analyze Stock Levels

The first two questions that you want your Inventory Report to answer are: *What is the current stock worth for each country?* and *How many products are currently in stock from each country?* To answer the first question, you will convert the inventory list to a Subtotals list; and to answer the second question, you will create a PivotTable and pie chart in the Pie Chart sheet. Before you can create a Subtotals list that will display the total worth of the video titles from each country, you need to sort the list alphabetically by country.

steps:

1. Click cell **D8** (contains **Country**), then click the **Sort Ascending button** 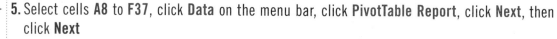 on the Standard toolbar
Now all the videos from Australia appear first. Next, create a Subtotals list.

2. Select cells **A8** to **F29**, click **Data** on the menu bar, then click **Subtotals**
The Subtotal dialog box appears. You need to calculate totals at each change in the Country field.

3. Click the **At each change in: list arrow**, click **Country**, compare the Subtotals dialog box to Figure P1-6, then click **OK**

4. Click cell **F39** and, if necessary, increase the column width so the total appears
The total worth of all the video titles currently stocked by Premium Videos is $5,069.00. You also now know the total worth of all the video titles from each country. For example, you have $1,064.00 worth of videos from the United States and $700.00 worth of videos from Japan. Next, create a PivotTable that counts how many videos are currently in stock from each country.

Hint

Click **No** to remove the Office Assistant.

5. Select cells **A8** to **F37**, click **Data** on the menu bar, click **PivotTable Report**, click **Next**, then click **Next**
A warning appears! You cannot create a PivotTable from a Subtotals list. You will need to abort the process and remove the subtotals from the list before you can create the PivotTable.

6. Click **OK**, click **Cancel**, click **Data** on the menu bar, click **Subtotals**, then click **Remove All**
You will display the Subtotals list again after you have created the PivotTable and pie chart.

7. Select cells **A8** to **F29**, click **Data**, click **PivotTable Report**, click **Next**, click **Next**, drag the **Country box** next to **COLUMN**, and the **Quantity box** above **DATA** as shown in Figure P1-7, click **Next**, click the **Existing Worksheet radio button**, click the **Pie Chart sheet tab**, click cell **A1**, then click **Finish**
The PivotTable appears in the Pie Chart sheet.

8. Select cells **J3** to **B2**, click the **ChartWizard button** on the Standard toolbar, click **Pie**, click **Next**, click **Next**, enter **Video Titles in Stock by Country** in the **Chart title box**, click the **Data Labels tab**, click the **Show Percent radio button**, then click **Finish**

9. Increase the chart size to fill the screen, right-click the legend, click **Format Legend**, click the **Font tab**, select a font size of **8**, click **OK**, right-click a data label, click **Format Data Labels**, select a font size of **8**, click **OK**, then change the font size of the chart title to **12 point**
Your completed pie chart should appear as shown in Figure P1-8. Next, go on to restore the Subtotals list and then select the products you need to order because of low stock levels.

FIGURE P1-6: Subtotals dialog box

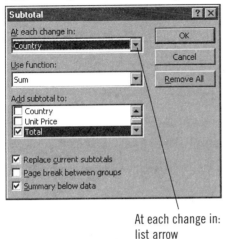

At each change in:
list arrow

FIGURE P1-7: PivotTable Step 3 of 4 dialog box

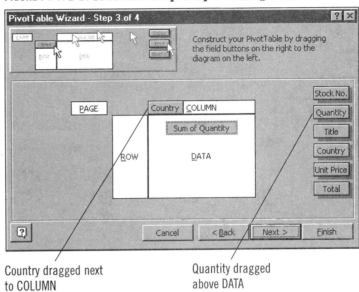

Country dragged next
to COLUMN

Quantity dragged
above DATA

FIGURE P1-8: Completed pie chart

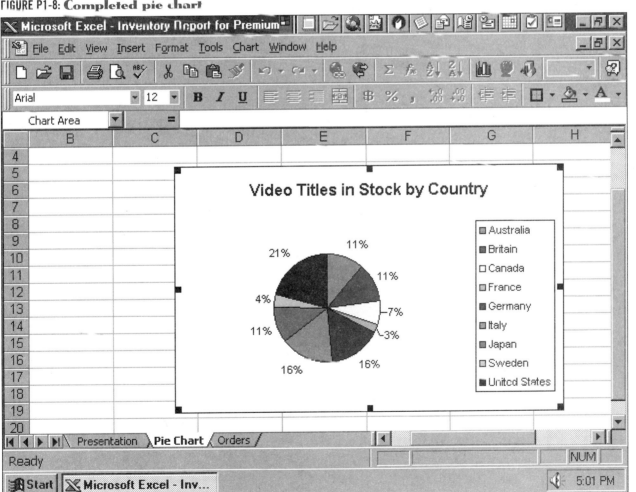

activity:

Select Videos to Order

You have decided to order only those titles with stock levels of less than 10. You will set up a criteria range and then use the Advanced Filter function to create a list that includes only the titles with stock levels of less than 10. You use the Advanced Filter function instead of the AutoFilter function because you want to display the filtered list in a new location on the Presentation worksheet. Once you have created the list of videos to order, you will create a complex criteria range to select only the videos from Italy, Japan, and the United States that have stock levels higher than 10 and a total worth of more than $200.

steps:

1. Click the **Presentation tab**, click **Data**, click **Subtotals**, click **OK**, then save the workbook

2. Click the **Orders tab**, enter **Quantity** in cell **A1**, enter **<10** in cell **A2**, then press **[Enter]**

You have set up the criteria range that the Advanced Filter function will use to create a list that displays all the videos with stock levels of less than 10.

3. Click the **Presentation tab**, click any cell in the Subtotals list (e.g., cell **C9**), click **Data** on the menu bar, click **Filter**, then click **Advanced Filter**

When you click a cell in the Subtotals list, Excel automatically enters the range of cells that make up the entire list in the Advanced Filter dialog box.

4. Click the **Copy to another location radio button** to select it, select the contents of the box next to **List Range**, select cells **A8** to **F39** in the worksheet, select the contents of the box next to **criteria range**, select cells **A1** and **A2** in the Orders sheet, click the box next to **Copy to:**, type **A44**, then compare the Advanced Filter dialog box to Figure P1-10

Trouble

If only one item appears in the list, repeat Steps 3 and 4. Make sure your dialog box appears exactly as shown in Figure P1-10 before you click OK.

5. Click **OK**, then drag the scroll bar down until you can see the list beginning in cell **A44**

As you can see, the list extends from cell A44 to cell F57. Next, create a complex criteria range to list only videos from Italy, Japan, and the United States with stock levels higher than 10 and a total worth of more than $200.00.

6. Click the **Orders tab**, click cell **A5**, then enter the labels and values as shown in Figure P1-10

You have set up a complex criteria range for an Advanced AutoFilter sort. Next, perform the sort.

7. Click the **Presentation tab**, click any cell in the Subtotals list, click **Data** on the menu bar, click **Filter**, then click **Advanced Filter**

8. Click the **Copy to another location radio button**, then use your mouse to select the required ranges for the Advanced Filter dialog box as follows: List range: Presentation!A8:F39; Criteria range: Orders!A5:C8; Copy to: A63

Note that the easiest way to enter the List Range and criteria range is to delete the current contents and then select the appropriate cells (e.g., cells A8 to F39 in the Presentations sheet and cells A5 to C8 in the Orders sheet).

9. Click **OK**, drag the scroll bar down until you can see the list beginning in cell **A63** as shown in Figure P1-11, then save the workbook

As you can see, only three videos conform to the criteria you set. Next, go on to display all the elements you have created in an attractively formatted report.

FIGURE P1-9: Advanced Filter dialog box

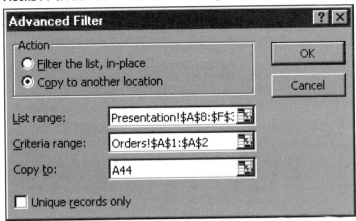

FIGURE P1-10: Complex criteria range in cells A5 to C8

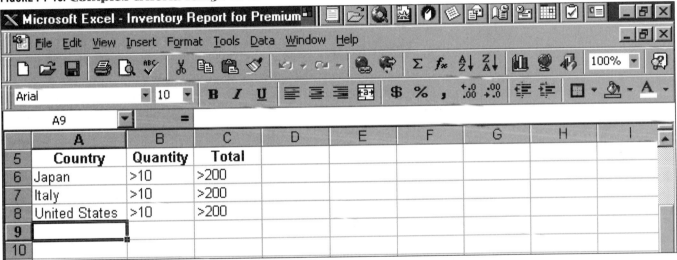

FIGURE P1-11: Advanced Filter list in cells A63 to F66

	Stock No.	Quantity	Title	Country	Unit Price	Total
64	PV-149	12	*Fellini's Eight and a Half*	Italy	$30.00	$360.00
65	PV-159	12	*Seven Samurai, The*	Japan	$35.00	$420.00
66	PV-143	13	*Citizen Kane*	United States	$28.00	$364.00

activity:

Format and Print the Inventory Report

You need to format the three lists in the Presentation sheet, insert the pie chart from the Pie Chart sheet, and then add text boxes so that your completed inventory report appears on two pages as shown in Figure P1-12. You will first format row 1 in the Subtotals list attractively and then apply this formatting to the remaining two lists.

steps:

1. Select cells **A8** to **F8**, click the **Borders list arrow** ▦ ▾ on the Formatting toolbar, select the **Heavy Outside Border** (lower right corner), click the **Color list arrow** 🅰 ▾ on the Formatting toolbar, click a **light gray box**, double-click the **Format Painter button** 🖌 on the Standard toolbar, select cells **A44** to **F44**, select cells **A63** to **F63**, then click the **Format Painter button** to deselect it

   Next, insert some blank rows above the list of videos to order.

2. Select the **43** to **44** on the worksheet frame, click the **right mouse button**, click Insert, then insert additional rows, until the Orders list begins on row 58

   Next, copy the pie chart to the presentation.

3. Click the **Pie Chart tab**, click the pie chart to select it, click the **Copy button** 📋 on the Standard toolbar, click the **Presentation tab**, click cell **B42**, then click the **Paste button** 📋 on the Standard toolbar

4. Insert several rows above the Subtotals list so that the list starts at row **15**, click the **Drawing button** 🔲 to display the Drawing toolbar if necessary, click the **Text Box button** 🔲 on the Drawing toolbar, draw a text box as shown in Figure P1-12, enter the text required, click the **3-D button**, then select **3-D Style 3**

5. Insert new rows where required, then insert and modify the remaining three text boxes as shown in Figure P1-12

   Note that if you insert new rows under the pie chart or a text box, the object will "grow." Just reduce the size of the object.

6. Click the **Print Preview button** 🔍 on the Standard toolbar, click **Setup**, click the **Margins tab**, click the **Horizontally** and **Vertically** check boxes, click the **Header/Footer tab**, create a Custom Header and Footer that appear as shown in Figure P1-12, click **OK**, then click **OK**

7. Click the **Page Break Preview button**, click **OK** to remove the message box, scroll up to find the first page break, drag the page break up so that it occurs after the Subtotals list, scroll down to find the next page break, then drag the page break down so that it occurs after the list of three items

   A dashed line may appear above the second page break. You need to delete selected rows in the worksheet so that the dashed line appears at the bottom of the worksheet.

8. Click **View** on the menu bar, click **Normal** to return to the normal worksheet view, display **50% view**, then delete rows and modify the sizes of the pie chart and text boxes so that the entire worksheet fits over two pages and the text boxes and pie chart are centered in relation to each other

   Refer to Figure P1-12 as you work.

9. Click the **Print Preview button**, click **Next** to view page 2, close the print preview screen, make any further sizing and positioning adjustments required, print a copy of the Presentation sheet, then save and close the workbook

   You may need to switch between Print Preview and Normal view a few times to check the positions and sizes of the pie chart and text boxes.

FIGURE P1-12: Completed Inventory Report

Page 1

Premium Videos
Inventory Report

As of [enter the current date], Premium Videos has the videos listed below in stock. The average price for a video from Premium Videos is $25.00. The total worth o the videos currently in stock is $5,069.00. We stocked 20 videos of each title two months ago; therefore, the current stock levels reflect sales over the past two months.

Stock No.	Quantity	Title	Country	Unit Price	Total
PV-150	9	Gallipoli	Australia	$20.00	$180.00
PV-155	12	My Brilliant Career	Australia	$25.00	$300.00
			Australia Total		**$480.00**
PV-147	2	Dr. Strangelove	Britain	$30.00	$60.00
PV-153	10	Kind Hearts and Coronets	Britain	$20.00	$200.00
PV-157	3	Rocky Horror Picture Show	Britain	$30.00	$90.00
PV-158	6	Scarlet Pimpernel, The	Britain	$25.00	$150.00
			Britain Total		**$500.00**
PV-146	7	Dr. Bethune	Canada	$30.00	$210.00
PV-154	6	Mon Oncle Antoine	Canada	$20.00	$120.00
			Canada Total		**$330.00**
PV-148	5	Entre Nous	France	$25.00	$125.00
			France Total		**$125.00**
PV-140	15	Aguirre: The Wrath of God	Germany	$35.00	$525.00
PV-145	14	Das Boot	Germany	$25.00	$350.00
			Germany Total		**$875.00**
PV-141	10	Bicycle Thief, The	Italy	$25.00	$250.00
PV-149	12	Fellini's Eight and a Half	Italy	$30.00	$360.00
PV-151	7	Garden of Finzi-Continis, The	Italy	$30.00	$210.00
			Italy Total		**$820.00**
PV-159	12	Seven Samurai, The	Japan	$35.00	$420.00
PV-160	8	Woman in the Dunes	Japan	$35.00	$280.00
			Japan Total		**$700.00**
PV-144	7	Cries and Whispers	Sweden	$25.00	$175.00
			Sweden Total		**$175.00**
PV-142	8	Casablanca	United States	$30.00	$240.00
PV-143	13	Citizen Kane	United States	$28.00	$364.00
PV-152	8	Gone with the Wind	United States	$35.00	$280.00
PV-156	9	Night at the Opera	United States	$20.00	$180.00
			United States Total		**$1,064.00**
			Grand Total		**$5,069.00**

Page 2

The pie chart displayed below illustrates the percentage of videos currently in stock from each country. At present, the majority of titles are from Britain, the United States, and the western European countries. Efforts are currently underway to obtain more titles from Japan, Australia, and Canada.

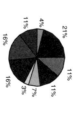

Video Titles in Stock by Country

Legend: ■ Australia ■ Britain ■ Canada □ France ■ Germany ■ Italy ■ Japan ■ Sweden ■ United States

(21%, 11%, 11%, 7%, 3%, 16%, 16%, 4%, 11%)

The list below displays the video titles that will shortly be ordered from our suppliers. Premium Videos will replenish stock levels to 20 videos for each title.

Stock No.	Quantity	Title	Country	Unit Price	Total
PV-150	9	Gallipoli	Australia	$20.00	$180.00
PV-147	2	Dr. Strangelove	Britain	$30.00	$60.00
PV-157	3	Rocky Horror Picture Show	Britain	$30.00	$90.00
PV-158	6	Scarlet Pimpernel, The	Britain	$25.00	$150.00
PV-146	7	Dr. Bethune	Canada	$30.00	$210.00
PV-154	6	Mon Oncle Antoine	Canada	$20.00	$120.00
PV-148	5	Entre Nous	France	$25.00	$125.00
PV-151	7	Garden of Finzi-Continis, The	Italy	$30.00	$210.00
PV-160	8	Woman in the Dunes	Japan	$35.00	$280.00
PV-144	7	Cries and Whispers	Sweden	$25.00	$175.00
PV-142	8	Casablanca	United States	$30.00	$240.00
PV-152	8	Gone with the Wind	United States	$35.00	$280.00
PV-156	9	Night at the Opera	United States	$20.00	$180.00

In general, video titles from Italy, Japan, and the United States are selling well. Only the three titles listed below have not sold as well as expected. Premium Videos plans a marketing campaign to promote these titles and acquire new titles with similar themes.

Stock No.	Quantity	Title	Country	Unit Price	Total
PV-149	12	Fellini's Eight and a Half	Italy	$30.00	$360.00
PV-159	12	Seven Samurai, The	Japan	$35.00	$420.00
PV-143	13	Citizen Kane	United States	$28.00	$364.00

Customer Profile for Travel France

As the Sales Manager of Travel France, a travel service that advertises exclusively on the World Wide Web, you have decided to analyze information about the clients who have purchased tours to France in June 1998. You will use the information you obtain to help you plan additions to your web page that will target the type of customers who have purchased the most tours. To create the Customer Profile for Travel France, you will **Set Up the Customer List**, **Analyze the List**, and then **Format the Customer Profile**.

activity:

Set Up the Customer List

The list shown in Figure P2-2 contains information about all the clients who purchased a tour from Travel France during June 1998.

steps:

1. Open a blank Excel workbook, click the **Text Box button**, draw a text box from cell **A1** to **G6**, then enter and enhance the three lines of text as shown in Figure P2-1
Next, enhance the text box with a shadow border and a textured fill.

2. Click the **Shadow button** 📷 on the Drawing toolbar, select **Shadow Style 13**, right-click the text box border, click **Format Text Box**, click the **Colors and Lines tab**, click the **Color list arrow**, click **Fill Effects**, click the **Texture tab**, click the **top left texture box**, click **OK**, then click **OK**
The completed text box appears as shown in Figure P2-1.

3. Save your workbook as **Customer Profile for Travel France**

4. Click cell **A8**, enter the labels in cells **A8** to **H8** as shown in the printout in Figure P2-2, select cells **A8** to **H8**, click the **right mouse button**, click **Format Cells**, click the **Alignment tab**, click the **Wrap Text check box**, click **OK**, center and bold the labels, then adjust the column widths as shown in Figure P2-2

5. Click cell **A9**, type **230**, press **[Enter]**, type **231** in cell **A10**, select cells **A9** and **A10**, then drag the corner handle down to cell **A24**

6. As shown in Figure P2-2, enter the records in cells **B9** to **H24**, then format the dollar amounts in cells **H9** to **H24** in the Currency style

7. Double-click the **Sheet1 tab**, type **List**, press **[Enter]**, change the name of the **Sheet2 tab** to **Chart**, change the name of the **Sheet3 tab** to **Ranges**, then save the workbook
Next, go on to analyze the list to produce the information you require for your Customer Profile.

FIGURE P2-1: Completed text box

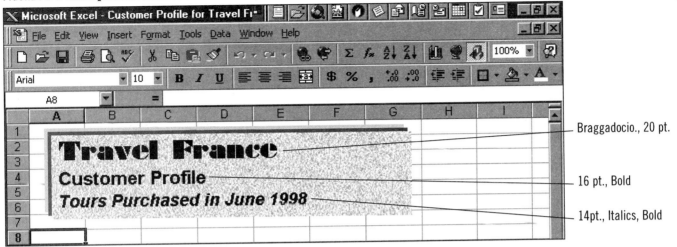

Braggadocio., 20 pt.

16 pt., Bold

14pt., Italics, Bold

FIGURE P2-2: Printout of field names and records for the customer list

	A	B	C	D	E	F	G	H
8	Order No.	Name	No. of Adults	Average Age	No. of Children	Home Country	Tour Name	Total Cost
9	230	Eliot, Marianne	2	50	0	United States	Ancient Brittany	$ 5,500.00
10	231	Mah, Raymond	4	35	2	Hong Kong	Loire Chateaux	$ 8,200.00
11	232	Tamaka, Hiromi	4	60	0	Japan	Loire Chateaux	$ 10,500.00
12	233	Bourne, Peter	2	65	0	Canada	Gourmet France	$ 9,500.00
13	234	Friesen, Helga	2	40	1	Germany	Light of Provence	$ 9,600.00
14	235	Lussier, Pierre	2	65	0	Canada	Light of Provence	$ 7,500.00
15	236	Holburn, James	3	62	0	United States	Gourmet France	$ 8,400.00
16	237	Kuratsu, Tsutomu	2	55	2	Japan	Loire Chateaux	$ 9,800.00
17	238	Nagata, Takashi	2	60	0	Japan	Light of Provence	$ 8,200.00
18	239	Palanio, Maria	4	63	0	Italy	Parisian Dreams	$ 5,600.00
19	240	Rosario, Renaldo	2	50	3	United States	Light of Provence	$ 11,700.00
20	241	Thiessen, Edvard	2	60	0	Germany	Light of Provence	$ 6,000.00
21	242	Hesse, Greta	2	64	0	Germany	Parisian Dreams	$ 7,500.00
22	243	Tasaka, Ayako	2	60	0	Japan	Light of Provence	$ 9,400.00
23	244	Mizumo, Mari	4	40	2	Japan	Parisian Dreams	$ 14,300.00
24	245	Kamei, Yoshi	2	42	2	Japan	Parisian Dreams	$ 12,700.00

activity:

Analyze the List

First, you want to know the total number of clients from each home country. You will create a PivotTable to count the number of clients from each home country and then use the data in the PivotTable to create a doughnut chart. You will then create a Subtotals list to calculate the total amount of money spent by customers in each home country. Finally, you will set up two complex criteria ranges to produce lists that focus on clients with children and clients over 60 years of age.

steps:

1. Click the List tab, select cells A8 to H24, click Data on the menu bar, click PivotTable Report, click Next, click Next, drag the Home Country box next to COLUMN, drag the No. of Adults box above DATA, drag the No. of Children box above DATA, click Next, click the Existing worksheet radio button, click the Chart tab, type A1, then click Finish

2. Select cells G5 to B3 of the PivotTable, then click the AutoSum button Σ on the Standard toolbar

3. Click a blank cell below the PivotTable, click the ChartWizard button 📊 on the Standard toolbar, click Doughnut, click Next, click the Collapse button to the right of the Data range box, select cells B5 to G5, click the Restore button, click the Series tab, click the Collapse button to the right of the Category labels box, select cells B2 to G2, then click the Restore button

4. Click Next, enter Breakdown of Clients by Country as the chart title, click the Data Labels tab, click the Show percent radio button, then click Finish

5. Increase the chart size so that it fills the screen, right-click one of the data labels (e.g., 19%), click Format Data Labels, click the Patterns tab, click the Automatic radio button in the Border and Area sections, click the Font tab, select a font size of 8 point, click OK, right-click the Legend, click Format Legend, click the Font tab, select a font size of 8 point, click OK, click the chart title, then change its font size to 12 point

   Your chart appears as shown in Figure P2-3. Next, return to the List sheet and create a Subtotals list.

6. Click the List tab, click cell F8, click the Sort Ascending button ↓ on the Standard toolbar, select cells A8 to H24, click Data on the menu bar, click Subtotals, click the At each change in: list arrow, click Home Country, then click OK

   You should see $144,400.00 in cell H31. Next, go on to set up a complex criteria range and then use the Advanced Filter function to list only those clients from the United States and Japan with children.

7. Click the Ranges tab, then enter the labels and values in cells A1 to B3 and cells A5 and A6 as shown in Figure P2-4

8. Click the List tab, click anywhere in the Subtotals list, click Data on the menu bar, click Filter, click Advanced Filter, click the Copy to another location radio button, click the Criteria Range box, click the Ranges tab, select cells A1 to B3, click the Copy to: box, type A35, then click OK

9. Use the Advanced Filter function to create a list of clients starting in cell A41 of the List sheet who are 60 years of age or older from the criteria range in cells A5 and A6 of the Ranges sheet, then save the workbook

   Cells A36 to G50 appear as shown in Figure P2-5.

FIGURE P2-3: Completed doughnut chart

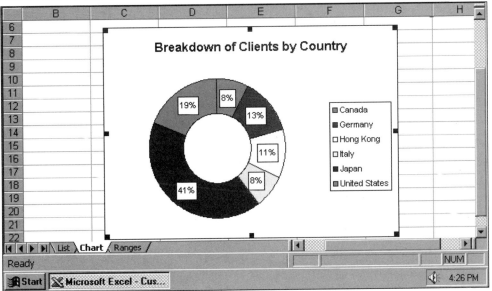

FIGURE P2-4: Criteria ranges

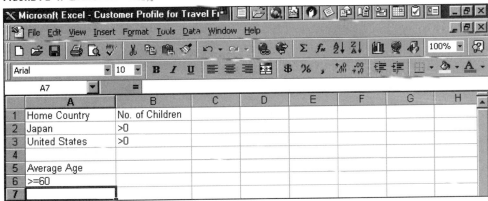

	A	B
1	Home Country	No. of Children
2	Japan	>0
3	United States	>0
4		
5	Average Age	
6	>=60	
7		

FIGURE P2-5: Advanced Filter lists in cells A36 to G50

	A	B	C	D	E	F	G
36	237	Kuratsu, Tsutomu	2	55	2	Japan	Loire Chateaux
37	244	Mizumo, Mari	4	40	2	Japan	Parisian Dreams
38	245	Kamei, Yoshi	2	42	2	Japan	Parisian Dreams
39	240	Rosario, Renaldo	2	50	3	United States	Light of Provenc
40							
41	Order No.	Name	No. of Adults	Average Age	No. of Children	Home Country	Tour Name
42	233	Bourne, Peter	2	65	0	Canada	Gourmet France
43	235	Lussier, Pierre	2	65	0	Canada	Light of Provenc
44	241	Thiessen, Edvard	2	60	0	Germany	Light of Provenc
45	242	Hesse, Greta	2	64	0	Germany	Parisian Dreams
46	239	Palanio, Maria	4	63	0	Italy	Parisian Dreams
47	232	Tamaka, Hiromi	4	60	0	Japan	Loire Chateaux
48	238	Nagata, Takashi	2	60	0	Japan	Light of Provenc
49	243	Tasaka, Ayako	2	60	0	Japan	Light of Provenc
50	236	Holburn, James	3	62	0	United States	Gourmet France
51							

activity:

Format the Customer Profile

You need to format the customer profile on one page in landscape orientation so that it appears as shown in Figure P2-6.

steps:

1. Click the **Print Preview button** 🔍 on the Standard toolbar, click **Setup**, click the **Page tab**, click the **Landscape radio button**, click the **Fit to radio button**, click **OK**, study the appearance of the worksheet in the Print Preview screen, then click **Close**

You first need to move the bottom advanced filter list so that it appears to the right of the top advanced filter list. You will work most comfortably in 50% view.

2. Click the **Zoom Control list arrow**, click **50%**, select cells **A41 to H50**, click the **Cut button** ✂️, click cell **J35**, then click the **Paste button** 📋

Next, insert the doughnut chart to the right of the Subtotals list.

3. Click the **Chart tab**, select the pie chart, click the **Copy button**, click the **List tab**, click cell **J11**, click the **Paste button**, increase the size of the chart, click away from the chart, then click 🔍 to see how your worksheet appears

As you can see, you need to increase the width of selected cells in the second advanced filter list.

4. Click **Close**, display **100% view**, adjust the column widths of the second Advanced Filter list (cells **J35 to Q44**) so that all the data is visible, then reduce the size of column I so that it is only about ¼" wide

5. Select cells **C36 to C40**, click the **AutoSum button** Σ on the Standard toolbar, enter, bold, and right-align **Total** in cell **B40**, bold the total in cell **C40**, calculate the total number of children and the total tour costs in the first Advanced Filter list and the total tour costs in the second Advanced Filter list, then add and enhance labels and bold the totals as shown in Figure P2-6

6. Center the values in the **No. of Adults**, **Average Age**, and **No. of Children** columns for all three lists, then bold all the country totals in the Subtotals list as shown in Figure P2-6

Hint

Draw the text boxes in 50% view, then switch to 100% to enter the text required.

7. Display **50% view** again, insert **6 rows** above the Subtotals list, create the text box as shown in Figure P2-6, insert **6 rows** above the two advanced filter lists, then create the two text boxes as shown in Figure P2-6

8. As shown in Figure P2-6, create a text box above the doughnut chart, slightly increase the size of the doughnut chart, move the chart slightly to the right so that it appears centered under the text box, then center the heading text box

9. View your worksheet in the Print Preview screen, click **Setup**, click the **Margins tab**, click the **Horizontally** and **Vertically check boxes**, click the **Header/Footer tab**, create a custom header as shown in Figure P2-6, close the Print Preview screen, make any positioning adjustments necessary, print a copy of the List worksheet, then save and close the workbook

FIGURE P2-6: Completed Customer Profile for Travel France

Customer Profile for Travel France

[Your name]

In June, 1998, Travel France sold a total of 53 tours for a total revenue of $144,400. The list displayed below shows that the most revenue ($64,900) was generated from clients in Japan, followed distantly by $25,600 from clients in the United States and $23,100 for clients in Germany.

Travel France
Customer Profile
Tours Purchased in June 1998

Order No.	Name	No. of Adults	Average Age	No. of Children	Home Country	Tour Name	Total Cost
233	Bourne, Peter	2	65	0	Canada	Gourmet France	$ 9,500.00
235	Lussier, Pierre	2	65	0	Canada	Light of Provence	$ 7,500.00
					Canada Total		**$ 17,000.00**
234	Friesen, Helga	2	40	1	Germany	Light of Provence	$ 9,600.00
241	Thiessen, Edvard	2	60	0	Germany	Light of Provence	$ 6,000.00
242	Hesse, Greta	2	64	0	Germany	Parisian Dreams	$ 7,500.00
					Germany Total		**23,100.00**
231	Mah, Raymond	4	35	2	Hong Kong	Loire Chateaux	8,200.00
					Hong Kong Total		**8,200.00**
239	Palanio, Maria	4	63	0	Italy	Parisian Dreams	5,600.00
					Italy Total		**5,600.00**
232	Tamaka, Hiromi	4	60	0	Japan	Loire Chateaux	10,500.00
237	Kuratsu, Tsutomu	2	55	2	Japan	Loire Chateaux	9,800.00
238	Nagata, Takashi	2	60	0	Japan	Light of Provence	8,200.00
243	Tasaka, Ayako	2	60	0	Japan	Light of Provence	9,400.00
244	Mizumo, Mari	4	40	2	Japan	Light of Provence	14,300.00
245	Kamei, Yoshi	2	42	2	Japan	Parisian Dreams	12,700.00
					Japan Total		**64,900.00**
230	Eliot, Marianne	2	50	0	United States	Ancient Brittany	5,500.00
236	Holburn, James	3	62	0	United States	Gourmet France	8,400.00
240	Rosario, Renaldo	2	50	3	United States	Light of Provence	11,700.00
					United States Total		**$ 25,600.00**
					Grand Total		**$ 144,400.00**

The chart below shows that 41% of the clients in June were from Japan. To attract more clients from this market, our site will shortly include a Japanese-language version.

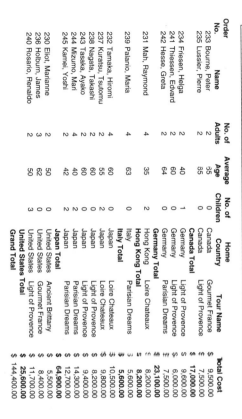

Breakdown of Clients by Country

- Canada
- Germany
- Hong Kong
- Italy
- Japan
- United States

19%
8%
13%
11%
8%
41%

Over half of our clients are 60 years of age or over. This market continues to grow. Efforts are underway to build links from our site to seniors-related sites worldwide.

Order No.	Name	No. of Adults	Average Age	No. of Children	Home Country	Tour Name	Total Cost
233	Bourne, Peter	2	65	0	Canada	Gourmet France	$ 9,500.00
235	Lussier, Pierre	2	65	0	Canada	Light of Provence	$ 7,500.00
241	Thiessen, Edvard	2	60	0	Germany	Light of Provence	6,000.00
242	Hesse, Greta	2	64	0	Germany	Parisian Dreams	7,500.00
239	Palanio, Maria	4	63	0	Italy	Parisian Dreams	5,600.00
232	Tamaka, Hiromi	4	60	0	Japan	Loire Chateaux	10,500.00
238	Nagata, Takashi	2	60	0	Japan	Light of Provence	8,200.00
243	Tasaka, Ayako	2	60	0	Japan	Light of Provence	9,400.00
236	Holburn, James	3	62	0	United States	Gourmet France	8,400.00
						Total Tour Costs	**$ 72,600.00**

Four of the clients traveled with their families. Revenue for these tours totaled $48,500—over one-third of the total revenue. A new page will be added to our World Wide Web site to focus specifically on family-oriented tours.

Order No.	Name	No. of Adults	Average Age	No. of Children	Home Country	Tour Name	Total Cost
237	Kuratsu, Tsutomu	2	55	2	Japan	Loire Chateaux	$ 9,800.00
244	Mizumo, Mari	4	40	2	Japan	Parisian Dreams	14,300.00
245	Kamei, Yoshi	2	42	2	Japan	Parisian Dreams	12,700.00
240	Rosario, Renaldo	2	50	3	United States	Light of Provence	11,700.00
	Total	10		**Total** 9		**Total Tour Costs**	**$ 48,500.00**

Research Report on Internet Providers

As part of a report you have written on Internet providers in Toronto, you want to include the research statistics you analyzed and formatted in Excel. To create this worksheet, you will **Create and Analyze the List**.

activity:

Create and Analyze the List

You will first enter the fields and records for the list of local Internet providers and then you will use various database functions to analyze the list.

steps:

1. Open a blank Excel workbook, name the **Sheet1** and **Sheet2** tabs **List** and **Calculations**, display the List sheet, create a 3-D text box for the heading, enter the text as shown in Figure P3-1, fill the text box with the **White marble** texture, click cell **A7**, type **ID**, enter and enhance the field names and records in cells **A7** to **G18** (to \$.30 for Web Spiders) as shown in Figure P3-1, then save the workbook as **Research on Internet Providers**

You will calculate the cost for 50 hours in Step 2. Note that Base Hours refers to the Internet time purchased by the monthly rate. The Add'l Hourly Rate refers to the cost of Internet time beyond the Base Hours.

2. Click cell **H7** (the blank cell to the right of Add'l Hourly Rate), enter **Cost for 50 Hours**, bold, center and wrap the text, click cell **H8** (the blank cell below the label you just entered), enter the formula to calculate the cost for 50 hours, copy the formula down to cell **H18**, then apply the currency format

The formula required to calculate the cost for 50 hours is =Monthly Rate + (50-No. of Hours)*Add'l Hourly Rate. Presuming the list begins in cell A7, the required formula is =E8+(50-F8)*G8. Next, you need to copy selected columns to the Calculations sheet, enter an IF formula to rank the companies, then create the pie chart and copy it into the List sheet.

Hint

The formula will appear in the formula bar as =IF(B2>40,"Over $40",IF(B2>=30,"$30–$40","Under $30")).

3. Select cells **B7** to **B18** (the list of company names), copy them to cell **A1** in the **Calculations sheet**, select cells **H7** to **H18** (the costs for 50 hours) in the **List sheet**, copy them, right-click cell **B1** in the **Calculation sheet**, click **Paste Special**, click **Values**, click **OK**, enter **Rank** in cell **C1** in the Calculations sheet, enter an **IF formula** in cell **C2** that ranks the 50-hour cost for each company according to the following scale: Over \$40, \$30–\$40, and Under \$30, then copy the formula down to cell **C12**

4. Create a PivotTable in cell **A14** of the **Calculation sheet** that counts the number of companies in each rank, then create a pie chart from the PivotTable data and copy it into the **List sheet**

Your completed pie chart should appear as shown in Figure P3-1.

Hint

Start the criteria range in cell A35 in the Calculations sheet, enter Lines in cell A35, Connect Success in cell B35, Cost for 50 Hours in cell C35, >30 in cell A36, >80% in cell B36, and <$30 in cell C36.

5. Create a complex criteria range in the **Calculations sheet** that you can use to list all the companies that have more than 30 lines, a connect success of more than 80%, and a 50-hour cost of less than \$30

6. Use the Advanced Filter function to create the list of companies that conform to the criteria you entered in the **Calculations sheet**

Only one company will be listed as shown in Figure P3-1.

7. Add text boxes, center the values in columns **C**, **D**, and **F**, format the **List sheet** for printing, print a copy, compare your completed version to Figure P3-1, then save and close the workbook

Internet Providers   [Your name]

Analysis of Toronto Internet Providers
[Current Date]

ID	Company Name	Lines	Connect Success	Monthly Rate	No. of Hours	Add'l Hourly Rate	Cost for 50 Hours
100	Internet Plus	50	90%	$ 25.00	30	$ 0.50	$ 35.00
101	Quest	100	80%	$ 18.00	25	$ 0.25	$ 24.25
102	Marvel Internet	75	75%	$ 30.00	30	$ 0.50	$ 40.00
103	Connect!	150	80%	$ 35.00	30	$ 0.30	$ 41.00
104	WebMasters	50	50%	$ 20.00	40	$ 0.25	$ 22.50
105	Ace Internet	200	85%	$ 25.00	25	$ 0.75	$ 43.75
106	Good Times Plus	100	60%	$ 15.00	15	$ 1.00	$ 50.00
107	Surf Dude	75	75%	$ 10.00	12	$ 0.75	$ 38.50
108	Web Mate	150	90%	$ 35.00	40	$ 0.75	$ 42.50
109	Easy Net	40	55%	$ 18.00	25	$ 0.40	$ 28.00
110	Web Spiders	250	85%	$ 22.00	35	$ 0.30	$ 26.50

As shown in the pie chart displayed below, 36% of the Internet providers charge less than $30 for 50 hours of connection time.

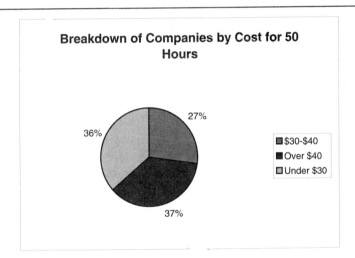

Breakdown of Companies by Cost for 50 Hours

Only one company conformed to the criteria required for an acceptable Internet provider: that the provider offered more than 200 lines, had a connect success rate higher than 80%, and charged less than $30 for 50 hours of connected time. I recommend Web Spiders as the most cost-effective and efficient Internet provider currently operating in Toronto.

ID	Company Name	Lines	Connect Success	Monthly Rate	No. of Hours	Add'l Hourly Rate	Cost for 50 Hours
110	Web Spiders	250	85%	$ 22.00	35	$ 0.30	$ 26.50

Independent Challenges

INDEPENDENT CHALLENGE 1

You run a small, home-based business that sells a product of your choice. Your business is starting to grow. Orders are coming in from local distributors, and your client base is increasing. You have decided to use Excel to create an inventory list of all the products you have on hand to sell and then use the database functions to analyze the list and identify products that are selling well, products that are overstocked, etc. You will present the finished report to your bank manager as part of your application for financing.

1. Identify the type of products you wish to sell. For example, you could make and sell craft items such as candles, costume jewelry, or handmade clothing, or you could sell homemade jams and preserves. Write the type of product (e.g., gourmet foods, textile products, crafts, etc.) you would like to sell from a home-based business in the box below:

> **Product type:**

2. List 10 specific products that you will include in your inventory list. Your inventory list will contain at least 20 products, but for now, you just want to get an idea of product variations. For example, if you choose to sell jams and preserves, you could list products such as Mango Chutney, Raspberry-Peach Jam, Grape Preserves, etc. List 10 specific products in the box below:

> 1.
> 2.
> 3.
> 4.
> 5.
> 6.
> 7.
> 8.
> 9.
> 10.

3. Give your company a name, and then write a brief description in the box below. For example, you could call a company that makes and sells uniquely designed children's clothing "Kid Gear," and then describe the company as a small, home-based operation that designs and sews sturdy, colorful play clothes for children aged 2 to 10.

> **Company Name:**
> **Description:**

4. List three questions you will ask in order to analyze your inventory list. For example, you could ask *How many jars of preserves do I have in each of three categories: sweet, savory, and sweet/sour?* or *What is the total worth of each type of clothing I stock (e.g., preschool boys, preschool girls, school-age boys, school-age girls, etc.)?* To answer the first question, you would create a PivotTable that counts the number of records in each category and then create a pie chart that shows the breakdown of your products by category. To answer the second question, you would create a Subtotals list. In the table form below, list three questions you need to ask and identify the method you would use to answer each question.

Question:	Method:
1.	1.
2.	2.
3.	3.

5. Create an inventory list that includes at least 20 items. Include field names such as Item No., Quantity, Product Name, Category, and Price. The field names you include will depend, in part, on the questions you will ask. For example, if you plan to

create a subtotals list that displays the total worth of each product category, you must include a field for Price. If you plan to create an AutoFilter list that includes only those products that cost less than $5.00 and have fewer than 10 items in stock, you will need to include a field for both Price and Quantity.

6. Use the database functions to answer the questions you have identified. If necessary, use additional sheets to contain PivotTables and criteria ranges and then copy the results into the sheet that contains your inventory list.

7. Format your inventory report attractively for printing. Include some text boxes to explain the significance of the various charts and lists you have created. Keep in mind the *purpose* of your inventory report (that is, to secure more financing for your business). Include information that you feel will help identify the strengths of your business and indicate how additional financing will help your business increase its profits. For ideas, refer to the inventory report you created for Project 1.

8. Save your inventory report as Inventory Report for [Name of Company], then print a copy. You will probably need to print the report over two pages, depending on how many lists and charts you have included.

INDEPENDENT CHALLENGE 2

Create a list of 30 or 40 customers and the products or services they have purchased from a company of your choice. When you have completed the list, ask questions and then use the database functions to answer the questions and create an attractively formatted Customer Profile.

1. Determine the name of your company and the type of products it sells. For example, you could run a catering service called "Six O'Clock Solution" that specializes in preparing and delivering meals to customers who do not have time to cook.

2. Create a list of 30 or 40 customers who have purchased your product or service in the past month. For example, the list of customers who have purchased meals from Six O'Clock Solution could include fields such as Date, Customer Name, Age Range (e.g., Under 30, 30 to 50, Over 50, etc.), Number of Meals, Type of Meal (e.g., Vegetarian, Cajun, Oriental, etc.), Gender, Amount Spent, etc. The field names you include will depend upon the type of information you wish to include in your customer profile. For example, if you want to find out how many of your customers in a specific age range spent over $75 and ordered more than two Vegetarian meals, you will need to include field names for Age Range, Meal Type, and Amount.

3. Determine two or three questions to ask regarding the information in your list and then use the database functions to create the lists and charts that will answer the questions.

4. Add text boxes to explain the significance of the charts and lists you have created. You will need to think about why you have created the various lists and charts. For example, you may wish to determine new target markets (for example, males over 50 or women over 30 who spend more than $50 on an order). The information you include in your customer profile will depend upon the nature of your business and your reasons for analyzing the customer list.

5. Save your Customer Profile as "Customer Profile of [Company Name]".

6. Format the worksheet attractively for printing on one or two pages, then print a copy.

INDEPENDENT CHALLENGE 3

Create a list of your 15 all-time favorite TV shows—both new and old. Include the following fields in your list: ID No., Title, Genre, Length, Year Ended (you may need to approximate for old shows), and Rating (e.g., three stars, four stars, etc.). Use the list illustrated in Figure IC-1 as your guide.

FIGURE IC-1: Sample list of TV shows

My Top 15 TV Shows					
ID No.	Title	Genre	Length	Year Ended (Approx.)	My Rating
VI-01	Due South	Drama	60 min.	1995	****
VI-02	Seinfeld	Comedy	30 min.	Current	***
VI-03	Hawaii Five-O	Drama	60 min.	1981	***
VI-04	Civilisation	Documentary	60 min.	1980	****
VI-05	I Love Lucy	Comedy	30 min.	1960	****
VI-06	Fawlty Towers	British	30 min.	1979	****

1. Create a PivotTable in Sheet2 that counts all the records in each genre, and then create a pie chart from the PivotTable data.
2. Ask three questions regarding the information in your list. Examples include: *Which TV shows are comedy, produced in the 1980s or earlier, and have a rating of three stars?* or *Which TV shows are drama, produced currently, and have a rating of four stars?* Enter the three questions you will ask in the box below:

Question 1: ....

....

Question 2: ....

....

Question 3: ....

....

3. Create criteria ranges in Sheet3 that contain the field names and criteria required to answer each question (you will need to create three criteria ranges), and then use the AutoFilter function to create the three new lists under your original list in Sheet1.
4. Add text boxes to explain the significance of your original list and the three AutoFilter lists, format Sheet1 attractively for printing, save the workbook as My Top 15 TV Shows, then print a copy.

INDEPENDENT CHALLENGE 4

You are trying to make up your mind about what photocopier to buy based on three criteria: price, copy speed, and the number of multiple copies you can make. You will first create a list of photocopiers and then you will use the appropriate database functions to answer the questions provided. Note that the list includes only the model numbers of the 10 photocopiers so that you can make your decision without being influenced by brand-name loyalty.

1. Create the list as shown in Figure IC-2.

FIGURE IC-2: **List of photocopiers**

Model	Max. Size	Reduce/ Enlarge	Speed	Max. Copies	Price
4030Z	11" X 17"	Yes	18 cpm	99	$ 3,500.00
4120Z	10" X 14"	Yes	21 cpm	50	$ 2,550.00
5130P	10" X 14"	Yes	18 cpm	99	$ 2,200.00
5330C	11" X 17"	Yes	10 cpm	10	$ 1,200.00
3089C	8.5" X 11"	No	10 cpm	20	$ 1,500.00
4033Z	8.5" X 11"	Yes	5 cpm	50	$ 1,800.00
3078C	8.5" X 11"	No	5 cpm	20	$ 900.00
4099X	10" X 14"	No	18 cpm	99	$ 2,800.00
2870C	8.5" X 11"	Yes	8 cpm	50	$ 1,000.00
4080X	10" X 14"	No	15 cpm	25	$ 1,500.00

2. Create a PivotTable in Sheet 2 that counts the number of photocopiers in each Max. Size category (e.g., 11" X 17", 10" X 14", and 8.5" X 11"), then create a pie chart that appears as shown in Figure IC-3.
3. Sort the list in ascending order by the Max. Copies category, then create a Subtotals list that counts the number of photocopiers in each Max. Copies category. In the Subtotals dialog box, you need to select Max. Copies for At Each Change In and Count for the Use Function. Your completed Subtotals list should appear as shown in Figure IC-3.
4. Set up a criteria range in Sheet2 that will select all the photocopiers that cost less than $3,000, allow a maximum size of 10" X 14", have a speed of 10 or more cpm (copies per minute), and allow reduction and enlargement.
5. Create an Advanced Filter list starting in cell A40 in Sheet1 from the criteria range you set up on Sheet2.
6. Add text boxes and format Sheet1 for printing so that it appears as shown in Figure IC-3. Note that you will need to supply the text in the text boxes.
7. Save the workbook as Photocopier Comparison, then print a copy of Sheet1.

FIGURE IC-3: Completed worksheet

Excel 97

Photocopier Comparison   [Your Name]

Photocopier Comparison Shopping

Explain the significance of the Subtotals list by noting the number of
copiers with maximum copies of 50 or more. Note that this feature is
important to your business.

Model	Max. Size	Reduce/ Enlarge	Speed	Max. Copies	Price
5330C	11" X 17"	Yes	10 cpm	10	$ 1,200.00
				10 Count	1
3089C	8.5" X 11"	No	10 cpm	20	$ 1,500.00
3078C	8.5" X 11"	No	5 cpm	20	$ 900.00
				20 Count	2
4080X	10" X 14"	No	15 cpm	25	$ 1,500.00
				25 Count	1
4120Z	10" X 14"	Yes	21 cpm	50	$ 2,550.00
4033Z	8.5" X 11"	Yes	5 cpm	50	$ 1,800.00
2870C	8.5" X 11"	Yes	8 cpm	50	$ 1,000.00
				50 Count	3
4099X	10" X 14"	No	18 cpm	99	$ 2,800.00
4030Z	11" X 17"	Yes	18 cpm	99	$ 3,500.00
5130P	10" X 14"	Yes	18 cpm	99	$ 2,200.00
				99 Count	3
				Grand Count	10

Describe the information displayed in the pie chart and note your
company's preference for the largest maximum original size possible
within your price range of under $3,000.

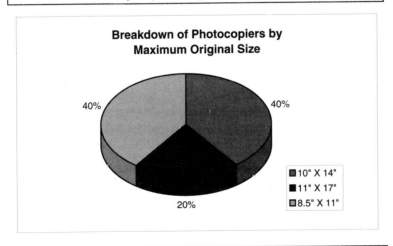

**Breakdown of Photocopiers by
Maximum Original Size**

40%   40%   20%

- 10" X 14"
- 11" X 17"
- 8.5" X 11"

State which of the two photocopiers listed below you will purchase and
why, keeping in mind that high speed is important to your business.

Model	Max. Size	Reduce/ Enlarge	Speed	Max. Copies	Price
4120Z	10" X 14"	Yes	21 cpm	50	$ 2,550.00
5130P	10" X 14"	Yes	18 cpm	99	$ 2,200.00

Visual Workshop

You have been given a list of inventory items stocked by The Learning Place, a retail operation that sells children's educational toys at various locations in the United Kingdom. Open a blank Excel workbook then, create the list shown in Figure VW-1. To display the prices in UK pounds, select cells G2 to G20, click Format, click Cells, click Accounting, click the Symbol list arrow, then select £ English (British). Calculate the required totals (Quantity X Price), then use the appropriate database functions to answer the questions provided. Save the workbook as The Learning Place, then format and print a copy of the worksheet after you have created the various elements required to answer the questions. Include text boxes in the completed worksheet that explain the elements and add "The Learning Place: Inventory Analysis" as the title.

FIGURE VW-1: Inventory List for The Learning Place

	A	B	C	D	E	F	G	H
1	Stock No.	Quantity	Description	Store Location	Category	Age Group	Price	Total
2	265	20	Cuddletime Book	Oxford	Book	Toddler	£ 4.50	
3	266	15	Big Block Builders	London	Construction	Preschool	£ 10.00	
4	267	18	Annie Anatomy Doll	Reading	Character	Toddler	£ 15.00	
5	268	15	Mechanix	Exeter	Construction	School Age	£ 25.00	
6	269	6	Chatty Friends	Exeter	Character	Toddler	£ 8.50	
7	270	8	Science Plus Cards	London	Academic	School Age	£ 6.00	
8	271	23	Annie Anatomy Doll	London	Character	Toddler	£ 15.00	
9	272	16	Big Block Builders	Newcastle	Construction	Preschool	£ 10.00	
10	273	9	Chatty Friends	Exeter	Character	Toddler	£ 18.00	
11	274	20	Annie Anatomy Doll	Manchester	Character	Preschool	£ 15.00	
12	275	21	Cuddletime Book	Exeter	Book	Toddler	£ 4.50	
13	276	12	Science Plus Cards	Reading	Academic	School Age	£ 6.00	
14	277	16	Prehistoric Adventures	Oxford	Academic	School Age	£ 5.00	
15	278	17	Prehistoric Adventures	Newcastle	Academic	School Age	£ 5.00	
16	279	21	Science Plus Cards	London	Academic	School Age	£ 6.00	
17	280	19	Cuddletime Book	London	Book	Toddler	£ 4.50	
18	281	12	Science Plus Cards	London	Academic	School Age	£ 6.00	
19	282	22	Mechanix	Oxford	Construction	School Age	£ 25.00	
20	283	18	Annie Anatomy Doll	Manchester	Character	Preschool	£ 15.00	

1. What percentage of items are Character toys, and what percentage are Academic toys? Create a pie chart to display this information.

2. What is the total worth of all the Toddler toys?

3. Which items have less than 20 items in stock at the London store and are priced at less than £15.00? Note that the Currency style is not used in the list because the currency required is UK pounds, not dollars. Keep all prices and totals in the Comma style.

4. Which School Age toys have more than 10 items in stock at the Oxford and Exeter stores?

Microsoft
► Excel
Projects

Predictions

In This Unit You Will Create:

 ► **Sales Forecast**

 ► **Sales Report**

 ► **Home Renovation Project**

You use Excel's powerful Scenario function to make predictions based on a current set of data. You can then use these predictions to plan business and sales ventures, analyze current sales patterns, and create sales forecasts. For example, you can create one scenario that displays your projected income and expenses should favorable conditions occur (e.g., your clientele increases and your expenses remain fixed) and another scenario that displays your income and expenses should unfavorable conditions occur (e.g., your sales drop by 30% and your rent doubles). You also can use the Goal Seek function to make predictions. For example, you can determine how much money you can afford to spend on Advertising when you want all your expenses for a particular month to total $5,000. The Goal Seek function will find the best option for the Advertising expense, based on the amounts you have entered for all your other expenses. Finally, you can use the Solver function to predict optimal sales levels based on the specific *constraints* you supply. For example, suppose you own a car dealership and want to know how many Nissans and Toyotas you must sell in order to make a profit of $50,000 when you can sell no more than 500 cars and 40% of the cars you sell must be Toyotas. Solver uses complex mathematical formulas to solve this problem and provides you with the number of Nissans and Toyotas you should sell at a specific price, given the constraints you have specified. ► In this unit, you will use the Scenario, Goal Seek, and Solver functions to solve problems based on various sets of worksheet data.

OVERVIEW

Sales Forecast for Books 'n Beans

Books 'n Beans is a small bookstore and coffee shop located two blocks from Mississippi Plaza, a newly revitalized heritage district in downtown St. Louis. Business at Books 'n Beans has decreased dramatically in recent months as tourists and locals have flocked to the chic restaurants and boutiques in Mississippi Plaza. As the owner of Books 'n Beans, you need to know whether you should risk relocating to Mississippi Plaza, where you will pay at least double your current rent but could increase your sales. To help you decide, you will create three kinds of scenarios: Current, Best Case, and Worst Case. Three activities are required to complete these scenarios for Books 'n Beans.

Project Activities

Create the Current Scenarios

The Current scenarios consist of the income generated and the expenses incurred by Books 'n Beans from July to December 1998. You will first create the income and expenses worksheet, calculate the required totals, and then use the Scenario Manager to create Current scenarios from the values for the current gross income and the expenses for Rent, Advertising, and Operating Costs. To create a scenario, you select the cells that contain the values you will change and then assign a scenario name to the current data. Figure P1-1 shows the Current scenarios of the income and expenses, along with a bar chart that shows the monthly net income.

Create the Best and Worst Case Scenarios

You are thinking of relocating to Mississippi Plaza, where the rent is double your current rent. If all goes well, you project that your advertising costs and some of your operating costs will be lower and your net income much higher if you relocate. To help you make a decision, you *change* the values for the current gross revenue and the expenses for Rent, Advertising, and Operating Costs to reflect your *projections* for the next six months, should you relocate. You then assign a new scenario name (Best Case scenario) to each set of new values. Figure P1-2 displays the worksheet and bar chart that appear when you apply the Best Case scenarios. However, if you relocate to Mississippi Plaza, your rent could more than double, your gross revenue may not increase as much as you hope, and your operating and advertising costs could be higher. You change the values in the worksheet again to reflect your worst case predictions and then assign "Worst Case scenarios" to each set of new values. Figure P1-3 displays how the worksheet and bar chart will appear when you assign the Worst Case scenarios.

Format and Print the Scenarios

Finally, you will add the bar chart displayed in Figures P1-1, P1-2, and P1-3. This bar chart will appear differently, depending on which scenario is "active." Once you have created the bar chart, you will format the worksheet for printing, apply the Current scenarios, and then print a copy. You will then apply the Best Case scenario and print a copy, and then apply the Worst Case scenario and print a copy. You always work with the same worksheet. However, you can quickly change the values and the appearance of the bar chart just by applying any combination of scenarios.

FIGURE P1-1: Current Scenario

Current Scenarios   [Your name]

Books 'n Beans
Income and Expenses: July to December, 1998

	July	August	September	October	November	December	Totals
REVENUE							
Gross Coffee Revenue	$ 9,760.16	$ 7,640.50	$ 6,973.46	$ 8,465.12	$ 7,840.30	$12,460.89	$ 53,140.43
Gross Book Revenue	5,420.00	3,460.45	6,780.46	7,880.50	6,207.80	11,608.90	41,358.11
Less Returns	455.40	333.03	412.62	490.37	421.44	722.09	2,834.96
NET SALES	$14,724.76	$10,767.92	$13,341.30	$15,855.25	$13,626.66	$23,347.70	$ 91,663.58
Less Cost of Goods Sold	9,108.10	6,660.57	8,252.35	9,807.37	8,428.86	14,441.87	56,699.12
GROSS PROFIT ON SALES	$ 5,616.66	$ 4,107.35	$ 5,088.95	$ 6,047.88	$ 5,197.80	$ 8,905.82	$ 34,964.46
EXPENSES							
Salaries	2,500.00	2,500.00	2,500.00	2,500.00	2,500.00	2,500.00	15,000.00
Rent	1,200.00	1,200.00	1,200.00	1,200.00	1,200.00	1,200.00	7,200.00
Advertising	300.00	300.00	300.00	300.00	300.00	300.00	1,800.00
Operating Costs	450.00	450.00	450.00	450.00	450.00	450.00	2,700.00
Total Expenses	$ 4,450.00	$ 4,450.00	$ 4,450.00	$ 4,450.00	$ 4,450.00	$ 4,450.00	26,700.00
NET INCOME	$ 1,166.66	$ (042.65)	$ 638.95	$ 1,597.88	$ 747.80	$ 4,455.82	$ 8,264.46

Current Net Income

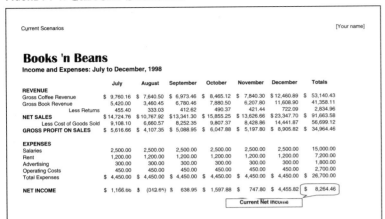

Current Monthly Net Income

FIGURE P1-2: Best Case Scenario

Best Case Scenario   [Your name]

Books 'n Beans
Projected Six Month Revenue: Best Case Forecast at Mississippi Plaza Location

	January	February	March	April	May	June	Totals
REVENUE							
Gross Coffee Revenue	$10,581.40	$11,639.54	$12,803.49	$14,083.84	$15,492.23	$17,041.45	$ 81,641.96
Gross Book Revenue	9,456.60	9,929.43	10,425.90	10,947.20	11,494.56	12,069.28	64,322.97
Less Returns	601.14	647.07	696.88	750.93	809.60	873.32	4,378.95
NET SALES	$19,436.86	$20,921.90	$22,532.51	$ 24,280.11	$ 26,177.18	$ 28,237.41	$ 141,585.98
Less Cost of Goods Sold	12,022.80	12,941.38	13,937.64	15,018.62	16,192.07	17,466.44	87,578.95
GROSS PROFIT ON SALES	$ 7,414.06	$ 7,980.52	$ 8,594.88	$ 9,261.48	$ 9,985.11	$10,770.97	$ 54,007.02
EXPENSES							
Salaries	2,500.00	2,500.00	2,500.00	2,500.00	2,500.00	2,500.00	15,000.00
Rent	2,400.00	2,400.00	2,400.00	2,400.00	2,400.00	2,400.00	14,400.00
Advertising	200.00	200.00	200.00	200.00	200.00	200.00	1,200.00
Operating Costs	300.00	300.00	300.00	300.00	300.00	300.00	1,800.00
Total Expenses	$ 5,400.00	$ 5,400.00	$ 5,400.00	$ 5,400.00	$ 5,400.00	$ 5,400.00	$ 32,400.00
NET INCOME	$ 2,014.06	$ 2,580.52	$ 3,194.88	$ 3,861.48	$ 4,585.11	$ 5,370.97	$ 21,607.02

Best Case Net Income
Coffee and Book revenue is increased by 25% of the October 1998 sales in the first month and then increased by 10% each month thereafter.

Best Case Forecast

FIGURE P1-3: Worst Case Scenario

Worst Case Scenario   [Your name]

Books 'n Beans
Projected Six Month Revenue: Worst Case Forecast at Mississippi Plaza Location

	January	February	March	April	May	June	Totals
REVENUE							
Gross Coffee Revenue	$ 8,888.38	$ 9,510.56	$10,176.30	$10,888.64	$11,650.85	$12,466.41	$ 63,581.14
Gross Book Revenue	8,274.53	8,853.74	9,473.50	10,136.65	10,846.21	11,605.45	59,190.08
Less Returns	514.89	550.93	589.49	630.76	674.91	722.16	3,683.14
NET SALES	$16,648.01	$17,813.37	$19,060.31	$ 20,394.53	$ 21,822.15	$ 23,349.70	$ 119,088.08
Less Cost of Goods Sold	10,297.74	11,018.58	11,789.88	12,615.18	13,498.24	14,443.11	73,662.73
GROSS PROFIT ON SALES	$ 6,350.27	$ 6,794.79	$ 7,270.43	$ 7,779.36	$ 8,323.91	$ 8,906.59	$ 45,425.35
EXPENSES							
Salaries	2,500.00	2,500.00	2,500.00	2,500.00	2,500.00	2,500.00	15,000.00
Rent	3,000.00	3,000.00	3,000.00	3,000.00	3,000.00	3,000.00	18,000.00
Advertising	700.00	700.00	700.00	700.00	700.00	700.00	4,200.00
Operating Costs	800.00	800.00	800.00	800.00	800.00	800.00	4,800.00
Total Expenses	$ 7,000.00	$ 7,000.00	$ 7,000.00	$ 7,000.00	$ 7,000.00	$ 7,000.00	$ 42,000.00
NET INCOME	$ (649.73)	$ (205.21)	$ 270.48	$ 779.36	$ 1,323.91	$ 1,906.59	$ 3,425.35

Worst Case Net Income
Coffee and Book revenue is increased by 5% of the October 1998 sales in the first month and then increased by 7% each month thereafter.

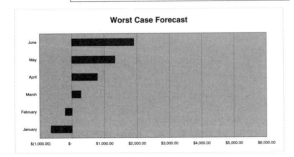

Worst Case Forecast

activity:

Create the Current Scenarios

You need to enter the labels and values for the six-month income and expenses statement for Books 'n Beans; calculate your total revenue, expenses, and net income; and then create the current scenarios.

steps:

1. Open a blank Excel workbook, enter **Books 'n Beans** in cell **A1**, enhance it with the **Britannic Bold font** and a font size of **24 point**, enter **Income and Expenses: July to December, 1998** in cell **A2**, enhance it with a font size of **12 point** and **Bold**, then save the workbook as **Sales Forecasts for Books 'n Beans**

   Next, enter the labels for the months of the year from July to December.

2. Click cell **B4**, type **July**, drag the corner handle of cell **B4** to cell **G4** to enter the remaining months, then click the **Bold** $\boxed{\text{B}}$ and **Center buttons** $\boxed{\equiv}$ on the Formatting toolbar

3. Enter the remaining labels and values, adjust the column widths as required, and format selected cells so that your worksheet appears as shown in the printout in Figure P1-4

   Next, you need to calculate the required totals. Start by calculating the returns, net revenue, cost of goods sold, and gross profit on sales.

4. Click cell **B8**, enter a formula that calculates **3%** of the sum of cells **B6** and **B7** (455.40), fill cells **C8** to **G8** with the formula, click cell **B9**, enter a formula that subtracts cell **B8** from the sum of cells **B6** and **B7** (14,724.76), fill cells **C9** to **G9** with the formula, click cell **B10**, enter a formula that calculates **60%** of the sum of cells **B6** and **B7** (9,108.10), fill cells **C10** to **G10** with the formula, click cell **B11**, enter a formula that subtracts cell **B10** from cell **B9** (5,616.66), then fill cells **C11** to **G11** with the formula

   Next, calculate the net income and the totals in column H.

5. Select cells **B14** to **G18**, click the **AutoSum button** $\boxed{\Sigma}$ on the Standard toolbar, click cell **B20**, enter a formula that subtracts the total expenses in cell **B18** from the gross profit on sales in cell **B11** (1,166.66), fill cells **C20** to **G20** with the formula, select cells **B6** to **H20**, then click the $\boxed{\Sigma}$

6. Switch to **75%** view, then widen the columns and format selected cells in the Comma or Currency styles, as shown in Figure P1-5

   Note that the total net income for the six months is $8,264.46—a value that is primarily attributable to the effect of Christmas sales on the business. Your monthly net income for July to November is not so promising. You are more convinced than ever that you should think about moving to Mississippi Plaza.
   Next, create a current scenario of the values entered in the Coffee Revenue row.

7. Return to **100%** view, select cells **B6** to **G6**, click **Tools** on the menu bar, click **Scenarios**, click **Add**, type **Current Coffee Revenue**, click **OK**, then click **OK** again to accept the values currently entered in cells B6 to G6

   Next, add current scenarios of the values entered in the Gross Book Revenue, Rent, Advertising, and Operating Costs rows.

8. Click **Add**, type **Current Book Revenue**, press [Tab] to move to the box under **Changing Cells**, type **B7:G7**, click **OK**, click **OK**, then add the next three scenarios as shown in the table below:

Scenario Name	Cells
Current Rent	B15:G15
Current Advertising	B16:G16
Current Operating Costs	B17:G17

9. Compare the Scenario Manager dialog box to Figure P1-6, click **Close** to exit the Scenario Manager dialog box, then save the workbook

   Next, go on to create the Best Case and Worst Case scenarios.

Hint

Use the [Ctrl] key to select all the Currency style rows, then click the Currency Style button. Use the same method to apply the Comma style to selected rows.

FIGURE P1-4: Printout of worksheet setup

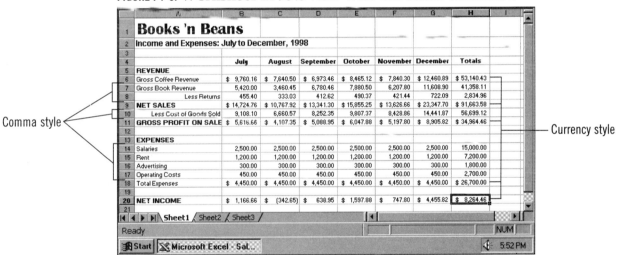

	A	B	C	D	E	F	G	H
1	**Books 'n Beans**							
2	**Income and Expenses: July to December, 1998**							
3								
4		**July**	**August**	**September**	**October**	**November**	**December**	**Totals**
5	**REVENUE**							
6	Gross Coffee Revenue	$ 9,760.16	$ 7,640.50	$ 6,973.46	$ 8,465.12	$ 7,840.30	$12,460.89	
7	Gross Book Revenue	5,420.00	3,460.45	6,780.46	7,880.50	6,207.80	11,608.90	
8	Less Returns							
9	**NET SALES**							
10	Less Cost of Goods Sold							
11	**GROSS PROFIT ON SALES**							
12								
13	**EXPENSES**							
14	Salaries	2,500.00	2,500.00	2,500.00	2,500.00	2,500.00	2,500.00	
15	Rent	1,200.00	1,200.00	1,200.00	1,200.00	1,200.00	1,200.00	
16	Advertising	300.00	300.00	300.00	300.00	300.00	300.00	
17	Operating Costs	450.00	450.00	450.00	450.00	450.00	450.00	
18	Total Expenses							
19								
20	**NET INCOME**							

Enter and enhance "Totals" in Cell H4

Currency style

Comma style

Right-align cells A8 and A10

FIGURE P1-5: Worksheet in 75% view with the totals calculated

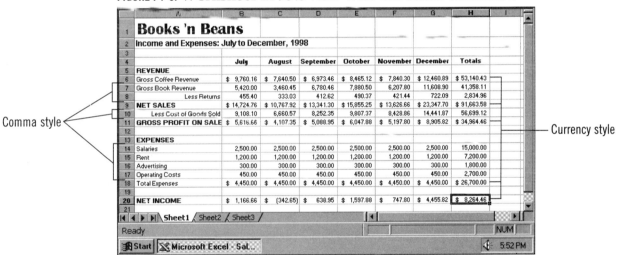

Comma style

Currency style

FIGURE P1-6: Scenario Manager dialog box

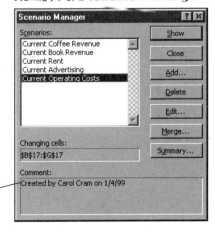

Your name and the current date will appear here

SALES FORECAST FOR BOOKS 'N BEANS

activity:

Create the Best and Worst Case Scenarios

You need to change the values in the worksheet to reflect your Best Case predictions should you relocate to Mississippi Plaza, and then change the values again to reflect your Worst Case predictions. Start by creating a Best Case scenario for the revenue generated from coffee sales. You predict that your monthly coffee revenues at Mississippi Plaza will be 25% higher than the current revenue in October in the first month and then will increase by 10% every month thereafter.

steps:

1. Click cell **B6**, enter the formula **=8465.12*1.25**, press **[Enter]**, click cell **C6**, enter the formula **=B6*1.1**, drag the corner handle across to cell **G6**, then widen the columns, if necessary

   You should see $119,310.06 in cell H9. Next, increase your gross book revenues by 20% of the October sales in the first month and then 5% for the following months.

2. Click cell **B7**, enter the formula: **=7880.50*1.2**, press **[Enter]**, click cell **C7**, enter the formula **=B7*1.05**, then copy the formula across to cell **G7**

   You should see $141,585.98 in cell H9. Next, create the Best Case scenario for the Gross Coffee Revenue row.

3. Click **Tools** on the menu bar, click **Scenarios**, click **Current Coffee Revenue**, click **Add**, type **Best Case Coffee Revenue**, then click **OK**

   A message appears telling you that at least one of the changing cells contains a formula.

4. Click **OK**, click **OK** again to accept the current value for each cell in the Best Case Coffee Revenue scenario, click **Current Book Revenue** as shown in Figure P1-7, click **Add**, type **Best Case Book Revenue**, click **OK**, click **OK** to accept the message, then click **OK** again

   Next, enter your projected values for the rent costs directly into the Scenario Manager.

5. Click **Current Rent**, click **Add**, type **Best Case Rent**, click **OK**, type **2400**, press **[Tab]**, enter **2400** for cells **C15** to **G15**, as shown in Figure P1-8, then click **OK**

6. Click **Current Advertising**, add a **Best Case Advertising** scenario that changes all the values in cells **B16** to **G16** to **200**, then click **Current Operating Costs** and add a **Best Case Operating Costs** scenario that changes all the values in cells **B17** to **G17** to **300**

   Next, show all the Best Case scenarios.

Hint

H20 now displays $21,607.02.

Hint

H9 now displays $119,088.08.

7. Click **Best Case Coffee Revenue**, click **Show**, click **Best Case Book Revenue**, click **Show**, show the remaining Best Case scenarios, then click **Close**

   Next, add the Worst Case scenarios. You will show the Current scenarios, then enter formulas to increase Coffee and Book Revenues by 5% of the current Revenue for October and 7% thereafter.

8. Click **Tools**, click **Scenarios**, click **Current Coffee Revenue**, click **Show**, show the remaining Current scenarios, click **Close**, check that cell H20 displays $8,264.46, click cell **B6**, enter the formula **=8465.12*1.05**, click cell **C6**, enter the formula **=B6*1.07**, copy it to cell **G6**, click cell **B7**, enter the formula **=7880.50*1.05**, click cell **C7**, enter the formula **=B7*1.07**, then copy it to cell **G7**

9. Click **Tools**, click **Scenarios**, click **Current Coffee Revenue**, click **Add**, type **Worst Case Coffee Revenue**, click **OK**, click **OK**, verify that the worst numbers are listed in the Scenario Values dialog box, click **OK** again, add the Worst Case Book Revenue scenario, add the Worst Case Rent, Advertising, and Operating Costs scenarios based on the values displayed below, show all the Worst Case scenarios, then close the Scenario Manager dialog box:

Worst Case Rent	Worst Case Advertising	Worst Case Operating Costs
3000/month	700/month	800/month

   The net income displayed in cell H20 is now $3,425.35 as shown in 75% view in Figure P1-9.

FIGURE P1-7: **Scenario Manager dialog box with Current Book Revenue selected**

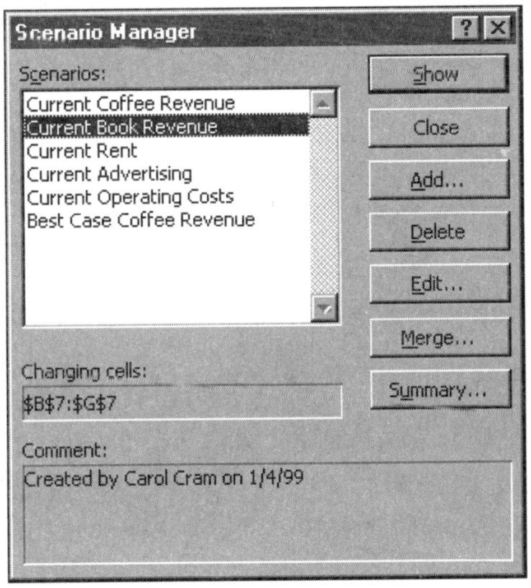

Scenario Manager ? X

Scenarios:
- Current Coffee Revenue
- Current Book Revenue
- Current Rent
- Current Advertising
- Current Operating Costs
- Best Case Coffee Revenue

Buttons: Show, Close, Add..., Delete, Edit..., Merge..., Summary...

Changing cells:
$B$7:$G$7

Comment:
Created by Carol Cram on 1/4/99

FIGURE P1-8: **Scenario Values dialog box**

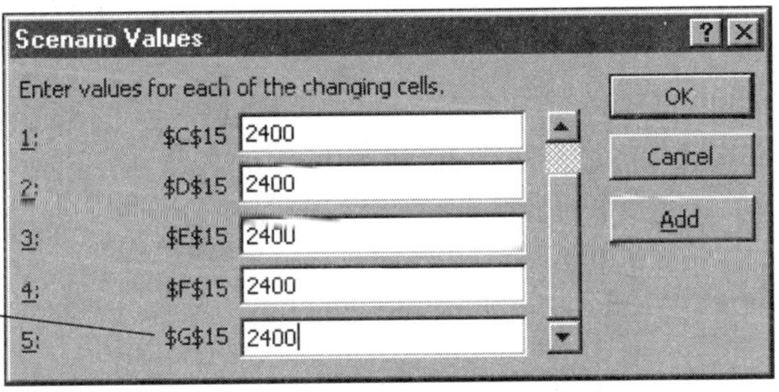

Scenario Values ? X

Enter values for each of the changing cells.

1:	$C$15	2400
2:	$D$15	2400
3:	$E$15	240U
4:	$F$15	2400
5:	$G$15	2400

Buttons: OK, Cancel, Add

Make sure $G$15 appears

FIGURE P1-9: **Worksheet in 75% view with Worst Case scenarios applied**

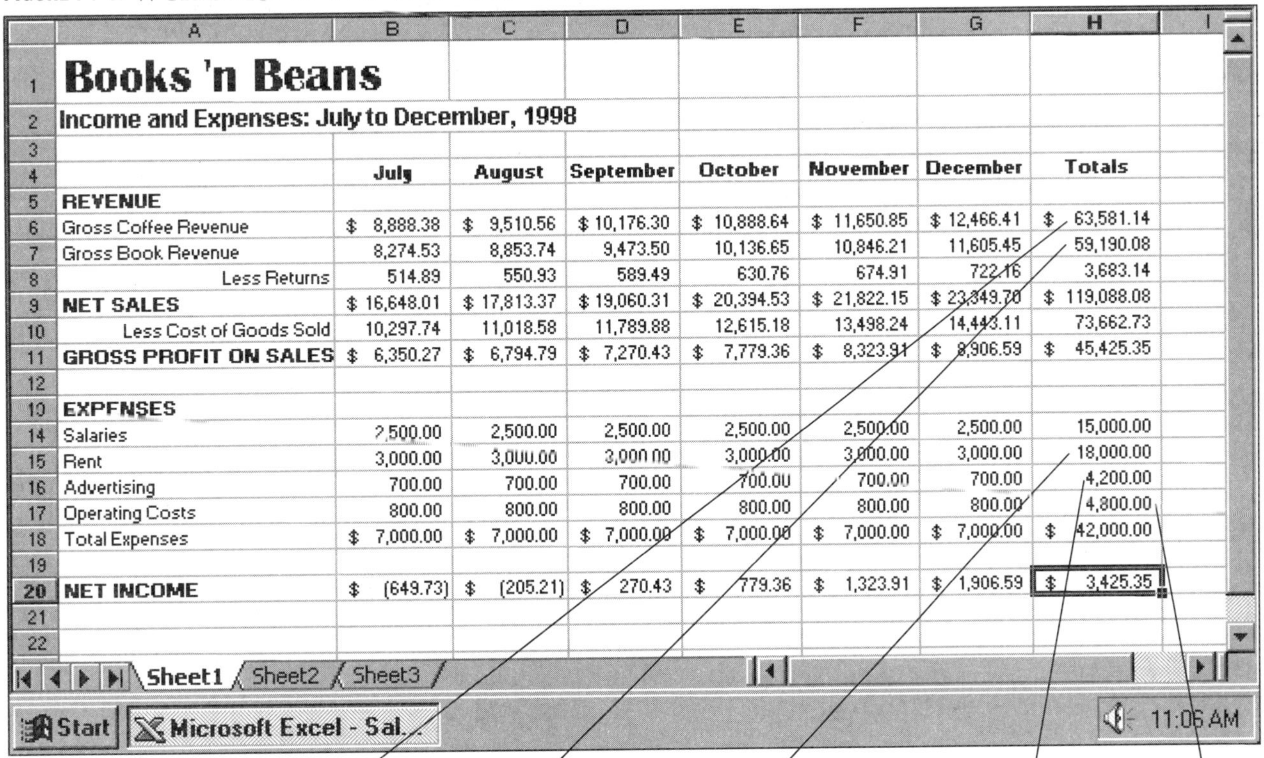

Books 'n Beans
Income and Expenses: July to December, 1998

	July	August	September	October	November	December	Totals
REVENUE							
Gross Coffee Revenue	$ 8,888.38	$ 9,510.56	$ 10,176.30	$ 10,888.64	$ 11,650.85	$ 12,466.41	$ 63,581.14
Gross Book Revenue	8,274.53	8,853.74	9,473.50	10,136.65	10,846.21	11,605.45	59,190.08
Less Returns	514.89	550.93	589.49	630.76	674.91	722.16	3,683.14
NET SALES	$ 16,648.01	$ 17,813.37	$ 19,060.31	$ 20,394.53	$ 21,822.15	$ 23,349.70	$ 119,088.08
Less Cost of Goods Sold	10,297.74	11,018.58	11,789.88	12,615.18	13,498.24	14,443.11	73,662.73
GROSS PROFIT ON SALES	$ 6,350.27	$ 6,794.79	$ 7,270.43	$ 7,779.36	$ 8,323.91	$ 8,906.59	$ 45,425.35
EXPENSES							
Salaries	2,500.00	2,500.00	2,500.00	2,500.00	2,500.00	2,500.00	15,000.00
Rent	3,000.00	3,000.00	3,000.00	3,000.00	3,000.00	3,000.00	18,000.00
Advertising	700.00	700.00	700.00	700.00	700.00	700.00	4,200.00
Operating Costs	800.00	800.00	800.00	800.00	800.00	800.00	4,800.00
Total Expenses	$ 7,000.00	$ 7,000.00	$ 7,000.00	$ 7,000.00	$ 7,000.00	$ 7,000.00	42,000.00
NET INCOME	$ (649.73)	$ (205.21)	$ 270.43	$ 779.36	$ 1,323.91	$ 1,906.59	$ 3,425.35

Sheet1 / Sheet2 / Sheet3

Start | Microsoft Excel - Sal... | 11:06 AM

Worst Case coffee revenues
Worst Case book revenues
Worst Case rent
Worst Case advertising
Worst Case operating costs

SALES FORECAST FOR BOOKS 'N BEANS

activity:

Format and Print the Scenarios

At present, all the Worst Case scenarios are displayed. You will show all the Current Scenarios and then create a bar chart. You will then format the worksheet for printing and print a copy. Finally, you will print copies of the worksheet with the Best Case and Worst Case scenarios applied.

steps:

1. Click **Tools** on the menu bar, click **Scenarios**, click **Current Coffee Revenue**, click **Show**, show all the remaining Current scenarios, then click **Close**

    You should see $8,264.46 in cell H20. Next, create a bar chart that shows the monthly net income.

2. Select cells **B4** to **G4**, press and hold the **[Ctrl]** key, select cells **B20** to **G20**, click the **ChartWizard button** 📊 on the Standard toolbar, click **Bar**, click **Next**, click **Next**, enter **Current Monthly Net Income** as the chart title, click the **Legend tab**, click the **Show legend check box** to deselect it, click **Finish**, switch to **75% view**, drag the chart down to row **27**, then resize the chart so that it extends from halfway across cell **A27** to cell **H50**

3. Right-click the **X-Axis**, click **Format Axis**, click the **Font tab**, change the font size to **8 point**, click the **Scale tab**, change the **Maximum** value to **6000**, click **OK**, right-click the **Y-Axis**, click **Format Axis**, click the **Font tab**, change the font size to **8 point**, click the **Patterns tab**, click the **Low radio button** in the **Tick mark labels** area, click **OK**, then change the font size of the chart title to **16 point**

    Next, use the drawing tools to highlight the current total net income.

4. Click cell **H20**, click the **Drawing button** 📝 to display the Drawing toolbar, click **AutoShapes** on the Drawing toolbar, click **Callouts**, select the **Rounded Rectangular Callout** (second from the left), draw the rectangular around cell **H20** as shown in Figure P1-10, right-click the border of the callout, click **Format AutoShape**, click the **Colors and Lines tab**, click the **Color List arrow**, click **No Fill**, click **OK**, click the **Text Box button**, then draw a text box and enter and enhance the text as shown in Figure P1-10

    Next, format and then print a copy of the worksheet.

5. Click the **Print Preview button** 🔍 on the Standard toolbar, click **Setup**, format the worksheet so that it fits on one page, is horizontally centered, and includes a Custom Header that displays **Current Scenario** at the left and your name at the right, click **OK**, click **OK**, then print the worksheet

    Next, apply the Best Case scenarios.

6. Make sure none of the drawing objects are selected, click **Tools** on the menu bar, click **Scenarios**, click each of the **Best Case** scenarios and **Show** in turn, then click **Close**

    Next, change the subtitle in cell A2, the months of the year, and the contents of the text box.

7. Click cell **A2**, enter the new subtitle as shown in Figure P1-11, click cell **B4**, type **January**, drag the corner handle across to cell **G4** to enter the remaining months, double-click the text box, enter the new text in **12 point** and increase the box size as shown in Figure P1-11, then change the chart title to **Best Case Forecast**, then click away from the chart

    Modify the header for the Best Case scenario worksheet.

8. Click 🔍, click **Setup**, click the **Header/Footer tab**, click **Custom Header**, change the text in the **Left box** to **Best Case Scenario**, then print a copy

    Finally, apply the Worst Case scenario and then format the sheet for printing.

9. Click **Tools**, click **Scenarios**, show all the **Worst Case** scenarios, click **Close** to exit the Scenario Manager dialog box, modify the subtitle, the text in the text box, and the chart title, as shown in Figure P1-12, modify the custom header so that **Worst Case Scenario** appears in the **Left** box, print a copy, then save and close the workbook

    You have printed copies of all three worksheets. Now you can "mix and match" scenarios to try out new predictions. For example, you could show the Current Advertising and Operating Costs scenarios along with the Best Case Rent Scenario, the Best Case Coffee Revenue scenario, and the Worst Case Book Revenue scenario. The net income in cell H20 changes with each combination.

Hint

The total net income in cell H20 is now $21,607.02.

FIGURE P1-10: Cell H20 enhanced with callout box in the Current Scenario worksheet

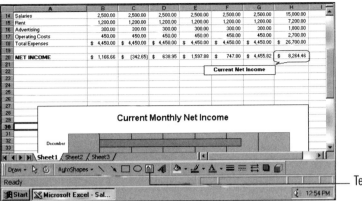

Text Box button

FIGURE P1-11: Best Case Scenario worksheet

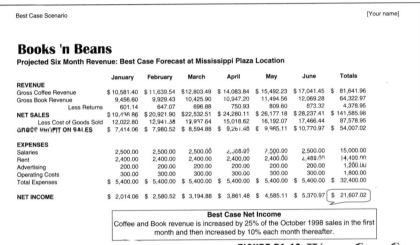

FIGURE P1-12: Worst Case Scenario worksheet

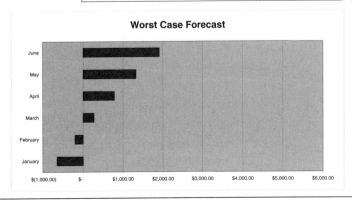

Sales Report for Island Resorts

Island Resorts manages resorts on four islands in the South Pacific: Fiji, Tahiti, Bali, and Pago Pago. As the sales manager for Island Resorts, you want to attract more guests to the resorts in the off-season months of April, May, and June. To determine your projected revenue and expenses should you attract more clients in these months, you will **Create a Sales Summary**, **Calculate Projected Sales**, and then **Use Solver to Calculate Maximum Sales**.

activity:

Create a Sales Summary

First, create the sales summary for April, May, and June 1998. You will use the data in this sales summary to make your sales projections.

steps:

1. Open a blank Excel workbook, click cell **A1**, enter and enhance your worksheet so that it appears as shown in the printout in Figure P2-1, then save the workbook as **Sales Report for Island Resorts**

   Next, make the required calculations to determine the totals required.

2. Click cell **B8**, enter the formula to multiply the **Average Cost per Room** by the **Total Number of Rooms Rented**, copy the formula across to cell **E8**, then increase the column widths, if necessary

3. Click cell **B13**, enter the formula to multiply the **Number of Rooms Available** by the **Operating Cost per Room**, then copy the formula across to cell **E13**

4. Click cell **B15**, enter the formula to add the **Total Operating Costs** to the **Advertising Costs**, copy the formula to cell **E18**, calculate the **Net Revenue** in cell **B17** as the **Total Expenses** subtracted from the **Total Room Rental Revenue**, then copy the formula to cell **E17**

   At present, the resorts in Fiji and Tahiti lose money in April, May, and June. Only the Pago Pago resort returns a respectable profit, while the Bali resort makes a modest profit. Next, enter the required totals in the Totals column.

5. Select cells **B7** to **F8**, click the **AutoSum button** Σ on the Standard toolbar, select cells **B13** to **F17**, click Σ, switch to **75% view**, compare your worksheet to Figure P2-2, then save it

   You should see $116,800.00 in cell F17. This amount represents your total profit in three months from the four resorts. Note that you don't total the Average Cost per Room, the Number of Rooms Available, and the Operating Cost per Room because these values don't relate to the revenue and expenses generated from the rental of hotel rooms. Next, go on to create a scenario to preserve the existing values in the worksheet and then use Goal Seek to determine how many rooms you need to rent to increase your net revenue.

FIGURE P2-1: Printout of worksheet setup

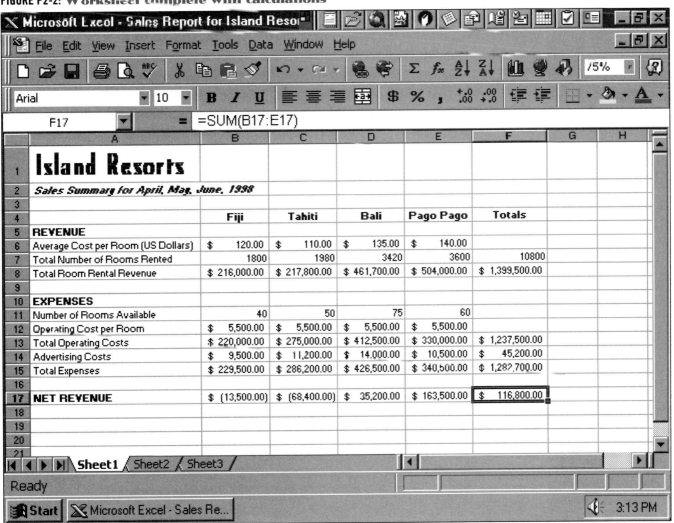

	A	B	C	D	E	F
1	**Island Resorts**					
2	*Sales Summary for April, May, June, 1998*					
3						
4		**Fiji**	**Tahiti**	**Bali**	**Pago Pago**	**Totals**
5	**REVENUE**					
6	Average Cost per Room (US Dollars)	$ 120.00	$ 110.00	$ 135.00	$ 140.00	
7	Total Number of Rooms Rented	1800	1980	3420	3600	
8	Total Room Rental Revenue					
9						
10	**EXPENSES**					
11	Number of Rooms Available	40	50	75	60	
12	Operating Cost per Room	$ 5,500.00	$ 5,500.00	$ 5,500.00	$ 5,500.00	
13	Total Operating Costs					
14	Advertising Costs	$ 9,500.00	$ 11,200.00	$ 14,000.00	$ 10,500.00	
15	Total Expenses					
16						
17	**NET REVENUE**					

— Kino MT, 28 pt., Bold

— Bold, Italics

FIGURE P2-2: Worksheet complete with calculations

X Microsoft Excel - Sales Report for Island Resor

File   Edit   View   Insert   Format   Tools   Data   Window   Help

Arial   10   B I U $ % ,

F17   = =SUM(B17:E17)

	A	B	C	D	E	F	G	H
1	**Island Resorts**							
2	*Sales Summary for April, May, June, 1998*							
3								
4		**Fiji**	**Tahiti**	**Bali**	**Pago Pago**	**Totals**		
5	**REVENUE**							
6	Average Cost per Room (US Dollars)	$ 120.00	$ 110.00	$ 135.00	$ 140.00			
7	Total Number of Rooms Rented	1800	1980	3420	3600	10800		
8	Total Room Rental Revenue	$ 216,000.00	$ 217,800.00	$ 461,700.00	$ 504,000.00	$ 1,399,500.00		
9								
10	**EXPENSES**							
11	Number of Rooms Available	40	50	75	60			
12	Operating Cost per Room	$ 5,500.00	$ 5,500.00	$ 5,500.00	$ 5,500.00			
13	Total Operating Costs	$ 220,000.00	$ 275,000.00	$ 412,500.00	$ 330,000.00	$ 1,237,500.00		
14	Advertising Costs	$ 9,500.00	$ 11,200.00	$ 14,000.00	$ 10,500.00	$ 45,200.00		
15	Total Expenses	$ 229,500.00	$ 286,200.00	$ 426,500.00	$ 340,500.00	$ 1,282,700.00		
16								
17	**NET REVENUE**	$ (13,500.00)	$ (68,400.00)	$ 35,200.00	$ 163,500.00	$ 116,800.00		
18								
19								
20								
21								

Sheet1 / Sheet2 / Sheet3 /

Ready

Start   X Microsoft Excel - Sales Re...   3:13 PM

activity:

Calculate Projected Sales

First, you will create a scenario to preserve the existing data and then you will use Goal Seek to determine how many rooms you should rent at the Fiji and Tahiti resorts to increase the net revenue from these resorts. Finally, you will format and print your projected sales analysis based on the values calculated by Goal Seek.

steps:

1. Select cells **B7** to **E7**, click **Tools** on the menu bar, click **Scenarios**, click **Add**, type **1998 Rentals**, click **OK**, click **OK**, then click **Close**

   Next, use Goal Seek to determine how many rooms you need to rent at the Fiji resort to increase the net revenue to $100,000.

2. Click cell **B17** (the net revenue for the Fiji resort), click **Tools**, click **Goal Seek**, click in the box next to **To value:**, type **100000**, click in the box next to **By changing cell:**, type **B7**, compare the Goal Seek dialog box to Figure P2-3, click **OK**, then click **OK** again

   As you can see, 2745.833333 appears in cell B7.

3. Click cell **B7**, click the **Comma Style button** [,], then click the **Decrease Decimal button** [.00] twice

   You need to rent 2,746 rooms at the Fiji resort to make a profit of $100,000. Next, calculate how many rooms you need to rent at the Tahiti resort to increase the net revenue to $120,000.

4. Click cell **C17**, click **Tools**, click **Goal Seek**, click in the box next to **To value:**, type **120000**, click in the box next to **By changing cell:**, type **C7**, click **OK**, click **OK** again, then format the values in cells **C7** to **F7** in the Comma style with no decimal places

   3,693 appears in cell C7. Next, create the Projected Revenue scenario from the values in row 7.

5. Click **Tools**, click **Scenarios**, click **Add**, type **Projected Rentals**, enter **B7:C7** as the changing cells, click **OK**, click **OK**, then click **Close**

   Next, create a bar chart to compare the current and projected revenue at the four resorts. Before you can create the bar chart, you need to have access to both scenarios. You will therefore copy the worksheet into Sheet2, then return to Sheet1 and show the 1998 Rooms scenario.

6. Name the three sheet tabs **1998 Rentals**, **Projected Rentals**, and **Solver Analysis**, copy the worksheet in the **1998 Rentals sheet** into the **Projected Rentals sheet**, click **Format** on the menu bar, click **Column**, click **AutoFit Selection**, return to the **1998 Rentals sheet**, then show the **1998 Rentals scenario**

   The net revenue in cell F17 of the 1998 Rentals sheet is again $116,800.00. Next, create a bar chart in the Projected Rentals sheet that compares the current and projected room sales.

7. Click the **Projected Rentals tab**, click cell **A20**, click the **ChartWizard button**, click **Bar**, click **Next**, click the **Collapse button**, click the **1998 Rentals sheet**, use the **[Ctrl]** key to select cells **B4** to **E4** and cells **B8** to **E8**, click the **Restore button**, click the **Series tab**, then click in the Name text box and type **Current Room Rentals**

8. Click **Add**, type **Projected Room Rentals**, click the **Collapse button** next to the **Values box**, select cells **B8** to **E8** in the **Projected Rentals sheet**, restore the dialog box, click **Next**, enter the chart title as shown in Figure P2-4, click the **Legend tab**, click the **Bottom radio button**, then click **Finish**

9. As shown in Figure P2-4, modify the size and position of the chart, reduce the font sizes of the chart title, Y-Axis, X-Axis, and Legend text, add the text box above the chart, add the two callout boxes next to the Tahiti and Fiji Projected Room Rentals bars, modify the subtitle, insert a header and footer, format and print a copy of the **Projected Rentals** worksheet, then save the workbook

FIGURE P2-3: **Goal Seek dialog box**

Goal Seek ? ✕

Set cell: `B17`

To value: `100000`

By changing cell: `B7`

[OK] [Cancel]

FIGURE P2-4: **Completed Projected Rentals worksheet**

Projected Rentals ——————————————————————— Modify the header

Island Resorts

Projected Sales Summary for April, May, June 1998 ——————————— Modify the subtitle

	Fiji	Tahiti	Bali	Pago Pago	Totals
REVENUE					
Average Cost per Room (US Dollars)	$ 120.00	$ 110.00	$ 135.00	$ 140.00	
Total Number of Rooms Rented	2,746	3,693	3420	3600	13,459
Total Room Rental Revenue	$ 329,520.00	$ 406,230.00	$ 461,700.00	$ 504,000.00	$ 1,701,450.00
EXPENSES					
Number of Rooms Available	40	50	75	60	
Operating Cost per Room	$ 5,500.00	$ 5,500.00	$ 5,500.00	$ 5,500.00	
Total Operating Costs	$ 220,000.00	$ 275,000.00	$ 412,500.00	$ 330,000.00	$ 1,237,500.00
Advertising Costs	$ 9,500.00	$ 11,200.00	$ 14,000.00	$ 10,500.00	$ 45,200.00
Total Expenses	$ 229,500.00	$ 286,200.00	$ 426,500.00	$ 340,500.00	$ 1,282,700.00
NET REVENUE	$ 100,020.00	$ 120,030.00	$ 35,200.00	$ 163,500.00	$ 418,750.00

In April, May, and June of 1998, both the Fiji and Tahiti resorts lost money. To increase revenue at the Fiji resort, we need to rent 2,746 rooms instead of the current 1,800 rooms. To increase revenue at the Tahiti resort, we need to sell 3,693 rooms instead of the current 1,980 rooms. By so doing, we will realize a net revenue of $100,000 from the Fiji resort and $120,000 from the Tahiti resort.

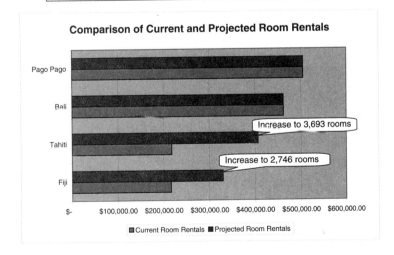

Comparison of Current and Projected Room Rentals

(Increase to 3,693 rooms)

(Increase to 2,746 rooms)

$- $100,000.00 $200,000.00 $300,000.00 $400,000.00 $500,000.00 $600,000.00

■ Current Room Rentals ■ Projected Room Rentals

—————— Modify the footer

[Your name]   [Current Date]

activity:

Use Solver to Calculate Maximum Sales

The Solver function uses advanced mathematical techniques to solve problems based on the *constraints* that you provide. You will use Solver to answer the following question: *How many rooms at each resort should I rent to make a gross profit of no more than $400,000 when no more than 30% of the rooms are rented at the Bali resort and no more than 4,000 rooms are rented at the Pago Pago resort?* First, you need to set up the Solver Analysis sheet.

steps:

Hint

Click **No** to remove the Office Assistant.

1. Click the **Solver Analysis tab**, then set up the worksheet so that it appears as shown in Figure P2-5
   Next, calculate the average cost per room based on the values in the 1998 Rentals sheet.

2. Click cell **B7**, click the **Paste Function button** [*fx*] on the Standard toolbar, select **Average** from the list of **Statistical** functions, click **OK**, click the **Collapse button** next to the **Number 1** box, click the **1998 Rentals tab**, select cells **B6** to **E6**, click the **Restore button**, then click **OK**
   The average cost per room is $126.25. Next, calculate the required totals.

3. Selects cells **B1** to **B5**, click the **AutoSum button** [Σ] on the Standard toolbar, click cell **B9**, enter the formula to multiply the **Total Rooms Rented** by the **Average Price**, click cell **B10**, enter the formula to calculate 80% of the **Total Rentals**, click cell **B11**, then enter the formula to calculate the **Gross Profit (Total Rentals - Less Cost of Rooms Rented)**, then display the values in cells **B9** to **B11** in the Currency style
   The total gross profit in cell B11 is $272,700.00. Next, use Solver to change the values in cells B1 to B4 to increase the gross profit in cell B11 to $400,000.

4. Click cell **B11**, click **Tools**, then click **Solver**
   The Solver Parameters dialog box appears. You need to tell Solver to change cells B1 to B4.

5. Click the box below **By Changing Cells**, then type **B1:B4**
   Next, add the constraints—that no more than 30% of the rooms are sold at the Bali resort, no more than 4,000 rooms are sold at the Pago Pago resort, and your gross profit is no more than $400,000.

6. Click **Add**, type **B3** in the box under **Cell Reference**, press [Tab] twice to move to the box under **Constraint**, type **B5*.3**, click **Add**, type **B4** in the box under **Cell Reference**, press [Tab] twice, type **4000**, click **Add**, type **B11** in the box under **Cell Reference**, press [Tab] twice, type **400000**, then click **OK**
   The Solver Parameters dialog box appears as shown in Figure P2-6. Next, solve the problem.

7. Drag the Solver Parameters dialog box down so that you can see the values in cells **B1** to **B4** (these are the values that will change), click **Solve**, check to ensure that the first four digits in cell **B1** are **3454**, then click **OK**

8. Display the values in cells **B1** to **B5** in the Comma style with no decimal places, then create a column chart that compares the Current and Projected Room Rentals as shown in Figure P2-7

9. Add the formatting and objects shown in Figure P2-7, format the **Solver Analysis** sheet for printing, print a copy, then save and close the workbook

FIGURE P2-5: Worksheet setup

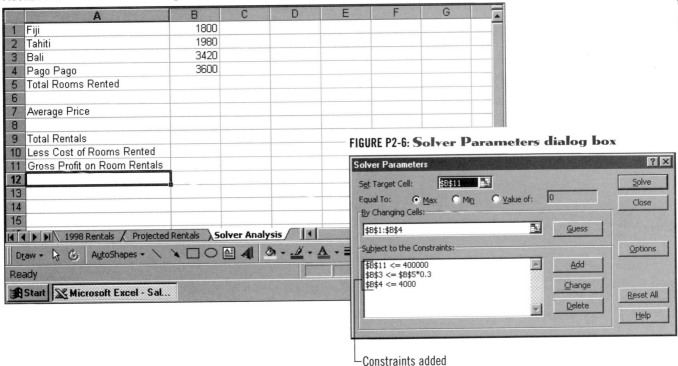

	A	B	C	D	E	F	G
1	Fiji	1800					
2	Tahiti	1980					
3	Bali	3420					
4	Pago Pago	3600					
5	Total Rooms Rented						
6							
7	Average Price						
8							
9	Total Rentals						
10	Less Cost of Rooms Rented						
11	Gross Profit on Room Rentals						
12							
13							
14							
15							

1998 Rentals / Projected Rentals \ Solver Analysis /

Draw ▾ ▸ ◡ AutoShapes ▾ \ ↘ □ ○ ▤ ▣ ◁ ▾ | ◊ ▾ ◢ ▾ ▲ ▾

Ready

🏁 Start | ✗ Microsoft Excel - Sal...

FIGURE P2-6: Solver Parameters dialog box

Solver Parameters   ? ✕

Set Target Cell: $B$11

Equal To: ● Max   ○ Min   ○ Value of: 0

By Changing Cells:
$B$1:$B$4

Subject to the Constraints:
$B$11 <= 400000
$B$3 <= $B$5*0.3
$B$4 <= 4000

Solve | Close | Guess | Options | Add | Change | Delete | Reset All | Help

└─ Constraints added

FIGURE P2-7: Completed Solver Analysis worksheet

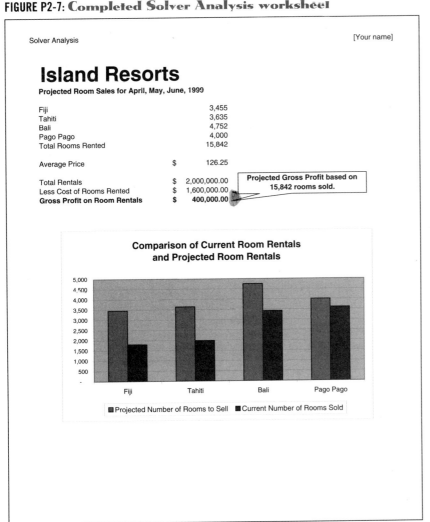

Solver Analysis   [Your name]

Island Resorts

Projected Room Sales for April, May, June, 1999

Fiji	3,455
Tahiti	3,635
Bali	4,752
Pago Pago	4,000
Total Rooms Rented	15,842
Average Price	$ 126.25
Total Rentals	$ 2,000,000.00
Less Cost of Rooms Rented	$ 1,600,000.00
Gross Profit on Room Rentals	**$ 400,000.00**

Projected Gross Profit based on 15,842 rooms sold.

Comparison of Current Room Rentals and Projected Room Rentals

■ Projected Number of Rooms to Sell   ■ Current Number of Rooms Sold

Home Renovation Project

As the owner of an older home, you decide that you need to renovate it so that you can increase its resale value and also improve your current living situation. You have received a quote for the work from a reputable contractor to add a new bathroom, modernize the kitchen, and build a sun deck. However, the price quoted ($25,500) exceeds your budget of $20,000 by $5,500. You need to find a way of completing the renovations within your budget. To complete the Home Renovation Project, you will **Use Solver to Reduce Labor Costs** and then **Use Solver to Calculate Cost Ranges**.

activity:

Use Solver to Reduce Labor Costs

steps:

1. Open a blank Excel workbook, enter and enhance the labels and values in cells **A1** to **D9** as shown in Figure P3-1, then save the worksheet as **Home Renovation Project**

2. Select cells **B5** to **D9**, click the **AutoSum button** Σ, click **Format** on the menu bar, click **Column**, then click **AutoFit Selection**

Next, copy cells A4 to D9 to cell A14 so that you can retain the original values after you have used Solver to change the values in the copied worksheet.

3. Select cells **A4** to **D9**, click the **Copy button** on the Standard toolbar, click cell **A14**, then click the **Paste Button** on the Standard toolbar

Next, use Solver to answer the question: How much should I reduce labor costs to spend a total of $20,000?

Trouble

If Solver does not appear on the Tools menu, see your instructor.

4. Click cell **D19**, click **Tools**, click **Solver**, type **C15:C17** in the box under **By Changing Cells**, click **Add**, enter **D19** as the **Cell Reference** and **20000** as the **Constraint** as shown in Figure P3-2, click **OK**, click **Solve**, then click **OK**

5. Save the worksheet, display **75% view**, then compare your worksheet to Figure P3-3

Next, go on to ask another Solver question and then format the worksheet for printing.

FIGURE P3-1: **Worksheet setup**

Select the font and font size you prefer

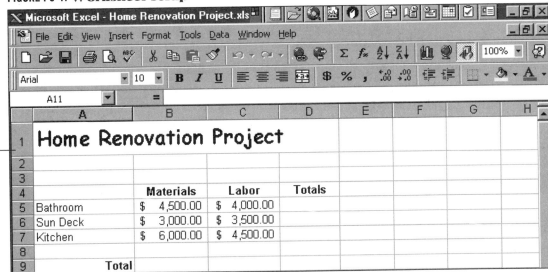

FIGURE P3-2: **Add Constraint dialog box**

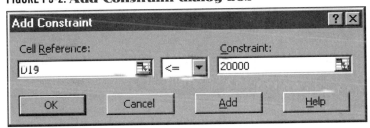

FIGURE P3-3: **Worksheet in 75% view**

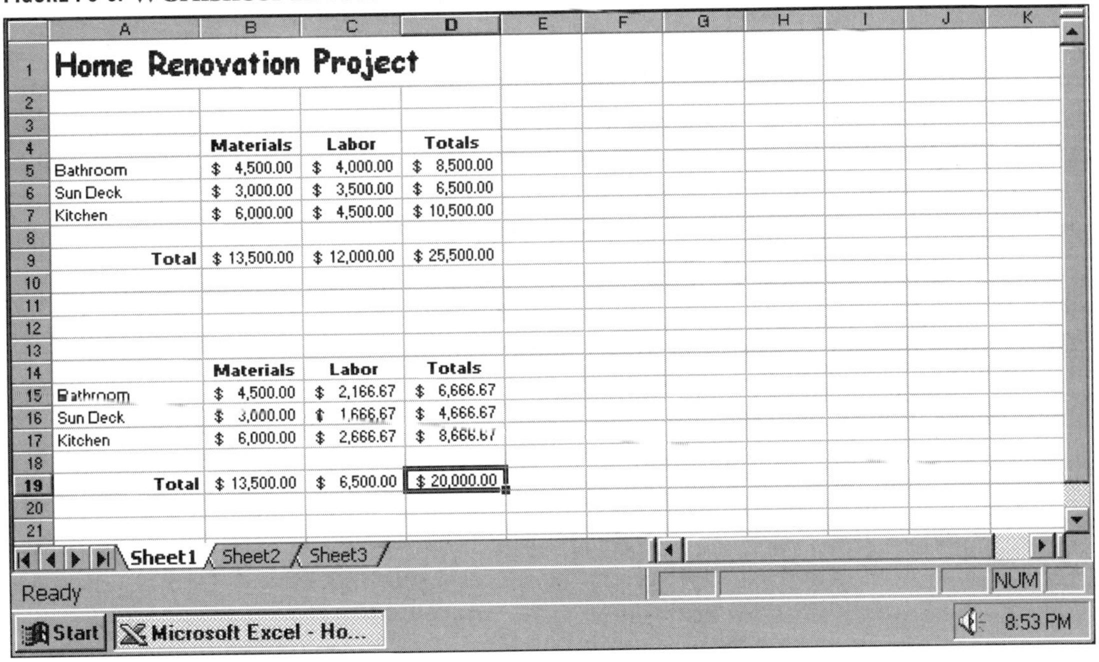

PROJECT 3

HOME RENOVATION PROJECT

activity:

Use Solver to Calculate Cost Ranges

You've already determined how much you can afford to spend on labor. However, this amount ($6,500 in cell C19) is almost half what the contractor will charge. You need to use Solver to determine the labor and materials costs if you do all but 20% of the labor yourself, but spend 40% more on materials for the extra tools you will need to buy.

steps:

1. Return to **100% view**, select cells **A14** to **D19**, click the **Copy button** 📋 on the Standard toolbar, click cell **A24**, then click the **Paste button** 📋 on the Standard toolbar

Next, use Solver to answer the question: How much will materials and labor cost if I spend 40% more on materials and spend only 20% of the total cost on labor?

2. Click cell **D29**, click **Tools**, click **Solver**, type **D29** in the box by **Set Target Cell**, then type **B25:C27** in the box under **By Changing Cells**

Next, you need to edit the current constraint to change the cell address to D29.

3. Click the constraints listed, click **Change**, type **D29**, then click **OK**

Next, you need to add six more constraints. The first three new constraints will tell Solver to make the values in cells B25 to B27 40% higher than the current values, and the next three constraints will tell Solver to make the values in cells C25 to C27 20% of the values in cells C5 to C7 (the labor costs quoted by the contractor). First, add the constraint that tells Solver to change cell B25 so that it is 40% more than 4500 (the value in cell B15).

4. Click **Add**, type **B25** in the **Cell Reference:** box, press **[Tab]** twice, type **4500*1.4** in the **Constraint** box, then click **Add**

Next, add the remaining constraints.

5. Add the next five constraints as shown below:

Cell Reference	Constraint
B26	3000*1.4
B27	6000*1.4
C25	4000*.2
C26	3500*.2
C27	4500*.2

6. Click **OK** after you enter the last constraint, then compare the Solver Parameters dialog box to Figure P3-4

Carefully check the Solver Parameters dialog box to ensure it matches Figure P3-4. Next, solve the problem.

7. Click **Solve**, then click **OK**

You should see $17,700.00 in cell B29 and $2,300.00 in cell C29. Next, insert a picture of a hammer next to the title.

8. Click cell **E1**, click **Insert** on the menu bar, click **Picture**, click **Clip Art**, click **OK** if a warning appears, select the **Hardware** category, select the picture of the **hammer**, click **Insert**, resize and position the hammer as shown in Figure P3-5, **right-click** the hammer, click **Format Picture**, click the **Colors and Lines tab**, click the **Line Color list arrow**, click **No Line**, then click **OK**

9. Add callout boxes and format the sheet for printing so that it appears as shown in Figure P3-5, print a copy of the worksheet, then save and close the workbook

Trouble

If Solver has *not* found a solution, click Cancel, then display the Solver Parameters dialog box and check that it matches Figure P3-4. If you find an error in a constraint, click Change and correct the error, then try solving the problem again.

FIGURE P3-4: **Solver Parameters dialog box**

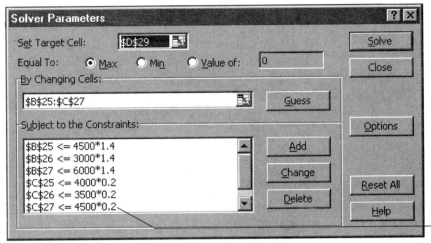

The D29 constraint appears below the C27 constraint

FIGURE P3-5: **Completed Home Renovation Project**

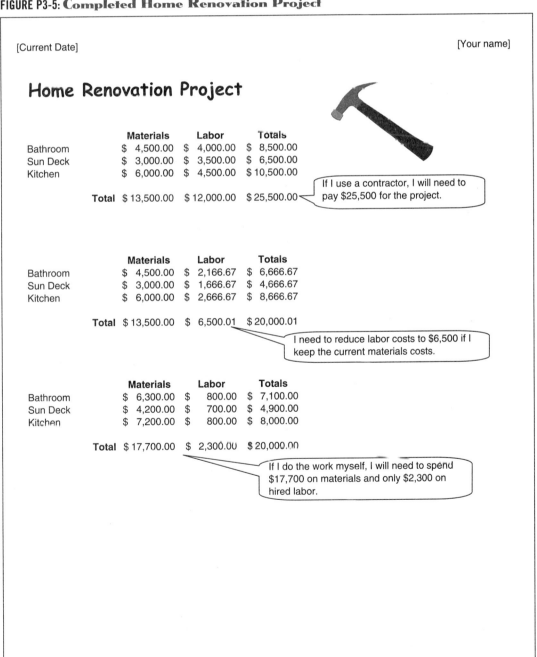

Independent Challenges

INDEPENDENT CHALLENGE 1

As the owner of a small business, you decide that you need to expand your operations in order to generate more income. To help you make an informed decision, you will use Scenario Manager to see the effect of your plans on a current income and expenses worksheet.

1. Determine the name of your company, the type of business it conducts, and your plans for expansion. For example, you could run a home-based catering service that has grown big enough to warrant moving the business out of your home and into a commercial location. Alternatively, you could run a desktop-publishing business from a small office and decide to move into a larger office and hire two assistants. Write the name of your company and a short description of your expansion plans in the box below:

Company Name: ....

Description of Expansion Plans: ....

....

....

2. Create an Income and Expenses statement that shows your income and expenses over a six-month period. Include labels for each of six months (e.g., January to June); labels for the various types of income you generate (e.g., Catering sales and Consulting), returns, and cost of goods sold; and labels for your various expenses such as Rent, Salaries, Advertising, and Operating Costs. Note that returns and cost of goods sold are calculated as a percentage of your gross revenue (usually 5% for returns and 60% to 70% for cost of sales). Calculate your monthly and total income and expenses.
3. Save the workbook as My Predictions for [Company Name].
4. Create Current scenarios from the data currently entered in the income and expenses statement. Note that you only need to create scenarios for the rows that contain the values you will change when you create a Best Case and Worst Case scenario.
5. Change the values in the income and expenses statement to reflect your best case predictions should you carry out your expansion plans. For example, if you decide to relocate, your Rent expense may increase, and if you hire an assistant, your Salaries expenses will increase. Make sure you also increase your income to reflect the increased revenue you expect after expanding.
6. Create Best Case scenarios from the new values you have entered in the income and expenses statement.
7. Change the values again to reflect your worst case predictions, should your expansion plans fail to proceed as well as you hope, then create Worst Case scenarios from the values that represent your worst case predictions.
8. Show the Best Case scenarios, highlight the new net income and explain its significance in a callout box, create a bar chart that displays the Best Case monthly income, change the month labels to display the next six months, then print a copy. Note the upper limit of the X-Axis in the bar chart. You want the bar charts you will print with the Current and Worst Case scenarios worksheets to display the same upper limit on the X-Axis so that the differences in the three charts are readily apparent.
9. Show the Current scenarios, change the title of the bar chart, change the upper limit on the X-Axis to the same upper limit displayed in the Best Case bar chart, format the worksheet for printing, then print a copy.
10. Show the Worst Case scenario, change the text in the callout box that points to the net income amount, change the title of the bar chart, change the upper limit on the X-Axis to the same upper limit displayed in the Best Case bar chart, then print a copy.
11. Save and close the workbook.

INDEPENDENT CHALLENGE 2

Use the Solver and Goal Seek functions to analyze a specific goal related to a company of your choice. For example, you could decide to increase your sales in two or three states or countries or increase the number of products of a certain type that you plan to sell. The guidelines provided will help you get started:

1. In the box below, write the name of your company and a short description of your business goal. For example, you could name your company "Luscious Landscaping," and describe your goal as increasing your sales of bedding plants.

Company Name: ....

Description of Business Goal: ....

....

2. Create a sales summary similar to the summary you created for Project 2. Note that you need to include two or three products or locations, the income generated from sales, and your various expenses. Use the summary you created for Project 2 as your guide.

3. Create a current scenario of the data that you will use Goal Seek to change. For example, if you decide to increase the total number of bedding plants you sell in May, you will need to create a current scenario of the sales data related to bedding plants.

4. Use Goal Seek to change the value in one of the cells (make sure the cell does *not* contain a formula) so that a cell that does contain a formula (e.g., the total) will equal a set value. For example, you can ask Goal Seek to calculate how many bedding plants you need to sell in May if you want your net income in May to equal $30,000.

5. Copy the sales summary into a new sheet, show the Current scenario in the original sales summary, then create a chart that compares the relevant values in the Current scenario with the new values generated by Goal Seek.

6. Ask a question related to your goal that you can use Solver to answer. For example, you could ask, *How many bedding plants should I sell at $1.98 per plant if I want bedding plants to constitute 40% of a total income of $100,000?* You will need to think carefully about a suitable Solver question. For ideas, refer to the Solver question you formulated in Project 2.

7. Set up a blank worksheet with the labels and values that Solver will use to answer the question. You will need to experiment with a variety of constraints. If the values that Solver finds appear unrealistic, cancel the Solver solution, and try changing your constraints. Remember that Solver will change the value in a specific cell based on the *constraints* that you specify.

8. Create a chart to display the data you generated after using Solver.

9. Format and print an attractive sales analysis. Include callout boxes to explain the significance of the various elements in your sales analysis. Think always in terms of the *practical* applications of the data you have determined. Ask yourself questions such as: *How does this data relate to my business? What actions should the business take?*

10. Save your sales analysis as "My Sales Analysis for [Company Name]," then print a copy of the analysis worksheet.

INDEPENDENT CHALLENGE 3

Think of a project that you will spend a specific amount of money on to complete and then use Solver to determine how much money you can spend on the two or three main project components. Project examples include: producing a short music video to promote a local band; producing and distributing a newsletter; or organizing a political rally, class party, or fund-raising event.

1. Specify a budget for your project. For example, you could have $10,000 available to produce a music video.

2. Break down the project cost into two or three categories. For example, cost categories for the music video could be Studio Time, Camera Purchase, and Videotape Production.

3. Set up a worksheet that displays your current cost estimates for the various project categories. The data for the music video project could appear as shown below.

	COST
Studio Time	$ 8,000.00
Videotape Production	$ 2,000.00
Video Camera	$ 2,000.00
Total	$ 12,000.00

4. Copy the labels and values in your cost estimate to a blank area of the worksheet, and then use Solver to answer a specific question. For the music video worksheet, you could ask Solver to determine how much you can spend on the video camera when you need to spend no more than $7,000 on studio time and can spend no more than $10,000 for the entire project.

5. Copy the labels and values in the Solver solution to a blank area of the worksheet, and then use Solver to answer another question that you feel more realistically reflects the cost breakdown for the project. For example, you may decide the amount that Solver determines you can spend for the video camera is not enough.

6. Format your worksheet attractively so that it displays all three versions of the project cost breakdown, add text boxes to explain the significance of the two Solver solutions, save the worksheet as "Project to [Description of Project]," and print a copy.

INDEPENDENT CHALLENGE 4

You run a sailboat rental business in the U.S. Virgin Islands that caters to adventure-bound travelers who rent sailboats for up to two weeks to explore the Caribbean Islands. During the previous summer, you failed to make a profit on the business. Now, you want to project sales for the coming summer months based on your plan to acquire more sailboats, increase advertising costs, and move into an attractive new boathouse.

1. Create the worksheet shown in the printout in Figure IC-1, then save the workbook as Current Summer Rentals.

FIGURE IC-1: Printout of Income and Expenses worksheet

	A	B	C	D	E	F
1	Tropical Breeze Boat Rentals					
2	Summer Rentals Projection					
3						
4						
5		June	July	August	Total	
6	Revenue					
7	Rental Income	$ 54,000.00	$ 62,000.00	$ 75,000.00		
8	Less Refunds: 4%					
9	Net Revenue					
10	Less Cost of Rentals: 75%					
11	Gross Profit on Rentals					
12						
13	Expenses					
14	Salaries	$ 8,200.00	$ 8,200.00	$ 8,200.00		
15	Rent	1,500.00	1,500.00	1,500.00		
16	Advertising	2,500.00	2,500.00	2,500.00		
17	Operating Costs	2,000.00	2,000.00	2,000.00		
18						
19	Total Expenses					
20						
21	Net Income					
22						
23						

2. Calculate the Refunds, Net Revenue, Cost of Rentals, Gross Profit on Rentals, Total Expenses, and Net Income.

3. Ensure that your total net income in cell E21 is (2,490.00). Note that you need to calculate the cost of rentals as 75% of the Rental Income, *not* the Net Revenue.

4. Create Current scenarios of the data for Rental Income, Rent, and Advertising. Call the scenarios "Current Rental Income," "Current Rent," and "Current Advertising."

5. Create the following Expansion scenarios for the Rental Income, Rent, and Advertising data:

Expansion Rental Income	Increase sales by 40% more than $75,000 in June (=75000*1.4) and then 30% more than the new June sales for July and 30% more than the new July sales for August (total rental income in cell E7: $418,950.00).
Expansion Rent	$2,200 per month
Expansion Advertising	$3,000 per month

6. Check that your net income in cell E20 is $41,779.50 after you have created and then displayed the three Expansion scenarios.

7. With the Expansion scenarios still displayed, create a bar chart that displays the monthly net income. Note the upper limit of the X-Axis.

8. As shown in Figure IC-2, add the graphic objects and the picture of the sailboat (in the Transportation category of the Clip Art gallery), insert a custom header, then format and print a copy of the worksheet.

9. Save the workbook as Projected Summer Rentals.

10. Display the Current scenarios, modify the header and the subtitle, modify the text in the text boxes, modify the chart title, then change the upper limit of the X-Axis to 25000 (so that it matches the bar chart that shows the Expansion net income).

11. Print a copy of the Current scenarios worksheet.

FIGURE IC-2: Projected Summer Rentals worksheet

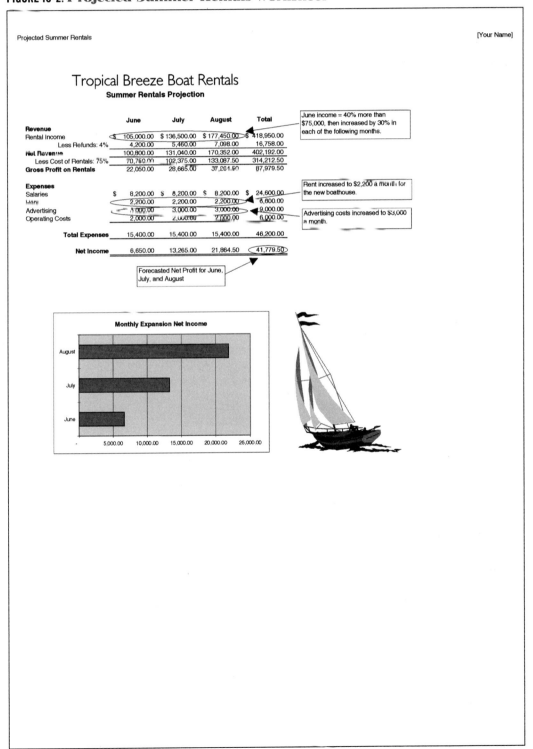

Visual Workshop

You and a friend have saved up $5,000 for a three-week car trip around North America. Now you want to determine how much you can afford to spend on the various expense categories (e.g., accommodations, gas, sightseeing, etc.), given a variety of constraints. Set up a worksheet so that it appears as shown in Figure VW-1 (enter formulas to multiply the number of days by the daily costs, then calculate the total expenses), then use Solver to answer the three questions provided. Save the worksheet as Trip Expenses, then save and print a copy of each Solver solution immediately after you create it.

FIGURE VW-1: Trip Expenses worksheet

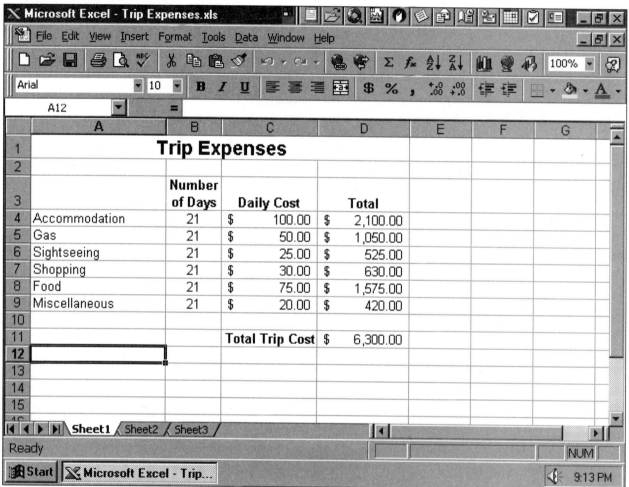

1. Use Solver to determine how much you can spend on accommodations each day, presuming that you will spend $30/day on gas and $40/day on shopping for souvenirs and not exceed your total trip budget of $5,000. Save the worksheet as Solver 1, then print a copy of the Solver solution.

2. Using the Solver solution you created in Question 1, use Solver to determine how much you can spend on accommodations each day if you reduce the total trip cost to $4,500 and spend $45/day on gas. Save the worksheet as Solver 2, then print a copy of the Solver solution.

3. Using the Solver solution you created in Question 2, use Solver to determine how much you can spend on food each day if you camp at a cost of $25 per night, spend only $15/day on sightseeing, and increase the total trip cost back up to $5,000. Save the worksheet as Solver 3, then print a copy of the Solver solution.

Index

S

► T

► V

► W